THE
Vermont
COUNTRY STORE®

COOKBOOK

RECIPES, HISTORY,
and LORE *from the*
CLASSIC AMERICAN
GENERAL STORE

Ellen Ecker Ogden
AND Andrea Diehl
WITH The Orton Family

FOOD PHOTOGRAPHY BY
Matthew Benson

THE
Vermont
COUNTRY STORE®

COOKBOOK

Copyright © 2015 by The Vermont Country Store, Inc., all rights reserved
The Vermont Country Store® is a registered trademark of the Vermont
Country Store, Inc. and may not be used or reproduced without the express
permission of the owner

Additional credits can be found on page 289

All rights reserved. In accordance with the U.S. Copyright Act of
1976, the scanning, uploading, and electronic sharing of any part
of this book without the permission of the publisher constitute
unlawful piracy and theft of the authors' intellectual property. If
you would like to use material from the book (other than for review
purposes), prior written permission must be obtained by contacting
the publisher at permissions@hbgusa.com. Thank you for your
support of the authors' rights.

Grand Central Life & Style
Hachette Book Group
1290 Avenue of the Americas
New York, NY 10104

GrandCentralLifeandStyle.com

Printed in the United States of America

Q-MA

First Edition: September 2015
10 9 8 7 6 5 4 3 2 1

Grand Central Life & Style is an imprint of Grand Central Publishing.
The Grand Central Life & Style name and logo are trademarks of Hachette
Book Group, Inc.

The Hachette Speakers Bureau provides a wide range of authors for
speaking events. To find out more, go to www.HachetteSpeakersBureau.com
or call (866) 376-6591.

The publisher is not responsible for websites (or their content) that are not
owned by the publisher.

Library of Congress Cataloging-in-Publication Data

Ogden, Ellen.
   The Vermont country store cookbook : recipes, history, and lore from the
classic American general store / Ellen Ecker Ogden and Andrea Diehl with
the Orton Family.—First edition.
      pages cm
   Includes index.
   ISBN 978-1-4555-5817-9 (hardcover)—ISBN 978-1-4555-5819-3 (ebook)
   1. Cooking, American—New England style. 2. General stores—Vermont.
I. Diehl, Andrea. II. Title.
   TX715.2.N48O375 2015
   641.5974—dc23   2015023085

BOOK AND JACKET DESIGN BY SHUBHANI SARKAR
sarkardesignstudio.com

TO THE MEMORY OF

VREST *and* MILDRED ELLEN ORTON

Founders of The Vermont Country Store,
pioneers of eating whole-grain foods,
and proponents of the Vermont way of life

CONTENTS

THE Vermont COUNTRY STORE® STORY

This issue is devoted to our own Vermont Country Store brand of fine foods, to tools and utensils for cooking and serving foods because all my life as a writer, publisher and editor I have done all I could to influence men's minds and nothing much came of it. Now I have decided to influence their stomachs.

—VREST ORTON
The Voice of the Mountains catalog, Summer 1949

I N THE FALL OF 1945, MY PARENTS, VREST AND MILDRED ORTON, MOTORED UP A GOLDEN VALLEY TOWARD MANCHESTER, VERMONT, THEN TOOK A DIRT ROAD UP INTO THE MOUNTAINS TO THE VILLAGE OF WESTON, TO MAKE REAL A DREAM INSPIRED BY A COFFEE AD.

Both had grown up in Vermont, she on a dairy farm south of Manchester and he in North Calais, where his father and grandfather ran a country store. Vrest had left to pursue a publishing career in New York, learning the ropes from H. L. Mencken. But Vermont beckoned, and he returned in the 1930s to his birth state, settled in Weston, and set up a print shop and publishing company in his garage. He met and married my mother in 1936, and I was born in September of 1941. When Pearl Harbor was attacked three months later and war duty called, my parents moved to Washington, D.C., where Vrest took a job with the Pentagon.

It was there that a chance encounter with a popular Chase & Sanborn Coffee advertisement triggered a memory for my father that would change all of our

lives. In the ad, four old men sit around a checkerboard balanced on a wooden barrel near a black iron potbellied stove; a hound sprawls on the floor nearby,

The Chase & Sanborn ad that launched a company.

Vrest's father's store in North Calais, Vermont.

36 Items you can buy now

14 FOR YOUR HOUSE
7 TO EAT
3 TO WEAR
12 TO READ
ALL FINE FOR GIFTS

Vermont headquarters for Vermont products

THE VERMONT COUNTRY STORE

VREST ORTON, *prop.*

SALES AGENTS FOR THE VERMONT GUILD
WHOLEGRAIN GRISTMILL PRODUCTS

Weston, Vermont

The first catalog, 1945.

while a shopkeeper pours sugar onto a large scale. This ad reminded him instantly and viscerally of his father's country store in North Calais. He vowed to return to Vermont and capture that feeling again through a store and a catalog.

"I wanted to revive an authentic, old-fashioned, rural operating store," wrote Vrest of that moment, "[with] the same merchandise: New England foods, store cheese and crackers, bolts of calico cloth, kitchen knives and cooking forks; and the atmosphere redolent with an evocative potpourri of wood smoke from the pot-bellied stove and of tobacco, peppermint sticks, freshly cut cheese, roasting coffee, nutmegs, cinnamon sticks and so many other nostalgic things I remembered."

My dad understood that during the war, nostalgia, a longing for the good old days, had already begun. And nostalgia would drive people to seek that simpler time, somehow. So, after the war was over, my parents packed up my baby brother, Jeremy, and toddler me and headed north. It was about six o'clock in the evening when they reached the village of Weston. The month was September. Maples blazed in the sunset. At last they were home.

Vrest and Mildred set to work on their first catalog, *The Vermont Country Store*, printing it on my father's printing press and mailing it to about a

thousand people on their expanded Christmas card list. This first issue was a modest brochure, three by five and a half inches in size, numbered only twelve pages, was printed on newsprint, and contained "36 Items you can buy now," as the cover proclaimed. But somehow, orders poured in and people wrote saying they couldn't wait to come to the store.

Problem was, there was no store.

Across the Village Green from my parents' house, however, there was an old building built in 1828 as a country inn that looked remarkably like Vrest's father's store in North Calais. They bought

Vrest's 1921 Model T Ford in front of the Store in the 1950s.

it, tracked down as many of the original fixtures as possible from the old abandoned store, and stocked it with goods. In late winter of 1946, Vrest and Ellen opened the doors of The Vermont Country Store to customers.

A 1952 *Saturday Evening Post* full-length story entitled "The Happy Storekeeper of the Green Mountains" really put the Store on the map. There was hardly a soul in America who did not read the *Post* in those days. As more and more people discovered the Store, we were obliged, in good New England style, to add on to the back of the original building every few years.

Some days during foliage season, the Store was so crowded that lines of people were required to wait outside. "We had to station a man at the door to let in two when two came out," wrote Vrest in one of the catalogs. Something had to be done. So in 1967, when the world was on the brink of a major change— think: Democratic convention, the assassinations of Robert Kennedy and Martin Luther King Jr.,

---

ᴐᴀ A SIGN OF THRIFTINESS

The first sign that hung over our store now hangs in the lobby of our main office. It's a big wooden sign, about twelve feet by three feet, and looks like something you'd see in an antique shop.

As there were no sign painters in Weston, Vermont, at the time—there were only 450 residents when we opened in 1946 (there are a whopping 600 now)—my father took up the brush and did all the lettering. In a small Vermont village in the 1940s, you had to figure things out for yourself more often than not.

That first sign read, "The Vermont Country Store, Founder, Vrest Orton, Prop.; Paul Orton, Mgr." A few years later, Dad painted over Paul's name after he moved on, with "Gardner Orton, Founder." When it was time to repaint, he would flip the big wooden sign over and paint it again.

I remember pounding out the nails so he could reuse them. He was a thrifty Vermonter, no doubt, and a practical one, too, since the nearest hardware store was miles down the mountain.

–LYMAN ORTON

⌘ THE RIGHT WAY

My grandfather Vrest was a bit of a perfectionist. He would find things, home in on them, and become an expert. He wrote books about the forgotten art of building a Rumford fireplace, the proper way to make cider, how to brew beer at home. He insisted on eggcups at breakfast and had rooster shears to properly cut the top off soft-boiled eggs. He was obsessive about making coffee: the right way of grinding it in the right grinder until it was the right grit (feels like sand), and used the original Chemex paper filter coffeemaker.

He had an exactness about the way things should be done, insisting that doing things right leads to better outcomes. He would only buy products that did it right, and he expected them to last (we still use my grandmother's Le Creuset cookware, now more than a half century old). All of which made him a proper, excellent storekeeper, proud of getting it just right.

My father, Lyman, certainly inherited those traits and applied them as he built the business. I turned forty in 2013 and have started to notice those same traits in myself, and I kid my dad about implanting a storekeeper microchip in me upon birth. All he says is, "DNA, my son!"

—ELIOT ORTON

Vrest Orton opens the Store, 1946.

Vrest and Lyman Orton, storekeepers,
around the potbellied stove in 1972.

Eliot, Gardner, Cabot, and Lyman—the new generation
of storekeepers—around the potbellied stove.

the whole hippie movement—we built a second store extolling a time when life was simpler, this one in Rockingham, Vermont.

Although I'd worked at the Weston store practically all my life, stamping checks at age six, then manning (or should I say, "boying") the candy counter, then working summers while I went to Middlebury College, my dad officially welcomed me into the business in 1964 when I graduated. Eleven years later, I became president—although Dad never officially retired, still laying out the catalogs and greeting customers at the Store. I loved running and expanding the business, and loved passing it on in 2010 to my own sons, this generation's purveyors of the practical and hard-to-find.

Today, hundreds of thousands of people, young and old, come from all over the nation and abroad to visit the Store, and our catalogs and website bring old-time products to hundreds of thousands more. The idea sparked by a coffee ad has become an icon, a destination for many of the Store's loyal customers, for which I'm grateful beyond words.

Since 1897, some Orton family member has been a storekeeper. I'm lucky to have known my grandfather Gardner Lyman, to have worked with my father, Vrest, and to have brought my sons, Cabot, Gardner, and Eliot, into the business. And I'm lucky to have walked through the doors of The Vermont Country Store most days of my life. If you haven't yet walked through those doors—and I hope you will—let me take you for a quick visit.

The jangle of a storekeeper's bell announces your arrival as you open the old wooden door. At eye level sit fifty-five glass canisters heaped with penny candy: saltwater taffy, licorice whips, fireballs, Mary Janes, watermelon fruit slices, Smarties, wax bottles, and Tootsie Rolls. You see hand-dipped chocolates by the pound and samples of Orton Family Fudge, along with Mallowbars, Wilbur Buds, Twin Bings, and Valomilk. Antiques hang from the rafters; goods

Mildred, Lyman, Gardner, Eliot, and Cabot cutting the fiftieth anniversary cake, 1996.

✍ DELIVERING, THEN AND NOW

When the *Saturday Evening Post* did an article on the Store in 1952, just six years after the Store's founding, it garnered an extraordinary response—more than eleven thousand people wrote in requesting a catalog; letters and orders increased tremendously. (No one called in those days—it was too expensive, and before credit cards, there was no way to pay over the phone!)

"The Happy Storekeeper of the Green Mountains" put The Vermont Country Store squarely on the map, in reality and in people's imaginations, and the business flourished after that. Our dad talks about getting letters after the article addressed to "Mr. Orton, Country Store, Somewhere in New England." Amazingly, all got delivered by the U.S. Postal Service!

When the *Today* show did a wonderful story on the Weston store recently, our website went crazy with orders and requests for catalogs. Of course, on the Internet you do need the right address: Anything other than VermontCountryStore.com—say, CountryStoreSomewhereinNewEngland.com—just plain won't get you there nowadays!

—GARDNER ORTON

Vrest Orton (second from left), owner of The Vermont Country Store in Weston, takes on neighbor Edwin Bolster at checkers. Alonzo Fuller, selectman, is to the right; Sam Waite is to the rear.

At the height of a successful career Vrest Orton decided he was doing the wrong thing and quit to start over in middle life. Now he does just what he enjoys most—and makes lots of money at it. No wonder so many people envy

The Happy Storekeeper of the Green Mountains

By EDWARD SHENTON

PHOTOGRAPHY BY FRANK ROSS

Weston's replica of the old grist mill that stood on the Wantastiquet River in 1791. Orton uses the mill to grind fourteen cereals and flours, which he sells in his store.

The inside of the shop, with Ace Waite behind the counter. Last summer, more than 75,000 tourists visited the store.

THE "NEW" STORE IN ROCKINGHAM, 1967

"I don't say that our new Vermont Country Store at Rockingham was erected only because of a bet," wrote Vrest Orton, "but I did have a bet with an old friend in Boston who claimed it couldn't be done. No one, he said and he'd bet on it, could reproduce a new store like the old one at Weston."

By the time Vrest was done salvaging two Victorian porte cocheres and a rococo ginger-bread-decorated porch from a house in nearby Chester, walnut counters and shelving from an old country store in Pennsylvania built before the Civil War, and Corinthian columns, cast-iron balustrades, and old curved-top windows from the soon-to-be-demolished Boston Public Library, the Store looked as if it had always been there. When Vrest's Boston friend came to visit, he took one look around and said, "You win the bet!"

THE VERMONT COUNTRY STORE

The Rockingham Store was built in 1967, but its real vintage fixtures and salvaged architectural features make it look as if it's been there forever.

Vrest and Mildred Orton in her kitchen, 1947.

extend far past where you can see. You absorb the scents of soap, sandalwood, and woodstove, notice the sounds of kids playing with games that never knew a joystick, and experience the nuanced tastes of Vermont Cheddar and chèvre.

Open tins of Vermont Common Crackers invite you to dip into a jar of heritage small-batch preserves, such as quince jelly or watermelon pickles. Samples of Vermont Cheddar send you to buy a wooden cheeseboard. Your search for a cast-iron skillet leads to a hand-cranked coffee mill just like your grandfather and mine used every morning to make coffee so strong you can smell it still.

When you walk into our stores, you may find your list is forgotten—while so much more is remembered. Because nostalgia is like that. We feel nostalgia for a real or imagined past, as my father knew, but we can also feel nostalgia for what we have now that we cherish—which, in Vermont, means fields, barns, landscapes, farmers' markets, good food,

and good company. We know we may not have it forever unless we work at preserving it.

This way of life is timeless, and therefore both deep-rooted and modern. It is place-based, human-based, emotion-based, and, for us, food-based. Which is why we present this cookbook: to share and to capture the essence of our store, the delicious food heritage of our dairies, farms, woods, streams, and fields, and the soul of the Vermont way of life—a self-reliant, rich life in the slow lane.

I'm lucky to have been a storekeeper all my life. I'm indebted to the amazing employees who make this all happen, a driven group who care deeply for their families, this company, our state, and our customers. Together, we decide how the company can give back to the communities in which we live, and support sustainability in our beautiful state.

I'm also lucky to have had long-lived parents (my father died at age eighty-nine, my mother at ninety-nine) and to be able to share their stories. The family archives we've conserved reveal fascinating friendships, a detailed history of the Store and catalogs, and hundreds of recipes handed down from both grandmothers and the great-aunts on my mother's side. These handwritten recipes, scribbled on the back of canceled envelopes and sheets of defunct stationery or collected in food-stained journals, form the foundation and inspiration for the recipes in this book.

Since I am a catalog person, I look at cookbooks as the modern equivalent of the old Sears Wish Book. People read a cookbook, imagine what they'd do, soak up the storytelling, taste the foods in their minds. Vermont has a lively food culture, which, combined with its lovely small-town stories, the family history of a family-run business, and the timeless charm of the general store, can become a lens through which we look at the appeal of all general stores, of all small towns, and of all good, authentic food.

This book—the first cookbook to come out of The Vermont Country Store since my mother's almost seventy years ago—is close to our hearts, as it is deep with family history, steeped in Vermont heritage, and represents our true personality as a family and a company: one of authenticity, tradition, hospitality, and welcome. I throw on my storekeeper's apron and welcome you to enter The Vermont Country Store any time you want through the pages of this cookbook.

—LYMAN ORTON

❧ A STOREKEEPER ALL MY LIFE

I started working at The Vermont Country Store at the ripe old age of six. My first job was to stamp the backs of checks with a rubber endorsement stamp—lots of fun for a six-year-old! By the time I was eight, my mother had taught me how to use an adding machine to add up the checks. She put the checks on the left and the adding machine on the right and taped a piece of paper over the right side of my face so I couldn't see the machine. If you're looking at the keys, you'll make mistakes.

I also worked in the Store, of course, bagging up candy and whole grains, waiting on customers, cutting cheese, working the register—stuff that kids could do. We had a school slate on the counter, and I'd add up customers' orders on the slate. By the time I was ten, I was a whiz at adding.

When I was old enough to drive, I'd take deposits with me on the way to school. In the morning I'd go to the bank with the checks and money all wrapped up in brown paper and tied with string and drop it into the outside deposit box. And on the way home I'd stop at the liquor store and pick up empty boxes to ship with. Recycling at its best, although some customers did write in objecting to receiving merchandise in a liquor carton.

—LYMAN ORTON

Lyman (at right) in his
storekeeper's apron in the 1950s.

CHAPTER 1

The DAIRY BARN

JUST SOUTH OF MANCHESTER, VERMONT, SPRAWLS a large dairy farm, a cluster of barns and houses with a stream flowing through the backyard. There, in 1911, Mildred Ellen Wilcox Orton was born, joining two brothers, her parents, aunts, and uncles all living together on the farm. (The family runs the dairy to this day, churning out Wilcox ice cream, served at Mildred's Dairy Bar at both of our stores and throughout Vermont since 1928.) The Wilcox clan delivered the key ingredients of a Vermont kitchen at the time: cheese, milk, butter, and eggs. Staples that still figure big in our cooking today.

BREAKFAST *and* BRUNCH

Vermont Cheese

FROM FARMHOUSE TO CO-OP AND BACK AGAIN

TWO HUNDRED YEARS AGO, EVERY FARM HAD AN average of a dozen cows and made its own butter and cheese. During the mid-1800s, farmers brought their milk to cheese co-ops—centrally located cheese-making factories. Practically every township (there were 248) had a cheese factory, so farmers in the days before refrigeration could quickly and safely get their milk in horse-drawn wagons to the local cheese maker before it spoiled. These co-ops turned milk into cheese, primarily Cheddar.

Today, only a few of the original cheese makers, such as Crowley Cheese (established 1824), Grafton Cheese (established 1892), and Cabot Creamery (established 1893), remain. Cheese making has again become a farmhouse activity, and farmstead and artisan cheese have a vibrant presence in Vermont.

FUN FACTS ABOUT CHEESE

7,000 years of cheesy goodness: Clay vessels with small holes found in Northern Europe in the 1970s stumped archaeologists for decades. New analyzation techniques reveal chemical evidence that these pots were Neolithic cheese strainers.

It takes ten pounds of cow milk, on average, to make one pound of cow cheese.

Fortifying the Pilgrims: What was in the hold of the *Mayflower* in 1620? Yes, cheese.

Nation's oldest: Built in 1882, the Crowley Cheese Factory in Healdville, Vermont, is the oldest cheese factory in the United States still in operation.

SHARP THOUGHTS ON CHEDDAR

TOURISTS COMING TO THE GREEN MOUNTAIN State have certainly obtained the unhappy impression from various articles about Vermont cheese, that *good* cheese must be sharp. They are told that the sharper the cheese, the better the cheese!

Nothing, of course, could be more misleading or further from the truth.

Richness and mellowness are qualities that make cheese good, never *sharpness*. Like famous European cheeses, the longer Vermont Cheddar is aged, the more delectable, tasty and highly prized it is, by real gourmets.

A carefully aged Vermont Cheddar Cheese...is rich, wholesome, delicious, and toothsome...Like fine wine it will exude a heady and satisfying *bouquet*, of great body, as they say of good aged wine. But it will never "smell" to high heaven, or taste *sharp*.

—VREST ORTON, *THE STORY OF THE VERMONT COUNTRY STORE*

"Here's a pound on the nose."–Lyman

I LEARNED THE CRAFT OF CUTTING CHEDDAR from Sam Waite, who worked at the Store for decades when I was growing up. Sam insisted I cut the cheese straight and clean and accurate.

Sam, who prided himself on cutting clean, also claimed he could cut precisely one pound of cheese on the nose every time. "I want a pound of Cheddar," a customer would say, and I'd watch as he sharpened his knife and took to the 35-pound wheel. One clean cut later, he wrapped the cheese in butcher's paper, pulled a length of country store string from the cone overhead, and wrapped the package. With a smooth one-handed move so fast you could barely catch the motion, he tied a Storekeeper's Knot using forefinger and thumb, and then, with a loop-wrap of the string around his left forefinger, snapped the string so it cut itself off—not against the finger but against the string itself.

Our Vermont-made Fairbanks platform scale had a balance beam at eye level so the customer could see. Sam moved the sliding weight to one pound. The tension built. He held the neat white packet of cheese over the platform and let it drop. The balance beam bounced a bit, settled down, and, as we watched, ended up right smack in the middle time after time. We never told the customer about Sam's thumb, which just may have helped it a bit either way.

Sam Waite cutting exactly one pound of Cheddar.

His pride was behind this cheeky move. Some customers got a bit over a pound and some a bit under, but we figured it all evened out. But when I started cutting and weighing cheese, my father told me in no uncertain terms, no thumb!

—LYMAN ORTON

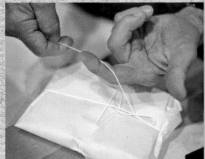

Lyman demonstrates the Storekeeper's Knot.

MAKE *Your Own* BUTTERMILK

Buttermilk is often used in baked goods because it helps the flour and baking powder to rise. Contrary to what many people think, buttermilk is not butter added to milk, but the liquid that's left after churning butter. No buttermilk on hand? Make your own by mixing 1 tablespoon white vinegar or lemon juice with 1 cup whole milk. Let it sit until it curdles, about 10 minutes. Stir and use in any recipe that calls for buttermilk.

BUTTERMILK DOUGHNUT PUFFS

Makes 12 DOUGHNUTS

—◆◆—

Th*ese delightful puffs are baked, not fried in the traditional way, and taste like a hybrid between spice cake and muffin, with a light, crisp blanket of cinnamon sugar. Kids enjoy rolling them in the butter and cinnamon sugar, then dunking them in a mug of warm apple cider. The hint of orange zest combined with the other fragrant spices gives this doughnut a tasty twist on an old-time Vermont favorite.*

PUFFS

8 tablespoons (1 stick)
unsalted butter, cut into 1-inch
pieces, plus more for the pan

1½ cups unbleached
all-purpose flour,
plus more for the pan

½ cup sugar

1 large egg,
at room temperature

1 teaspoon baking powder

½ teaspoon salt

¼ teaspoon freshly
grated nutmeg

Pinch of ground cloves

Pinch of ground ginger

1 teaspoon grated orange zest

½ cup buttermilk, at room
temperature

TOPPING

6 tablespoons (¾ stick)
unsalted butter, melted

½ cup sugar

1 teaspoon ground cinnamon

MAKE THE PUFFS: Preheat the oven to 350°F. Grease and lightly flour a 12-cup muffin tin or line it with paper muffin cups.

In a medium saucepan, melt the butter over medium-high heat and stir with a wooden spoon until browned and nutty smelling. Be careful not to let it burn—as soon as you see it browning, take it off the heat and stir for another minute to cool slightly.

Transfer the melted butter to the bowl of a stand mixer fitted with the paddle attachment, add the sugar, and beat on medium speed. Add the egg and continue beating until all are blended together.

In a separate bowl, stir together the flour, baking powder, salt, nutmeg, cloves, ginger, and orange zest. With the mixer on medium speed, gradually add the dry ingredients to the butter-sugar mixture, alternating with the buttermilk, until blended. Take care not to overbeat.

Spoon the batter evenly into the muffin cups and bake for 25 minutes, until golden brown.

MAKE THE TOPPING: In a small saucepan, melt the butter and remove from the heat. In a small bowl (or a brown paper lunch bag), combine the sugar and cinnamon.

When the puffs come out of the oven, use a knife to gently remove them from the muffin tin, and one by one, dip each puff in the melted butter, then roll it in the cinnamon sugar (or drop it into the paper bag, fold over the top, and shake). Transfer to a serving platter and serve warm.

CHEDDAR BREAKFAST POPOVERS

Makes 6 STANDARD POPOVERS OR 12 MINI POPOVERS

———— ❖ ————

Although seen most commonly as an accompaniment for roast beef, popovers are the ultimate breakfast treat: eggy, warm, and satisfying. Our recipe includes a hint of cheese to give them a little extra flavor. An authentic popover pan is deeper and heavier than a muffin tin, and should be preheated in a hot oven before the batter is added, to make sure the pastries rise and "pop over" the sides.

3 tablespoons unsalted butter

1½ cups unbleached all-purpose flour or rye flour

½ teaspoon salt

¼ teaspoon freshly ground black pepper

3 large eggs

1½ cups whole milk

½ cup finely grated Cheddar cheese

Butter and jam, for serving

Preheat the oven to 450°F. Dot each of 6 popover cups with ½ tablespoon of the butter and place in the hot oven to preheat while you mix the batter.

In a small bowl, stir together the flour, salt, and pepper. In a medium bowl, whisk together the eggs, milk, and cheese, then gradually add the flour mixture and whisk until smooth. (You can do this in a mixer, but whisking by hand produces more tender, lighter popovers.)

Carefully remove the popover cups (which will be smoking hot) and divide the batter evenly among the cups, filling each three-quarters full. Return to the oven and bake for 20 minutes. Reduce the oven temperature to 350°F and bake for 20 minutes more, until the popovers are golden brown. Remove from the oven and serve piping hot with butter and jam.

CINNAMON SWIRL WREATHS OR BUNS

Makes 2 WREATHS OR 12 BUNS

Who doesn't love cinnamon buns? Here we turn the rich, gooey goodness into wreaths, fragrant Christmas morning treats perfect before or after opening the stockings. The rich batter layered with maple cinnamon sugar and pecans yields enough to make two wreaths—one for your own family and the other to give to the neighbors. Of course, it makes beautiful buns, too, or you can make a wreath for Christmas morning and buns to last through New Year's morning (except they won't).

DOUGH

1 (¼-ounce) packet active dry
yeast (2¼ teaspoons)

¼ cup warm water
(105° to 115°F)

2 cups whole milk

8 tablespoons (1 stick)
unsalted butter

½ cup granulated sugar

1 teaspoon salt

7½ to 8 cups unbleached
all-purpose flour,
plus more for dusting

2 large eggs, lightly beaten

Vegetable oil, for greasing

FILLING

½ cup pure maple syrup

2 cups packed
dark brown sugar

2 tablespoons
ground cinnamon

4 tablespoons (½ stick)
unsalted butter,
at room temperature

2 cups pecans,
coarsely chopped

MAKE THE DOUGH: In a large bowl, sprinkle the yeast over the warm water and set it aside for 10 minutes to grow.

In a small saucepan, heat the milk to just before boiling. Turn off the heat; add the butter, sugar, and salt and stir to combine. Let cool to lukewarm. (You can test by dipping in your finger—if it is too hot to touch, it is too hot for the yeast. If you can just barely feel the heat, it is ready to combine with the yeast.)

Add the milk mixture to the bowl with the yeast. Add 3 cups of the flour and the eggs, mixing well with a wooden spoon or a handheld mixer fitted with a dough hook. Keep adding the flour, cup by cup, until a soft dough forms. Turn the dough out onto a lightly floured surface and knead until smooth, about 5 minutes. Test it by pressing in two fingers; if the indentation immediately fills, it is ready.

Place in a bowl lightly greased with the oil, turning once to coat the dough with the oil. Cover with plastic wrap (to keep the dough moist and warm) and let the dough rise in a warm place until doubled in volume, about 1½ hours.

MAKE THE FILLING: While the dough is rising, in a small bowl, stir together the maple syrup, brown sugar, and cinnamon.

Once the dough has doubled, punch it down and divide it in half. Cover and let rest again for 10 minutes. Roll each half into a 15 × 7-inch rectangle, about ½ inch thick. Rub with the softened butter and sprinkle evenly with the cinnamon-sugar mixture (reserving a few tablespoons) and the pecan pieces.

Beginning with one long side, roll up each rectangle. Seal the edge by pressing the dough together. Form each into a ring, and place each one on parchment paper set on a baking sheet. With scissors, cut 1-inch sections three-quarters of the way into the circles, keeping each piece intact at the center. Twist the pieces outward to show the swirl interior facing up to form a

ICING
(OPTIONAL)

1 cup confectioners' sugar

3 tablespoons whole milk

½ teaspoon pure vanilla
extract

wreath. Adjust the dough on the baking sheets to get it the way you will want it to look when baked. If you would like rolls instead, cut the pieces all the way through and place them swirl side up in a greased muffin tin.

Let everything rise again until almost doubled in volume (about 45 minutes). Just before baking, preheat the oven to 375°F.

Brush the wreaths or rolls with more softened butter and sprinkle with the reserved cinnamon-sugar mixture. Bake wreaths for 35 minutes and rolls for 30 minutes. Remove from the oven and let cool slightly on a rack before slicing and serving.

MAKE THE ICING, IF DESIRED: While the wreaths or rolls are cooling, in a small bowl, combine the sugar, milk, and vanilla and whisk until smooth. Drizzle over the top of the cinnamon wreaths or buns.

↬ GOING ORGANIC

For more than a decade, organic dairy has provided a profitable alternative for smaller Vermont dairy farms, which could not or would not get larger to compete in the conventional market. The fastest-growing agricultural segment in Vermont in the past two decades, certified organic dairy farms have increased in number from two in the early 1990s to two hundred in 2014, making up 20 percent of Vermont's dairy farms. Organic's success in Vermont is due not only to farmers dedicated to organic, but also to the Northeast Organic Farming Association (NOFA) of Vermont, which provides key technical support for Vermont farmers.

FARMHOUSE YOGURT

Makes 8 CUPS OR EIGHT (6-OUNCE) MASON JARS

O nce you get in the habit of making homemade yogurt, you may never go back to commercial brands. Our go-to recipe works every time. We prefer to start with a powdered culture (easy to find online and in some health food stores) because this guarantees it will work. We also make yogurt by adding a tablespoon of existing yogurt to each jar, and shaking. This works for the first few batches, but once you start getting runny yogurt, start another batch with the powdered culture to give it fresh oomph. We've given you the recipe both ways.

The only tricky thing about making yogurt is finding a place to keep it at 105°F to incubate the cultures. The warming drawer of the stove, a low oven with a pilot light, or inside an insulated cooler are all places we've found success. Place a candy thermometer that can register temperatures below 200°F in the yogurt and make sure the temperature of the yogurt does not go above 110°F, or the yogurt won't firm up.

8 cups whole milk
(for extra creaminess,
use part half-and-half or
cream)

1 packet live culture,
or ½ cup whole milk
plain yogurt

Pour the milk into a 4-quart saucepan and heat it over medium heat until it registers 180°F on a candy thermometer (just before a simmer) and a film forms on the top.

Turn off the heat, skim off the film, and transfer the milk to a large bowl. Clip the thermometer to the rim of the bowl and stir occasionally to help cool the milk to about 115°F; it will take about 20 minutes.

If using a powdered yogurt culture, add the specified amount of powdered culture to the warm milk; typically this is one full packet per batch. Gently stir with a wooden spoon. **If using yogurt as a starter culture,** add ½ cup to the heated milk and stir. Pour the warm milk into the jars, place the lids on top, secure, and place the jars in the bottom of the warming drawer, or in an oven heated to its lowest temperature, to keep the temperature at 105° to 110°F for 6 to 8 hours. Keep the candy thermometer in the drawer or oven to watch the temperature and if it gets higher than 110°F, open the drawer to release some heat.

After 6 to 8 hours, the yogurt will be firm, although a little more custardy than what you would find in the store. Eat a jar fresh and place the rest in the refrigerator to cool completely. The yogurt can be stored in the refrigerator for up to 2 weeks.

MILDRED'S
BUTTERMILK GRIDDLECAKES

Makes 16 TO 18 SMALL PANCAKES

*W*hen Mildred wrote this recipe almost a half century ago, buttermilk—the liquid left over after cream is churned into butter—was a staple in every Vermont kitchen. It is worth seeking out today in as unadulterated a form as possible. Thick and with a tangy, buttery flavor, it actually contains far less fat than regular milk, is loaded with vitamins, minerals, and probiotics, and has a shelf life long enough for lots of baking and Sunday mornings.

We are delighted to have discovered this recipe, because it has become our "go-to" favorite for pancakes. The cornmeal keeps the cakes crisp and firm, so it is easy to make tiny, delicate pancakes to stack several layers high. Serve with a side of applesauce (see page 144) or fresh raspberries and maple syrup.

1 large egg

1 cup buttermilk

2 tablespoons pure maple syrup, plus more for serving

2 tablespoons unsalted butter, melted

⅔ cup whole wheat flour

⅓ cup cornmeal

½ teaspoon baking soda

1 teaspoon baking powder

¾ teaspoon salt

1 teaspoon vegetable oil, plus more as necessary

In a medium bowl, whisk together the egg, buttermilk, maple syrup, and butter until combined. In a separate bowl, whisk together the whole wheat flour, cornmeal, baking soda, baking powder, and salt.

Slowly pour the flour mixture into the buttermilk mixture and blend just enough to moisten the flour and get rid of lumps. Take care not to overmix, or the batter will be tough.

Lightly oil a cast-iron griddle and heat it over medium heat until water flicked onto the surface skips across the top. Drop 2 tablespoons of the batter onto the hot griddle to make 3-inch cakes. When small bubbles appear on the surface (about 2 minutes), flip the cakes and cook for another minute or two, until golden brown on both sides. Transfer the griddle cakes to a plate and cover to keep warm, or keep warm in a low oven. Repeat with the remaining batter, oiling the griddle as necessary between batches.

Serve with warmed maple syrup.

❧ GRIDDLECAKE RITUALS

Pancakes were the breakfast of choice at my grandparents' house, just down the road from us when we were growing up. From our beds there, we could hear our grandparents setting the dining room table with the good dishes, the small stainless-steel server with hot water beneath, and the little sailor boy syrup pitcher, whose cap came off to pour.

Our grandmother made her pancakes on a soapstone griddle. Our grandfather Vrest was the pancake chef. To us, he seemed enormous, with a gruff voice and exacting manner. He'd pull up wooden stools so we could reach the counter. "Pay attention!" he'd order, as he showed us how to wait for the griddle to heat up and then throw a couple of drops of water on it. If the water "danced across the surface," the griddle was ready.

We loved Gram's thick, hearty griddlecakes, topped the Vermont way with homemade applesauce and plenty of maple syrup. And I've learned to appreciate my grandfather's precision, as I've become more like him: a bit anal-retentive, but appreciative of the art of things, the process. And so Julie and I make pancakes with our kids the exact same way, and we eat them with applesauce, just like Gram did.

—ELIOT ORTON

STRAWBERRY-RHUBARB
BREAKFAST STREUSEL

Makes ONE 9 × 13-INCH PAN; *Serves* 6 TO 8

When the first ruby red knobs of rhubarb begin to emerge in the spring, we know it is only a short few weeks before we can make this classic streusel. Easily adapted for all types of seasonal fruit, it shines in spring with rhubarb and strawberries, and is just as good when you substitute other berries available later in the summer. The nuts and sugar topping gives it a not-too-sweet flavor, with just the right balance of cake and crumb.

NOTE: *If you have buttermilk on hand, use that in place of the milk and vinegar. (Vinegar causes the milk to slightly curdle so the baking soda activates, but buttermilk does it naturally.)*

To preserve rhubarb for winter use, simply remove the leaves, chop the stalks into 1-inch pieces, and freeze in a resealable plastic bag.

CAKE

8 tablespoons (1 stick)
unsalted butter,
at room temperature,
plus more for the pan

2 cups unbleached
all-purpose flour,
plus more for the pan

4 large stalks rhubarb

1 pint strawberries
or raspberries

1 cup whole milk or
buttermilk (omit the vinegar
below if using buttermilk)

1 tablespoon
apple cider vinegar

1 teaspoon baking soda

1 teaspoon sea salt

1 cup packed light or
dark brown sugar

1 large egg

¼ cup plain yogurt

MAKE THE CAKE: Preheat the oven to 350°F and position a rack in the center. Lightly butter and flour a 9 × 13-inch baking dish, tapping out the excess flour.

Remove the leaves from the rhubarb and slice the stalks into ½-inch-thick pieces. Hull and quarter the strawberries. Place both in a bowl or a measuring cup. (You should have about 3 cups mixed rhubarb and strawberries.)

Combine the milk and vinegar and let stand until the milk curdles, about 5 minutes. In a small bowl, mix the flour, baking soda, and salt to combine. In the bowl of a stand mixer fitted with the paddle attachment, or in a medium bowl using a handheld mixer, cream together the butter and brown sugar until light and fluffy, about 3 minutes. Beat in the egg and the yogurt. Gradually add the flour mixture, alternating with the milk, until both are incorporated. By hand, fold in the rhubarb and strawberries. Spread the batter evenly in the prepared pan.

½ cup packed light or
dark brown sugar

½ cup chopped walnuts

¼ cup sunflower seeds

1 teaspoon ground cinnamon

½ teaspoon ground ginger

¼ teaspoon ground cloves

MAKE THE TOPPING: In a small bowl, mix together the topping ingredients until thoroughly combined and sprinkle the topping evenly over the batter. Bake for 35 to 45 minutes. Let cool in the pan on a wire rack and serve warm or at room temperature.

RHUBARB, *the* SWEETHEART *of the* GARDEN

The brilliant rosy color of the stalks and the flamboyant nature of the giant leaves are more characteristic of tropical plants found in the Caribbean than in Vermont, yet rhubarb is a true harbinger of spring here and belongs in every kitchen garden. The plants thrive in cool weather, will keep producing edible stalks all summer, and last for decades.

Rhubarb has a flavor both earthy and sour, with a distinct tartness not even tempting to eat raw—which is a good thing, considering it's slightly toxic, especially in large doses. (Don't worry, cooking reduces the deleterious effects.) Properly prepared, rhubarb has an ability that no other fruit can claim—it balances sweeter foods with a shivering tartness. But even though strawberry-rhubarb pies are popular for that reason, many of us in Vermont still favor straight rhubarb pie.

SUNDAY MORNING FRITTATA

Serves 4

◆◆◆

Start your Sunday morning—or any morning—with this tasty frittata, prettier than an omelet because of the colorful vegetables and the scattering of bright green basil on top. Pop it in the oven to finish cooking while you make the toast or heat the muffins. Although we like the visual and taste combination of zucchini and red bell pepper, you can use whatever vegetables you have on hand, either roasting them the night before or sautéing them until softened, as in this recipe.

We found a recipe for Indian Scramble, a scramble of eggs, corn, Cheddar, and bacon, in Mildred's old notebook. Julie Orton makes this more up-to-date version of the classic, and we highly recommend you try it with fresh corn kernels à la Mildred, if corn's in season.

4 slices bacon

2 tablespoons olive oil

½ red onion, coarsely chopped (¼ cup)

1 small zucchini, diced (about 1 cup)

½ red bell pepper, diced (about 1 cup)

4 large eggs

¼ cup whole milk

½ cup sour cream

¾ teaspoon minced fresh sage, or ¼ teaspoon dried

¾ teaspoon minced fresh thyme, or ¼ teaspoon dried

½ cup grated Cheddar cheese

8 leaves fresh basil, rolled and thinly sliced (about ½ cup)

Preheat the oven to 350°F.

Lay the bacon in a single layer on a rimmed baking sheet and place in the oven. Remove from the oven when almost fully cooked, 10 to 12 minutes (keep your eye on it, since thin-sliced bacon will cook more quickly than thick). Transfer to a paper towel to drain excess fat.

Meanwhile, heat the olive oil in an ovenproof 9-inch skillet over medium-high heat; add the onion and cook until soft, about 5 minutes. Add the zucchini and bell pepper and lightly sauté until soft, about 5 minutes. (If using preroasted vegetables, sauté until warmed through.) In a small bowl, whisk together the eggs, milk, sour cream, sage, and thyme and pour evenly over the vegetables in the pan. Roll the pan so the eggs cover the whole pan, and cook for less than a minute.

Crumble the cooked bacon and the cheese evenly over the egg mixture. Place the pan in the oven to bake for 10 minutes.

Remove from the oven and slide the frittata from the pan onto a cutting board. Neatly cut it into four even pieces. Top with the fresh basil and serve.

EGG LOVE

Americans' affection for eggs was at an all-time high in 1945, when the consumption per person was 405 eggs per year. Even though these days that's down to only 263 a year, that's still an average of five a week.

VERMONT MAPLE-LACED
BREAKFAST SAUSAGE

Makes 12 PATTIES

It's no surprise that a Vermont breakfast sausage would have just a touch of sweetness provided by Vermont maple syrup! This quick (remember to mix it together the night before) and easy recipe is a perfect accompaniment to Mildred's Buttermilk Griddlecakes (page 12) or to farm-fresh eggs.

1 pound ground pork

¾ teaspoon ground sage

½ teaspoon freshly ground white pepper

½ teaspoon freshly ground black pepper

1½ teaspoons ground fennel seeds

¼ teaspoon ground cloves

2 teaspoons salt

3 tablespoons pure maple syrup (make sure it's from Vermont!)

1 teaspoon vegetable oil

¼ cup apple juice, cider, or water (optional)

In a large bowl, combine the pork, sage, white and black pepper, fennel seeds, cloves, salt, and syrup and mix thoroughly with a wooden spoon or with your hands. Cover tightly with plastic wrap and refrigerate for at least 2 hours and up to 2 days.

Form the mixture into twelve patties and flatten them slightly. Heat the oil in a large skillet over medium heat, carefully add the patties, and cook until crispy on both sides, about 3 minutes per side. If your patties are thick, add the liquid of your choice—apple juice, cider, or water—to the pan after you flip to help cook them through. Your patties will be done when the liquid evaporates.

✃ JERSEY GIRLS

The iconic black-and-white Holstein, the sweet-eyed Jersey, the hardy Ayrshire, the almost dainty Guernsey, and the Brown Swiss, whose hooves and mouths seem designed for open grazing on Vermont's hillsides, are the most common purebred cows in Vermont. Jerseys, which arrived in the 1850s, loomed large in Vermont history, as the high levels of butterfat in Jerseys' milk (4.9 percent, in contrast to 2.5 to 3.6 percent in Holsteins) was preferred for making butter. Vermont Jerseys became internationally known when a West Randolph herd won first prize for its butter at the Paris Exposition in 1889 and again at the World's Columbian Exposition in 1893.

CRANBERRY-ORANGE COUNTRY SCONES

Makes 12 LARGE SCONES

———◆◆———

Lyman Orton recalls learning to ski as a young boy back in the bear-trap-binding-and-rope-tow days, coming home tired and happy to steaming hot chocolate and fortifying fresh-baked scones. Mildred's scones, due to the whole wheat flour, are rather dense and slightly serious; we found it necessary to eat them right away, as they did not keep for more than a half hour without becoming too heavy for today's tastes. We add a bit of levity and longevity to our scones with the tang of citrus and cranberries and the lightness of cream and all-purpose flour.

4 cups unbleached
all-purpose flour, plus more
for dusting

1 cup sugar,
plus more for sprinkling

1 teaspoon salt

2 tablespoons baking powder

¾ cup (1½ sticks)
unsalted butter, frozen

2 cups fresh cranberries

1 tablespoon
grated orange zest

½ cup heavy cream

½ cup fresh orange juice

2 large eggs

Whole milk, for brushing

Preheat the oven to 425°F. Line two baking sheets with parchment paper.

In a medium bowl, combine the flour, sugar, salt, and baking powder. Using the large holes of a box grater, grate the butter into the flour mixture. Mix with a fork to evenly distribute the butter. When the butter is generally absorbed, and the mixture resembles pea-size pieces, stir in the cranberries and orange zest.

In a separate bowl, stir together the cream, orange juice, and eggs. Slowly add the egg mixture to the flour mixture and stir until blended, just until a rough dough forms. Take care not to overmix.

Flour the surface of a wooden cutting board. Turn out the dough and gently shape it into a ball, then press it lightly into a rectangle 2 to 2½ inches high. Using a dough cutter or a knife, cut the dough crosswise into six smaller rectangles and then cut these into twelve equal triangles. Place the triangles evenly spaced about 2 inches apart on the prepared baking sheets and flatten them slightly.

Using a pastry brush, brush the scones lightly with milk and sprinkle the tops with sugar. Bake for about 20 minutes, or until lightly browned.

BLUEBERRY AND ZUCCHINI QUICK BREAD

Makes TWO 8½ × 4½-INCH LOAVES

In most gardens, the blueberries are ripening just as the zucchini is starting to get big, so the two are a natural combination for a tasty quick bread. The zucchini contributes moisture, while the berries add a sweet note, and the combination of the dark green zucchini shreds mixed with the blueberries creates beauty when the bread is sliced. Eat hot from the oven, or toast slices and smother with sweet blueberry syrup as a breakfast treat.

8 tablespoons (1 stick) unsalted butter, melted, plus 1 teaspoon for the pans

3 cups unbleached all-purpose flour, plus more for the pans

2 teaspoons ground cinnamon

1 teaspoon baking soda

¼ teaspoon baking powder

1 teaspoon sea salt

1½ cups sugar

3 large eggs

1 teaspoon pure vanilla extract

¼ cup plain yogurt

¼ cup vegetable oil

2 cups grated zucchini (about 1 medium zucchini)

1 pint fresh blueberries

Zest of 1 lemon (2 to 3 teaspoons)

Preheat the oven to 350°F and position a rack in the center. Lightly butter and flour two 8½ × 4½-inch loaf pans, tapping out the excess flour. (If they are nonstick, skip this step.)

In a large bowl, stir together the flour, cinnamon, baking soda, baking powder, and salt and set aside.

In the bowl of a stand mixer fitted with the whisk attachment, beat the sugar and melted butter on medium speed until blended, then add the eggs. Reduce the mixer speed to low and mix in the vanilla, yogurt, and oil. Gradually add the flour mixture. Add the zucchini and beat until blended. By hand, fold in the blueberries and the lemon zest with a spatula. Pour the batter into the prepared pans and spread it evenly.

Bake until a toothpick inserted into the center of each loaf comes out clean, 40 to 45 minutes. Let cool in the pan on a wire rack for 10 minutes before slicing and serving.

CHAPTER 2

The KITCHEN GARDEN

A S SURE AS LILAC TREES DECORATE THE FRONTS of old farmhouses in Vermont, a vegetable garden most likely grows in the back. Our soil sprouts rocks (stone walls aren't just picturesque), and our growing season is notoriously short. But we've inherited the tenaciousness of our ancestors, who only knew New England's rocky soil and fickle weather. Our abundant farmers' markets brim with the heirloom and organic vegetables and fruits we can grow here. In fact, we lead the country in the number of farmers' markets per capita—and that's with a growing season a mere four months long!

SOUPS, SALADS, *and* SIDES

Vermont Apples

A PERFECT FALL DAY FOR CIDER

LEO AND ELLA ORTON, NINTH-GENERATION VER-monters, know how to take advantage of a perfect fall day—and their father, Eliot.

They were helping peel apples for an apple pie, using a cool tool from the Store that peels the apple in one long strip while cutting it into perfect slices and, coring it to boot. They took turns cranking the handle and ate the long strips of peel like Lady and Tramp ate spaghetti, each taking an end and almost meeting in the middle. Giggles rang through the kitchen.

"We need more apples!" Leo shouted, and he ran out to the garage and hopped onto his miniature electric John Deere tractor. Ella popped onto the seat next to him, and off they drove down to the apple trees by the edge of the field. The sun shone brightly, and the air was as crisp as the big red apples weighing down the trees' branches.

As soon as they had a bucket full, Leo, a true Vermonter, suggested making apple cider. So Eliot pulled the cider press out of the garage and the kids loaded the apples into the wooden press while Eliot cranked. Minutes later, cool, golden cider flowed into a big glass mason jar, poised perfectly to catch every last delicious drop. You can't get more fresh—or more Vermont—than that!

(RIGHT) Ella, Leo, and Eliot Orton press cider from apples from their small orchard.

IF YOU FOLLOW THE BACK ROADS OUT OF WESTON, passing the cemetery and the white church on your right, head south and straight uphill, you will eventually find yourself in the small village of Landgrove. The town ordinance dictates no paved roads, so during the muddy season in April when snow melts, the ruts in the road can be so deep that cars are often left abandoned.

Before you enter the open valley, there is a small farm on the right, with groves of ancient apple trees, a few plum and pear trees among them. For more than fifty years, Dr. Karl Pfister cultivated these her-itage varieties and would often deliver his homemade cider to friends and neighbors.

If you have ever tasted fresh apple cider, you will never forget the sweet nectar, and Dr. Pfister's cider was especially good because it was pressed from thirteen varieties of apples: seven heirloom varieties: Gravenstein, Wealthy, Golden Russet, Maiden Blush, Northern Spy, Westfield Seek-No-Further, and Hyslop Crab; and six modern types: McIntosh, Cortland, Macoun, Spartan, Joyce, and Monroe. The charm that an old orchard holds goes hand in hand with the sublime taste of the heirloom fruit.

CURRIED ASPARAGUS SOUP

Serves 6

---

*I*n early spring, we can't get enough fresh asparagus, lightly steamed with butter and lemon juice or oiled and charred on the grill. Near the end of the asparagus season, once we have eaten it every night and frozen a few bags for a winter meal, we make this delicious soup. You'll find the Asian twist, with curry and coconut milk, a nice match for the asparagus. At the end of cooking, a fistful of spinach brings out a healthy, spring-bright green color, especially beautiful when garnished with asparagus tips and cream.

---

2 pounds asparagus
(about 16 spears)

2 tablespoons olive oil

1 medium onion, chopped

1 clove garlic, pressed or
finely chopped

2 tablespoons curry powder

2 tablespoons
light brown sugar

2 tablespoons creamy peanut
butter (optional)

1 russet potato, cut into
1-inch cubes (about 2 cups)

1 (8-ounce) can coconut milk

1½ to 2 cups packed
fresh spinach leaves

1 cup heavy cream,
plus more for finishing

½ teaspoon salt

¼ teaspoon freshly ground
black pepper

Snap the asparagus to remove the tough base and cut the stalks into 1-inch pieces, reserving some of the tips for garnish.

In a 2-quart stockpot, heat the oil over medium heat. Add the onion and garlic and cook, stirring, until soft and translucent, 5 to 8 minutes. Add the curry powder, brown sugar, and peanut butter and stir with a wooden spoon until fragrant. Add the asparagus (except for the reserved tips) and potato and continue to stir, allowing all the flavors to infuse, for about 5 minutes.

Pour in the coconut milk and 3 cups water and cook until the potatoes are tender, about 10 minutes. Add the spinach leaves during the last 5 minutes of cooking. Meanwhile, in a small saucepan, heat 1 inch of water. Set the reserved asparagus tips in a steamer basket and steam for 2 minutes, until tender but toothsome (alternatively, steam the asparagus tips in the microwave).

Using an immersion blender directly in the pot, puree the soup until smooth. Alternatively, transfer the soup to a blender in batches and puree—be careful, as the soup is hot. Return the soup to the pot, if necessary, add the cream, season with salt and freshly ground black pepper to taste, and heat just until hot—do not boil. Serve hot or cold. Garnish with a drizzle of cream and the reserved asparagus tips.

FARMERS' MARKET GAZPACHO, TWO WAYS

The farmers' market dazzles in late summer, and tables laden with ripe, juicy tomatoes in red, yellow, merlot, pink, and with green stripes and swirls stop us in our tracks. Piles of cucumbers and peppers in all colors beckon. On hot days, the thought of cold gazpacho cools and tempts.

A blender or food processor makes a smooth gazpacho with the quick push of a button, but the hand-chopped red tomato version has a more substantial texture that we find pleasing. For a colorful variation, try the golden gazpacho on page 28, sweetened with a peach or an orange and infused with sweet basil. This unconventional gazpacho can be as spicy or mellow as you wish, depending on the amount of hot sauce you use. Garnish with the most beautiful edible flowers you can find.

RED TOMATO GAZPACHO

Serves 8

4 large tomatoes, seeded and finely chopped (2½ cups)

1 large cucumber, peeled and finely chopped (1¾ cups)

1 red onion, finely chopped (1 cup)

1 medium red bell pepper, seeded and finely chopped (1 cup)

1 cup chopped arugula

½ cup chopped fresh sweet basil

½ cup chopped fresh flat-leaf parsley

2 cloves garlic, minced (1 teaspoon)

⅓ cup rice vinegar or red wine vinegar

3 tablespoons olive oil

Salt and freshly ground black pepper

Calendula petals or other edible flowers, for garnish

In a large bowl, mix the tomatoes, cucumber, onion, bell pepper, arugula, basil, parsley, garlic, vinegar, and olive oil (or, if you prefer a smooth gazpacho, combine the ingredients in a blender in batches and puree). Cover and refrigerate until well chilled, at least 4 hours and preferably overnight. Taste, and season with salt and pepper as desired. Serve the soup in chilled bowls, garnished with calendula petals.

YELLOW TOMATO GAZPACHO

Serves 8

1 navel orange or peach, peeled, seeded (or pitted), and cut into 1-inch pieces

4 medium yellow tomatoes, coarsely chopped (2 cups)

2 red, orange, or yellow bell peppers, coarsely chopped (2 cups)

1 medium cucumber, peeled and coarsely chopped (1½ cups)

½ sweet onion, finely chopped (½ cup)

1 clove garlic, minced (½ teaspoon)

¼ cup coarsely chopped fresh sweet basil leaves, plus sprigs for garnish

¾ cup olive oil

¼ cup sherry vinegar

¼ teaspoon fiery hot sauce or Tabasco

Salt and freshly ground black pepper

Crème fraîche, for garnish

In a blender or food processor fitted with the steel blade, combine the orange, tomatoes, bell peppers, cucumber, onion, and garlic and pulse to coarsely chop. Add the basil, olive oil, vinegar, and hot sauce and pulse to combine, either until smooth or keeping a few chunks for texture. Cover and refrigerate until well chilled, at least 1 hour. Taste and season with salt and pepper as desired. Serve the soup in chilled bowls, garnished with a swirl of crème fraîche and a sprig of basil.

HEARTY *vs.* SOFT GREENS

We're pretty wild about throwing greens in just about anything: eggs, pastas, risottos, soups. Their nutritional boost alone makes this a good idea; their bright color and intensity of taste up the ante.

But all greens are not created equal when it comes to cooking. Hearty greens, such as turnip, dandelion, chicory, mustard, and broccoli rabe, require some tender loving care to reduce their inherent bitterness: Blanch, shock in ice water, squeeze dry, and chop before adding these greens to a recipe. Kale and collard greens, also hearty, don't need such special treatment: Trim the tough stems, chop the leaves, and you're good to go. Soft greens, such as spinach, arugula, and watercress, just need to be washed and they're ready for use.

GREEN MOUNTAIN GREENS AND SAUSAGE SOUP

Serves 6 TO 8

—◆◆—

*E*verything about this soup is satisfying, from the sweet and spicy sausages to the hearty greens. We're big fans of healthy greens, and kale, spinach, and collards grow in most Vermont gardens long into fall. In this recipe, we've used collard greens, an overlooked leaf that deserves more attention, but feel free to use kale or spinach (just add the spinach at the very end). Collard's flat, open leaves are easy to prepare: Stack them and roll them up in a tube, then slice across the roll to cut the leaves into thin strips, or "chiffonade." If you use kale or spinach, rip off the tough ribs and slice the leaves into strips.

We've also added corn, fresh off the cob, to give a hint of sweetness. (We strip corn off the cob in the summer and freeze it so we can enjoy sweet corn all year long.) Serve this soup with fragrant herbed cheese bread (see page 157) and a pat of Vermont-made butter for a truly soul-satisfying meal.

---

4 tablespoons olive oil

3 hot Italian sausages, cut into ½-inch pieces

3 sweet Italian sausages, cut into ½-inch pieces

1 onion, finely chopped (about 1 cup)

4 cloves garlic, minced

¼ teaspoon red pepper flakes

Salt and freshly ground black pepper

2 pounds Yukon Gold potatoes (6 to 8), peeled and cut into ¾-inch pieces

4 cups chicken stock

1 pound collard greens, stacked and sliced into fine strips (about 6 cups)

1 cup corn kernels (preferably cut fresh from the cob)

Heat 1 tablespoon of the oil in an 8-quart stockpot over medium-high heat until shimmering. Add the hot and sweet sausages and cook, stirring occasionally, until lightly browned, 4 to 5 minutes. Transfer to a bowl and set aside.

Reduce the heat to medium and add the onion, garlic, and red pepper flakes. Season with a generous sprinkling of salt and black pepper. Cook, stirring frequently, until the onion is translucent, 3 to 5 minutes. Add the potatoes, stock, and 4 cups water and bring to a boil.

Reduce the heat to low and simmer for 10 minutes, until the potatoes are just tender.

With a measuring cup or soup ladle, transfer 1 cup of the vegetable solids and 1 cup of the stock to a blender. Add the remaining 3 tablespoons oil and blend until very smooth and well combined, about 1 minute. Set aside.

Add the collard greens to the pot with the soup and simmer for 5 minutes. Add the sausages and corn and continue to simmer until the greens are tender, 8 to 10 minutes more.

Stir the pureed soup mixture back into the pot, return everything to a simmer, and serve hot.

ROASTED CARROT AND BUTTERNUT SQUASH SOUP

Serves 6 TO 8

Roasting vegetables before adding them to a soup brings out deeper flavors, and the soup is ready in half the time. Roasting also makes it easier to peel the squash: Simply slice it in half, then in half again to form quarters, and roast. Once the squash is soft, it's a snap to scoop out the flesh.

This soup is a veritable feast for the senses: the exotic fragrances of the spices garnished with crème fraîche, lime zest, and fresh cilantro, the visual beauty of the finished soup, and the rich, deep taste of the roasted vegetables.

1 teaspoon vegetable oil

6 medium carrots, scrubbed

2 medium shallots, quartered

1 medium butternut squash, quartered lengthwise

2 tablespoons olive oil

2 tablespoons unsalted butter

2 cloves garlic, minced (2 teaspoons)

1 onion, coarsely chopped (1 cup)

1 teaspoon salt

2 tablespoons grated fresh ginger

½ teaspoon ground turmeric

1 teaspoon curry powder

½ teaspoon freshly ground black pepper

4 cups vegetable stock

GARNISH (optional)

5 sprigs fresh cilantro

½ cup crème fraîche, or whole milk plain yogurt

Zest of 1 lime

Preheat the oven to 400°F.

MAKE THE SOUP: Lightly oil a shallow 13 × 9-inch baking dish and spread the carrots, shallots, and squash in the dish in a single layer. Roast for 30 minutes. With a fork or tongs, transfer the carrots and shallots to a cutting board (they will cook faster than the squash) and bake the squash for 15 minutes more, until soft. Let the squash cool slightly, then scoop out the seeds and remove and discard the skin; set the flesh aside in a bowl. When cool enough to handle, slice the carrots into 1-inch lengths and coarsely chop the shallots.

Meanwhile, in a 4-quart stockpot, heat the olive oil and butter over medium heat. Add the garlic, onion, and salt. Reduce the heat to low and cook, stirring occasionally, for 5 minutes, until softened.

Stir in the ginger, turmeric, curry powder, and pepper. Cook for 5 minutes to allow the fragrant oils from the spices to release. Add the roasted carrots, shallots, and squash and cook, stirring occasionally, for 5 minutes more, so the vegetables absorb all the flavors.

Pour in the stock and 2 cups water and adjust the heat to maintain a simmer. Simmer the soup for about 25 minutes, until everything is tender. Test for doneness by spearing the larger pieces of squash with a sharp knife. Remove from the heat and use an immersion blender to puree the soup directly in the pot. Alternatively, transfer the soup to a blender or food processor and puree until smooth—be careful, as the soup is hot.

MAKE THE GARNISH: Chop the cilantro leaves and combine with the yogurt and the lime zest. Drop a large tablespoonful into the center of each bowl of hot soup just before serving.

FIRE-ROASTED TOMATO CHEDDAR SOUP
WITH CRUNCHY CHEESE STRAWS

Serves 6 TO 8

The combination of fire-roasted tomatoes and Vermont Cheddar is a time-honored favorite in these parts, with the cheese adding depth and smoothness to the smoky, rich tomatoes. Fire-roast your own fresh tomatoes as we do here, or substitute a can of fire-roasted tomatoes (we prefer Muir Glen Organic) for a quick, satisfying soup ready to ladle into bowls after less than half an hour of simmering on the stove. Serve with crunchy cheese straws (recipe follows).

6 firm ripe tomatoes
(or one 28-ounce can
fire-roasted tomatoes), halved

2 tablespoons
extra-virgin olive oil

1 medium onion,
coarsely chopped

2 cloves garlic, minced

1 tablespoon curry powder

4 cups chicken stock

1 cup half-and-half

1 teaspoon fresh thyme,
or ½ teaspoon dried

8 ounces Cheddar cheese,
coarsely grated (2 cups)

½ teaspoon salt

¼ teaspoon freshly ground
black pepper

TO FIRE-ROAST THE TOMATOES: Build a fire in a charcoal grill and let it burn until the coals are covered with white ash. Or, with a gas grill, turn all the burners to high and heat for 15 minutes. When the grill is ready, place the tomatoes skin side down on the grill. Cook until the skins are blackened, about 3 minutes. Let cool slightly, then peel the tomatoes, coarsely chop, and set aside in a small bowl. If using canned tomatoes, drain and coarsely chop the tomatoes.

MAKE THE SOUP: In a 2-quart stockpot, heat the oil over medium heat. Add the onion and cook, stirring, until soft and translucent, about 5 minutes. Add the garlic and curry powder and stir for another minute, until fragrant.

Add the tomatoes, stock, half-and-half, and thyme. With a wooden spoon, give it a stir and then bring to a gentle boil. Immediately adjust the heat to maintain a simmer and cook, stirring occasionally, for 15 minutes. Remove from the heat.

Add the cheese, one handful at a time, stirring with a wooden spoon until it is melted. Use an immersion blender to blend the soup directly in the pot until the ingredients have combined, yet are still somewhat chunky. Alternatively, transfer the soup in batches to a blender and pulse to combine— be careful, as the soup is hot. Season with the salt and pepper. Serve warm.

(Continued)

CRUNCHY CHEESE STRAWS

Makes ABOUT 60 CHEESE STRAWS

1⅔ cups unbleached
all-purpose flour,
plus more for dusting

½ teaspoon sea salt

1 teaspoon dry mustard

¼ teaspoon red pepper flakes

8 tablespoons (1 stick)
unsalted butter,
cut into ¼-inch slices,
at room temperature

8 ounces sharp Cheddar
cheese, grated (2 cups)

1 to 3 tablespoons ice water

1 egg yolk

2 tablespoons whole milk

2 tablespoons grated
Parmesan cheese

Thin, crisp pastry sticks with the tang of cayenne and sharp Cheddar, cheese straws are the perfect appetizer for cocktails or church socials alike, and a fine crunchy accompaniment to top the Fire-Roasted Tomato Cheddar Soup (page 33). The simple dough is rolled out and sliced into "straws." For a decorative touch, use a fluted ravioli cutter to achieve a crimped edge. A tin of cheese straws makes an excellent hostess gift.

Preheat the oven to 425°F.

In a medium bowl, whisk together the flour, salt, dry mustard, and red pepper flakes.

In the bowl of a stand mixer fitted with the paddle attachment, beat together the butter and Cheddar on medium speed until thoroughly combined.

With the mixer running on medium speed, slowly add the dry ingredients to the butter and cheese mixture and mix for 1 to 2 minutes. Add the ice water, 1 tablespoon at a time, allowing 30 seconds between each spoonful of water. Stop when the dough comes together into a ball (you may not need all the ice water).

Turn the dough out onto a lightly floured surface. Knead five or six times, just to bring it together into a cohesive ball. With a rolling pin, press the dough into a rectangle, ¼ inch thick. Cut strips ¼ inch wide and 10 to 12 inches in length with a ravioli cutter to give it fluted edges. (If you don't have a ravioli cutter, use a sharp knife.)

Transfer the strips to two ungreased baking sheets with a spatula, placing them ¼ inch apart to allow space for expansion. In a small bowl, whisk together the egg yolk and the milk to make an egg wash. Brush the straws with the egg wash and sprinkle lightly with the Parmesan.

Bake for 12 to 15 minutes, until the straws are just starting to look golden brown and crisp. Transfer to a wire rack to cool slightly. Serve while still hot or at room temperature, and store any extras in a resealable plastic bag or airtight container in the pantry for 1 to 2 weeks.

CORN AND CUCUMBER SUMMER SALAD

Serves 4 TO 6

———◆◆———

This sweet, chunky summer salad is at its best in July, when sweet corn rules the roadside stands. If the grill is hot, cook the corn on the cob over the hot coals rather than steaming it, to give it more flavor. The maple-balsamic vinaigrette will quickly become a staple, delicious on a variety of year-round salads.

If you are lucky enough to find smoked maple syrup (see sidebar on page 37), use it in this salad dressing to give a smoky flavor that is reminiscent of bacon. If you don't have it, you can make it without, but it does make a difference! A little goes a long way, so just add a teaspoon to the standard maple syrup and it will be plenty.

Salt

3 large ears fresh corn, husked

1 pint cherry tomatoes, halved

1 medium cucumber, cut into ½-inch cubes (about 1½ cups)

1 small red onion, thinly sliced into half-moons (about ½ cup)

½ cup finely chopped fresh flat-leaf parsley

½ cup finely chopped fresh cilantro

Juice of 1 lemon (about 3 tablespoons)

¼ cup Maple-Balsamic Vinaigrette, plus more as desired (recipe follows)

Freshly ground black pepper

Fill a large stockpot with 1 inch of water and add 1 teaspoon of salt. Place the corn in the pot in neat layers. Cover the pot and bring to a boil over high heat. Cook until the corn is tender, about 5 minutes. Drain in a colander and let cool enough to touch. Cut each ear in half and stand on one end to cut off the kernels. You should have about 3 cups kernels.

In a medium salad bowl, combine the corn kernels, tomatoes, cucumber, onion, parsley, and cilantro. Add the lemon juice and toss. Add some Maple-Balsamic Vinaigrette (page 37) and toss to coat, then add more if you like. Season with salt and pepper. Cover and refrigerate until chilled, at least 2 hours or up to overnight. Serve chilled. Reserve the balance of the dressing for another salad.

PICK-YOUR-OWN

Pick-your-own farm signs crop up around Vermont in early summer like mushrooms after a rainstorm. Since berries are seasonal and the season is short, folks flock to the farms to make the most of blueberry, strawberry, and raspberry time. Pick-your-own prices are half the retail cost of even farmers' markets; you pay by the honor system, weighing your berries, then pushing money into the slot of a locked cash box. It's great fun for kids, too. Leo and Ella, with stained lips and hands, climb happily back into our car and head home to help make a pie or two.

—ELIOT ORTON

MAPLE-BALSAMIC VINAIGRETTE

Makes ½ CUP

1 teaspoon Dijon mustard

1 large clove garlic, smashed
and minced (1 teaspoon)

2 tablespoons pure
maple syrup

1 teaspoon smoked maple
syrup, optional (see sidebar)

1 tablespoon fresh lemon juice

3 tablespoons balsamic
vinegar

1 tablespoon finely chopped
fresh basil

½ cup extra-virgin olive oil

¼ teaspoon salt

⅛ teaspoon freshly ground
black pepper

In a small bowl, combine the mustard, garlic, maple syrups, lemon juice, vinegar, and basil. Slowly stream in the olive oil while whisking to emulsify. Season with the salt and pepper.

❧ SMOKED MAPLE SYRUP–A NEW TWIST ON AN OLD FAVORITE

A few springs ago, after the sugaring season was finished for the year, Rob Hausslein, owner of Sugar Bob's Finest Kind in Landgrove, Vermont, decided to kick his operation up a notch. He built a fire in his pig roaster, located next to his sugarhouse, and began to smoke syrup.

The pig roaster is a backyard rig: concrete block foundations stacked three high, with a grill and a hood. There, Hausslein roasts a few pigs a year, mostly for charity events. To smoke the maple syrup, he fills a traditional evaporating tray with five gallons of syrup and places it on the grill, putting a piece of sheet metal between the flames and the bottom of the pan to send the smoke around the edges to season the syrup. Hausslein keeps this fire going for two weeks, throwing on logs throughout the day and into the evening.

Purists may think changing the flavor of maple syrup is sinful or at least unpatriotic–certainly un-Vermont. Hausslein maintains that smoked syrup has truly the most authentic flavor, since syrup has always been at least partially seasoned with the smoke that seeps around the edges of wood-fired evaporators.

Pop the top on a bottle of smoked syrup and the complexity of the sweet and smoky flavors is evident. It's easy to imagine possibilities for a creative cook: Barbecue sauce comes to mind, as does grilled salmon drizzled with smoked syrup, and a maple-balsamic vinaigrette (see recipe above). "It's not recommended on pancakes," says Hausslein, "but a fine, lacy drizzle on a side order of sausage and bacon can't be beat."

ROASTED VEGETABLE PLATTER

Serves 4 TO 6

Y*ou might think that a vegetable platter does not need a recipe, and, in theory, we agree. Yet too many cooks will mask vegetables with a fancy sauce, so we include this recipe to prove that vegetables, when slowly roasted, have extraordinary power to please. Not every vegetable can be roasted with success, however, and this recipe reflects our tried-and-true medley, with tiny young eggplant, colorful potatoes, wispy asparagus, and delicate endive alongside the usual suspects: zucchini, summer squash, and bell peppers.*

¼ to ½ cup extra-virgin olive oil

2 pounds assorted small potatoes, scrubbed

2 endive heads, halved lengthwise

1 small eggplant, cut into thick wedges

2 red or green bell peppers, halved and seeded

1 small zucchini, halved lengthwise

1 small yellow squash, halved lengthwise

1 bunch (1 pound) thin asparagus

2 sprigs fresh rosemary

2 sprigs fresh sage

1 teaspoon sea salt

½ teaspoon freshly ground black pepper

Sprigs of fresh thyme, oregano, or parsley, for garnish

Preheat the oven to 400°F and position a rack in the center.

Pour a small amount of olive oil over the bottom of a 13 × 9-inch baking pan and lay the vegetables flat, with the "cupped" side up to hold the oil you're about to drizzle. The whole pan will be full, but try to keep everything in one layer, tucking the vegetables close to one another so they remain succulent during the cooking process. This is key; otherwise, they may dry out. Since the asparagus is thin, push the stalks into a little pile or bunch; they tend to cook faster and this keeps them from wilting. Evenly drizzle the olive oil over the vegetables, starting with ¼ cup, though you may need a little more to give everything a light coating. Tuck the rosemary and sage sprigs around the vegetables and season with salt and black pepper. (We've given you a measurement, but use your own judgment for how much to use of each; we prefer to be liberal with both salt and black pepper, since this can really give the vegetables good flavor.)

Roast for 20 minutes. Remove the pan from the oven and flip the vegetables so they cook evenly. Reduce the oven temperature to 325°F, return the pan to oven, and roast for 30 minutes more, then check to see if the delicate vegetables are done. Remove any vegetables that are ready before the others, placing them on a serving dish and tenting loosely with foil. Return the pan to the oven for 10 minutes more, or until all the vegetables are done.

Serve on a platter, neatly and colorfully arranged. Garnish with sprigs of thyme, oregano, and/or parsley. We enjoy this as a main dish, a side dish, or served over ravioli, pasta, or polenta. Leftovers are perfect for our Roasted Vegetable Lasagna (page 174).

 CELEBRATING A TOWN'S ROOTS

If you visit Vermont in late October, don't miss the Gilfeather Turnip Festival in Wardsboro, Vermont (population: nearly 900), the town where the delectable tuber first saw the light of day. An official Vermont heritage vegetable with an intriguing story, the Gilfeather turnip can grow as big as a soccer ball and maintains an uncommon tenderness and sweetness that early Vermont frosts only improve.

The local turnip became part of Wardsboro lore in the early 1900s, when John Gilfeather experimented with hybridization at his hillside farm. The late Gilfeather was described as a "lanky bachelor of few words," and none of those words revealed the source of his seeds. When Gilfeather developed his singular, eponymous turnip, he jealously guarded its secret. He sold the turnips by the wagonload as far away as Northampton, Massachusetts—but he hoarded the seeds for himself, cutting off the tops and bottoms of his turnips so no one else could grow them!

After his death, neighbors managed to save a bottle of seeds. Now gardeners can order seeds through a few catalogs and local nurseries, and the curious can order three pounds of the genuine article at harvesttime from The Vermont Country Store.

At the Gilfeather Festival, admission is free. Enter and you're surrounded by all things turnip. Buy a turnip to take home and a T-shirt or two. Check out the ugliest turnip contest and the biggest (this year, twenty-five pounds). And sample what local cooks have created: turnip bread, carrot and turnip cake, mashed potatoes and turnips, and other turnip treats. Sip Gilfeather turnip soup or try a turnip doughnut. We like ours raw, sliced thin, with a dab of butter and flaky sea salt.

∽ KNOW YOUR POTATOES

Potatoes don't mind the cool air and rocky soil of Vermont. We even have one named after our own state—the Green Mountain—and gardeners grow many varieties in all colors and shapes.

To use potatoes properly, it helps to know what makes a good "baker" or "boiler." Good bakers are also called mealy or floury potatoes, and are characterized by a dry and delicate texture that readily crumbles. This dry texture is the result of high starch; when baked, the large starch granules swell up and separate, becoming ethereally light and fluffy.

High-starch potatoes like russets mysteriously absorb rich cream and butter without becoming cloying or heavy, which is why they are also perfect for mashing, thinly slicing for a gratin, or simply baking. The ability to absorb liquids and fats is part of their charm, and the floury texture rends to a soft and unctuous side dish.

Low-starch potatoes, on the other hand—common examples are red-skinned and new potatoes—are often described as waxy and have a higher moisture content and denser texture. Thin skins make them great for boiling without peeling; they'll hold their shape in recipes that ask for a little toothy quality such as potato salads or hash browns.

An all-purpose potato, such as the Yukon Gold or the Green Mountain, falls in between. These middle-of-the-road potatoes can be wrestled into service for either mashing or baking. When boiled, they become wonderfully soft without disintegrating, maintaining a bit of decorum. And yet they can absorb a good dash of olive oil infused with rosemary and can be trusted to bake in a hot oven until crisp.

GREEN GODDESS DRESSING
AND POTATO SALAD

Makes 1 CUP; Serves 4

———◆◆———

*B*efore bottled dressing, all good cooks made their own salad dressing, and often it would be a cooking oil blended with cider vinegar. For a creamier style, they would add buttermilk, still an excellent simple dressing. We've come a long way when it comes to recipes for dressing, and we love this lemony fresh herb dressing on almost anything. It's worlds apart from the bottled version, with which you may be familiar.

Serve it over fresh asparagus, as a dip for artichokes or a crudité platter, spooned over a pile of salad greens, or to dress up new potatoes in a cold salad as we've done here. The piquant herbs and the anchovies draw out the best in just about every vegetable we've tried. This recipe makes more than you'll need for one sitting—or maybe not!

DRESSING

½ cup mayonnaise

½ cup sour cream

3 tablespoons
extra-virgin olive oil

2 canned anchovy fillets

½ clove garlic, finely chopped

Juice of 1 lemon (3 tablespoons)

1 tablespoon
fresh tarragon leaves

1 tablespoon
fresh parsley leaves

¼ cup fresh basil leaves

Salt and freshly ground
black pepper

SALAD

Salt

2 pounds medium
new red potatoes (about 8)

½ red onion, finely chopped

1 head butterhead lettuce,
washed and dried

½ cup finely chopped
fresh chives

MAKE THE DRESSING: In a blender or food processor, combine the mayonnaise, sour cream, olive oil, anchovies, garlic, lemon juice, tarragon, parsley, and basil. Blend until smooth, 1 minute. Season with salt and pepper. Refrigerate until ready to use.

MAKE THE SALAD: Bring a pot of lightly salted water to a boil. Scrub the potatoes, leaving the skins on, and place them in a steamer basket. Set the steamer basket over the boiling water and cook until the potatoes are tender when pierced with a sharp knife, about 30 minutes, depending on size. When the potatoes are cool enough to handle, slice or quarter them.

Place the potatoes in a salad bowl along with the onion and spoon ¼ cup of the dressing over the top. Toss to fully coat, adding more dressing to taste. Chill and serve on a bed of soft butterhead lettuce leaves; garnish with chopped chives. Reserve the remainder of the dressing in a mason jar to use over the course of a week.

CREAMY SWEET CORN
PUDDING SOUFFLÉ

Serves 4 AS MAIN DISH, 6 TO 8 AS SIDE

Soufflés are satisfying, impressive, and easier to make than you might think. In the height of corn season, no one wants to turn on the oven, but this soufflé is worth it. Creamy and delicious, it's the perfect accompaniment to grilled chicken, steak, or a simple salad. You'll need fresh corn on the cob, or the corn kernels you so wisely froze in the summer; you can use commercially frozen corn, although the flavor will be compromised, but do not use canned. If you're feeling extravagant, substitute half-and-half or pure cream for some or all of the whole milk for a decadently rich soufflé. Serve as a main course with salad for a vegetarian kitchen table supper, or as a side dish for a real crowd-pleaser at a dinner party.

3 tablespoons unsalted butter, plus more for the baking dish

6 ears fresh corn, husked

1 cup whole milk

4 scallions or 1 small onion, finely chopped (¾ cup)

3 tablespoons unbleached all-purpose flour

1 tablespoon finely diced jalapeño

½ cup ricotta cheese

2 tablespoons pure maple syrup

½ teaspoon salt, plus more as needed

¼ teaspoon freshly ground black pepper

3 eggs, separated

Preheat the oven to 375°F. Generously butter a 1-quart ovenproof baking or soufflé dish.

Remove the kernels from the corncobs (you should have about 4 cups). In a food processor fitted with the steel blade, puree 2 cups of the corn kernels with the milk until smooth, 1 to 2 minutes. Set a fine sieve over a large bowl and pour in the corn puree. Press on the solids with a rubber spatula to extract all the liquid. Set aside both the liquid and the corn puree left in the sieve.

In a medium saucepan, melt the butter over low heat. As soon as you see it start to brown, add the scallions and cook for 1 minute, stirring with a wooden spoon to keep the butter from browning. Stir in the flour, then whisk in the corn-milk liquid and cook over medium heat, stirring continuously, for 5 minutes, until it starts to thicken. Remove from the heat, stir in the remaining corn kernels, corn puree, jalapeño, ricotta, maple syrup, salt, and pepper.

In a small bowl, slowly ladle a small amount of the hot liquid over the egg yolks while stirring vigorously. Once blended, pour everything back into the saucepan and briskly stir again. (This tempers the egg yolks and keeps them from curdling or cooking too quickly.) Continue stirring over low heat until well blended, then remove from the heat.

In the bowl of a stand mixer fitted with the whisk attachment, or in a large bowl using a handheld mixer, whip the egg whites until they hold firm peaks. Using a rubber spatula, slowly fold the egg whites into the corn-milk base, gently stirring to fully incorporate. Transfer the batter to the prepared

dish and set in a large roasting pan. Pour boiling water into the baking pan until it comes halfway up the side of the baking dish.

Bake for 55 minutes, or until the pudding is golden and puffy and is sturdy when jiggled, making sure that the center is firm. Bring to the table hot and serve warm.

KEEPS *on* CUTTING KERNELS

Kernel Corn-Cutter and Creamer

This ingenious corn-cutter provides the only known method of obtaining a truly cream style corn off the cob. The skin of the kernel remains on the cob. Or by a simple adjustment, it will also cleanly cut off the whole kernels so you can obtain kernel corn off the cob with ease and dispatch. Cuts, shreds and scrapes in one operation, eliminates labor and saves time and effort. Many people use this for home canning or preserving corn for freezing. Simply place the 17½ inches long wood tool over a dish and draw the ear of corn over the metal tool. Only $2.00 each. (Ship. wt. 1 lb.) (See page 30.)

Back in 1958, The Vermont Country Store introduced a Kernel Corn-Cutter and Creamer, a long wooden tool that cuts, shreds, or scrapes corn off the cob "with ease and dispatch." The ingenious kitchen tool not only is "the only known method of obtaining a truly cream style corn off the cob," but also quickly cuts kernels for freezing. The Store still sells this handy item today.

VERMONT CHEDDAR AND SPINACH CUSTARD

Makes FOUR 8-OUNCE RAMEKINS; *Serves* 4

*C*heddar and spinach are old friends and are beautifully paired in this delicate custard, which makes a fine brunch entrée when served on a bed of mixed greens. Baked in small ramekins, the custards are inverted onto plates like a crustless quiche. This custard is pure comfort food for all ages, and an elegant way to eat your greens. Delicious for breakfast, too!

If you are concerned about calories, switch out the cream for whole milk and you will still have delicious custard. Freshly grated nutmeg is a must with many an egg dish, and the nutmeg grater that was a top seller in The Vermont Country Store's first catalog is still sold in the Store today.

2 tablespoons unsalted butter, at room temperature

¼ teaspoon sea salt, plus more as needed

3 cups fresh spinach leaves

1 cup heavy cream

4 large egg yolks

1 cup shredded sharp Cheddar cheese

⅛ teaspoon freshly ground black pepper

⅛ teaspoon freshly grated nutmeg

Preheat the oven to 325°F. Generously butter four 8-ounce ramekins.

Bring a large pot of lightly salted water to a boil. Add the spinach and cook until tender, about 3 minutes. Drain and rinse under cold water. A handful at a time, squeeze out the excess moisture from the spinach. Chop coarsely. (You should have about 1 cup chopped spinach.)

In a medium bowl, whisk together the cream and egg yolks until well combined. Stir in the cooked spinach, cheese, salt, pepper, and nutmeg. Divide the custard evenly among the ramekins and place them in a roasting pan. Pour boiling water into the roasting pan until it comes halfway up the sides of the ramekins.

Bake for 35 minutes, or until the custard is set when given a slight shake or a sharp knife inserted into the center comes out clean. Remove the ramekins from the roasting pan and let stand for 5 minutes. Run a knife around the inside of each ramekin and invert onto separate plates to unmold, or serve directly from the hot oven to the table in the ramekins (be careful, as they'll be hot!).

CHAPTER 3

Small
FAMILY FARMS

MORE THAN A CENTURY AFTER MILDRED WAS born on a small family farm, we still value our working landscape, so much so that Vermont was ranked first in the country for local food production and consumption in a recent USDA census. Our numerous farmers' markets abound with heirloom and organic vegetables and fruits, grass-fed poultry, heritage pork, and creamy goat cheese.

In her late nineties, Mildred kept wanting to go "back to the farm," that idyllic place that celebrated the deeply Vermont way of life of the farmer. All across the country, and especially in Vermont, we're trying to go back to the farm in our cooking, too. ◆

CHICKEN, TURKEY, *and* PORK

Vermont Farm Life

THE SMELL OF A WORKING LANDSCAPE

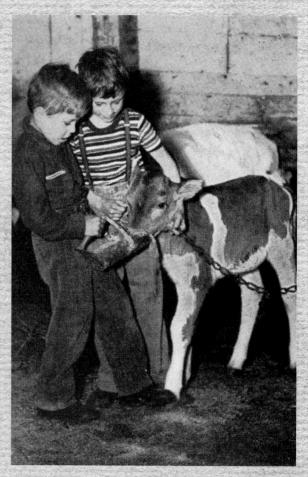

Lyman Orton and his pal Calvin Walker at Walker farm, 1947.

THE SENSE OF SMELL EVOKES MEMORY AND EMOTION in a way no other sense can. Growing up in Weston, I was surrounded daily by the strong, distinct smells of a working landscape, which even now connect me irrevocably to the farms, forests, and open fields of Vermont.

We had a couple of wood-product manufacturing businesses in the village, the Weston Bowl Mill on one end of town and the Weston Toy Shop on the other. I recall the odors of sawdust, linseed oil, and piles of rough-sawn timber. Just one whiff brings back a forgotten scene as sharp as a photograph.

The several working farms on either side of the village have been there since my father was a boy. The Walker farm to the north (where Lyman spent his youth milking cows) and the Foster farm to the south smelled of animals, feed, manure, machinery, the welcoming waft of old barns, the tang of fresh-cut hay.

Driving to Weston in the spring, down-country visitors recoil and roll up their windows at the pungent smell of manure-covered fields. Vermonters breathe it in, knowing it means sweet corn in July.

—ELIOT ORTON

FARMERS' MARKETS ENLIVEN COMMUNITIES from New England's rocky shores to the coast of California. With the abundance of small family farms here in Vermont, we are lucky enough to have scores of summer markets and a good smattering of year-round ones, too, to feed our need for fresh-grown food.

One of our favorites is Londonderry's West River Farmers' Market, just down the road from our store in Weston. Farmers and vendors arrive early every Saturday with bushels of fresh-picked organic and locally grown produce, and some of the best meats, baked goods, artisan cheese, and arts and crafts around. Soon the market is buzzing with activity, turning it into one of the best weekly social events of the summer.

Knowing who actually grows our food, where it was grown, and what it was grown with—or, more crucially, without—is increasingly important to us. And there's nothing like the taste of a tomato or zucchini that was picked the same morning it was put on the table for dinner. It's as nourishing for the spirit as it is for the body.

—GARDNER ORTON

ALONG THE RIDGE OF THE GREEN MOUNTAINS the soil was shallow and the growing season for crops was three months and sometimes less. This kind of farming was a struggle against nature's handicaps. The fact that our stalwart and rugged Vermonters mastered these hazards for over 200 years and prospered is a tribute to their great character, which factor gave the nation more national leaders per capita than from any other state.

By "prospered," however, I do not mean the accumulation of dollar bills. They prospered by the building of character. The greater the challenge, the greater the response.

—VREST ORTON, *THE STORY OF THE VERMONT COUNTRY STORE*

WE *Support* LOCAL FOOD

As a company that celebrates the joys of a simpler time, The Vermont Country Store is proud to support the Vermont Cheese Council, Slow Food Vermont, and Vermont Fresh Network. At the Bryant House, we source our cheeses, meats, smoked products, and ice cream from no fewer than nineteen local farms and farmers!

❧ LIFE OF A FARM GIRL

Growing up on a dairy farm, with four hundred acres to roam over and a great barn full of hay and warm milking cows, touched all aspects of Mildred's life. She worked hard, gathering eggs and feeding the chickens, helping her dad deliver the milk, and making maple bonbons with her mother, which they sold by the side of the road. And she played, swimming with her brothers in a dammed-up brook and feeding her pet crow.

When she was a child, her father, Erwin Edgar but known to all as E.E., drove her the five miles to school in a horse-drawn wagon or sleigh, delivering milk, cream, cheese, and butter along the way. He paid the school's tuition with products from the farm; one receipt reads: "two lambs, five chickens, 12 dozen eggs."

Life on the Wilcox farm was hard work, and hearty meals were the highlight of each day. Nearly everything the family ate came from its own gardens and pastures, so all the food was local and seasonal, and nothing went to waste. The only preservatives in those days were vinegar for pickling, salt for curing, and wood smoke for drying. White flour and white sugar were luxuries reserved for confections. Margarine was unthinkable when sweet, fresh butter was at hand. Growing up a farm girl, Mildred learned by osmosis the advantages of real food.

Sustaining AGRICULTURE

Turns out that small-scale agriculture is alive and well in Vermont. We've added hundreds of new farms to the landscape since the millennium, the majority of which are between ten and fifty acres (small compared to many of the huge farms in the Midwest); and encouragingly, more young people are becoming farmers. What is happening in our state now—more acreage in agriculture, more farms, an increase in the overall value of our agricultural products—is how we can ensure our working landscape will thrive for generations to come.

NUMBER One

With all the local farms and farmers' markets, newly implemented GMO labeling laws, and countless opportunities for outdoor activities, it's no wonder that Vermont has been ranked number one in health out of all states by the United Health Foundation for four years running.

ROASTED HERB CHICKEN
WITH LEMON

Serves 4

---

*N*othing beats the aroma of a fresh chicken roasting in the oven. Once reserved for Sunday night family dinner, roast chicken was on the dinner menu when an older laying hen could be culled from the flock. Today, most supermarket chickens are youngsters, and it's hard to find a flavorful hen. A free-range bird will be most reminiscent of old-fashioned flavor.

Herb salt sprinkled inside the cavity releases natural juices that are infused with a hint of citrus to make a delicious natural gravy. Prepare the herb salt in advance and pack it away in an airtight container to use liberally in a range of other recipes, too. This roast chicken will quickly become a favorite; it's simple, yet it will always feel special.

---

1 (5- to 6-pound) free-range
roasting chicken

¼ cup Fragrant Herb Salt
(recipe follows)

4 sprigs fresh thyme

4 sprigs fresh tarragon

4 sprigs fresh sage

4 lemons: 2 whole, 2 halved

4 tablespoons (½ stick)
unsalted butter,
at room temperature

4 heads garlic,
halved crosswise

Preheat the oven to 375°F and position a rack in the lower third.

Remove the giblets and any excess fat from the cavity of the chicken; pat the outside dry. Place the chicken in a large roasting pan, pat the inside dry, and liberally salt the inside with 2 to 3 tablespoons of the herb salt. Stuff the cavity with the fresh thyme, tarragon, and sage.

Puncture the 2 whole lemons with a small knife in as many places as you can, about thirty punctures per lemon. Insert the lemons into the cavity of the chicken and tie the legs together with kitchen twine, tucking the wing tips under the body of the chicken.

Brush the outside of the chicken all over with the softened butter. Sprinkle with the remaining herb salt to cover the bird evenly. Scatter the garlic and lemon halves around the base. Roast for 1½ hours. Every 30 minutes or so, open the oven door, pull out the rack, and baste the outside of the bird with the pan juices.

To test the doneness of the chicken, wiggle the drumstick to see if it moves easily. Remove the chicken from the oven and tent with aluminum foil; let rest for 10 to 15 minutes. Transfer to a serving platter and thinly slice, starting by removing the legs and thighs, then slicing the breast. Serve each piece with a spoonful of the herb-infused juices poured over the top and half a head of the roasted garlic so guests can squeeze out the soft cloves and enjoy.

FRAGRANT HERB SALT

½ cup coarse sea salt

¼ cup mixed dried herbs (see list at right)

½ teaspoon dried lavender

Herb salt dresses up any dish and is a good way to use up the end of the jars of dried herbs in your cupboards so you can replace them with a fresher batch.

If you have traveled to France, you will find these herbs in a collection known as herbes de Provence, but you can also make your own by combining classic culinary herbs such as parsley, sage, rosemary, thyme, savory, tarragon, and basil, and always just a light touch of culinary lavender, which accentuates the flavors of the other herbs.

Place the salt and the herbs in a food processor fitted with the steel blade and pulse until fine. Transfer to an airtight container. The herb salt will keep indefinitely at room temperature.

CHICKEN SCRATCH

Breeding chickens became a popular hobby in the seventeenth century, producing a range of unusual species. Now, though, production birds are limited to just a few breeds, and the majority of commercial egg farms concentrate on the common white Leghorn that produces American's favorite white eggs. New Englanders still prefer brown eggs, largely produced by Rhode Island Reds and Plymouth Rock breeds. And more and more of us are raising Araucana breeds, which deliver the loveliest pale blue, soft green, or light pink eggs—colors so beautiful that Martha Stewart based a paint line on them.

HERBED CHICKEN THIGHS
WITH CIDER SAUCE

Serves 4 TO 6

If you are new to cooking with fresh herbs, start with the six classic culinary herbs: parsley, thyme, tarragon, chives, sage, and rosemary. If you have space for a garden, these will grow easily and reward you with ample seasoning.

In this simple chicken dish, we combine fresh herbs with apple cider to accentuate the aromatic qualities of the herbs. Authentic apple cider is important, so try to make this dish in the fall, when apples are abundant and your herb garden is still flourishing. Fresh herbs are ideal, but dried herbs work well if it is the middle of winter. This dish is quick to make for a hungry family, with a savory sauce that calls out for something to soak it all up, like rice or couscous. Serve a simple vegetable like steamed broccoli with a squeeze of lemon alongside.

⅔ cup unbleached all-purpose flour

1 tablespoon finely chopped fresh thyme, or 1 teaspoon dried

1 tablespoon finely chopped fresh tarragon, or 1 teaspoon dried

1 tablespoon finely chopped fresh rosemary, or 1 teaspoon dried

½ teaspoon fine sea salt

¼ teaspoon freshly ground black pepper

6 boneless skinless chicken thighs

2 tablespoons unsalted butter

2 tablespoons olive oil

2 cups apple cider

Fresh parsley sprigs, for garnish

In a medium bowl, mix the flour, thyme, tarragon, rosemary, salt, and pepper. Dip each chicken thigh into the herbed flour, patting to help the flour adhere, and shake off the excess.

In a large Dutch oven, melt the butter with the oil over medium-high heat. Add the chicken in a single layer and cook until brown on both sides, about 5 minutes per side. Pour in the apple cider and bring to a boil. Cover, reduce the heat to medium-low, and simmer until the chicken is cooked through when pierced with the tip of a sharp knife and the sauce has thickened, about 20 minutes.

Taste and season the sauce with salt and pepper as desired. Serve hot, sprinkled with fresh sprigs of parsley.

SAUTÉED CHICKEN BREASTS
ON CREAMY LEEKS

Serves 4

———◆———

*T*his is the perfect "elegant meal in a hurry" dish, and it tastes far more complicated than it is to prepare. *When you start off with naturally sweet leeks and sauté them in creamy butter with a touch of sharp tarragon, you just can't go wrong. In fact, the creamy leeks work equally well as a base for a salmon fillet.*

Since the chicken is flattened, it cooks quickly. Once you've prepared the leeks and the chicken has been sautéed, prepare the sauce. While it simmers, set the kitchen table with a tablecloth and light some candles, then heat the plates so everything can be served warm and delicious. No one will know how easy this delectable dish is.

---

8 tablespoons (1 stick) unsalted butter

3 good-size leeks, white parts only, cleaned and chopped into ½-inch sections (about 3 cups)

Salt and freshly ground black pepper

3 pounds boneless skinned chicken breast, divided into 4 portions

½ cup dry white wine

2 cloves garlic, smashed and finely minced

3 tablespoons crème fraîche or heavy cream

1 tablespoon chopped fresh tarragon

In a nonstick 12-inch skillet, melt 4 tablespoons of the butter. Add the leeks and season with salt and pepper. Cover and simmer, stirring often, to soften and lightly caramelize, about 20 minutes. Transfer to a bowl and set the skillet aside, unwashed.

Place the chicken in a plastic bag or between two sheets of waxed paper and gently pound with a wooden mallet to flatten. It doesn't have to be super flat, just enough to break the muscle and tenderize, and to get the fillets to the same thickness, about ½ inch thick. Lightly season the chicken with salt and pepper.

Place the chicken breasts in the same skillet you used to cook the leeks, adding a touch of butter or oil, if necessary. Gently brown the chicken over medium heat, about 5 minutes per side. Transfer to a warm platter and tent with aluminum foil, or keep warm in a low oven.

Add the wine and garlic to the skillet, scraping the sides and all the brown bits from the chicken and leeks with a wooden spoon; simmer over medium-high heat until the wine has reduced by two-thirds, about 5 minutes. Reduce the heat to low and whisk in the crème fraîche or heavy cream. Cut the remaining butter into small pieces and add one piece at a time to the saucepan, stirring with a whisk until smooth and slightly thickened, about 5 minutes. Add the tarragon, cover, and keep warm.

To serve, divide the caramelized leeks among four (warmed) plates. Spoon a generous amount of the sauce over the leeks, then place a chicken fillet on top of each. Drizzle with more sauce and serve.

❧ JOHN DEERE, VERMONT'S NATIVE SON

Tractors are almost sacred items in Vermont, and many folks speak of theirs with the soft tones of love usually reserved for children or dogs. Tractor parades, with scores of tractors of all sizes lit up and decorated for the holidays, roll through villages like Dorset and Manchester soon after Thanksgiving and draw admiring crowds. And no tractor is more common here than the ubiquitous yellow-and-green one invented by Vermont's native son, John Deere.

It hardly matters that John Deere didn't invent the steel self-scouring plow until he moved to the Midwest in 1837 and encountered rich soil that clogged plows accustomed to the light, sandy soil of Vermont. He was born in Rutland in 1804, came of age in Middlebury, trained as a blacksmith here, working in Burlington, Vergennes, and Leicester, and married a Vermont woman with whom he had nine children. He was endowed with unconquerable energy, determined will, a drive for self-made success, and the inclination for hard practical work that we see as a particularly Vermont virtue, and we're claiming him.

TRADITIONAL ROAST TURKEY
WITH APPLE-SAGE DRESSING

Serves 6 TO 8

———◆———

Every year, there's a different newfangled way to cook turkey, from brining it in salted water overnight to dropping it into a deep fryer. We grew up with this recipe for traditional Thanksgiving turkey with a New England stuffing and prefer its simplicity and the way it infuses the house with a delicious aroma as it slowly cooks. Some people prefer to add sausage to their stuffing; here, we stick to a simpler style, with chopped apples and fragrant herbs that are naturally moistened from the turkey drippings. We use our Farmhouse Whole Wheat Honey Bread (page 148), but any good honest loaf of country bread will do.

Grandmother Wilcox's trick to keeping the turkey meat moist and evenly cooked was to cover it with cheese-cloth saturated with melted lard (we use butter or olive oil), as described in this recipe. Always select a fresh, free-range turkey from a nearby farm—the taste is completely worth it.

1 loaf Farmhouse Whole Wheat Honey Bread (page 148), or a bag of dried stuffing

1 (12- to 15-pound) fresh turkey

2 tablespoons Fragrant Herb Salt (page 59) or coarse sea salt

1 stick (8 ounces) unsalted butter, plus 1 cup (2 sticks) unsalted butter, melted, or 1 cup heated olive oil

2 large yellow onions, coarsely chopped (2 cups)

6 stalks celery, cut into ¼-inch slices (1½ cups)

3 Cortland apples, unpeeled, cored, and cut into ¼-inch cubes (2 cups)

1 teaspoon dried thyme

1 teaspoon dried sage

2 teaspoons table salt

1 teaspoon freshly ground black pepper

2 cups chicken stock

The day before you plan to make the stuffing, slice the loaf and cut the bread into ½-inch cubes (you should have about 8 cups bread cubes). Spread out the cubes on a rimmed baking sheet to dry and harden. If you want to dry the cubes on the day of cooking, place them in a preheated 250°F oven for 20 minutes, stirring halfway through.

An hour before roasting, take the turkey out of the fridge. Remove the bag of giblets and pat dry inside and out with paper towels. Sprinkle the interior with the herb salt and set the turkey breast side up on a roasting rack in a large roasting pan. This will help the meat cook more evenly because it dries out the skin, which promotes browning and crisping.

Preheat the oven to 425°F.

In a large skillet, melt 8 tablespoons of the butter over medium heat. Add the onions and sauté until translucent, about 10 minutes. Add the celery and the apples and cook for 5 minutes more, then add the herbs, table salt, and pepper. Transfer the bread cubes to a large bowl, add the mixture from the pan, and toss with a wooden spoon or both hands to mix well.

Spoon the stuffing into the turkey, pressing to fill, but be careful not to stuff it too full—the stuffing will expand as it cooks. Truss the legs together with kitchen twine and tuck the wings under the bird. Cut off a piece of cheesecloth that will cover the bird and be long enough to rest in the pan. In a small saucepan, heat the stock with the 1 cup melted butter.

(Continued)

Immerse the cheesecloth in the stock and butter, then evenly spread it over the bird, tucking the edges alongside the bird. Pour the remaining stock-butter mixture over the bird, keeping the edges of the cheesecloth immersed while it cooks. The juices will wick up through the cotton weave, to crisp up the skin and turn it a beautiful deep golden brown, while keeping the meat moist and evenly cooked.

Roast the turkey for 45 minutes, then reduce the oven temperature to 350°F. Baste the turkey every 45 minutes, tilting the pan to capture the stock and butter juice, and with a turkey baster, scooping up the liquids and releasing them on top of the turkey.

The rule of thumb for cooking a turkey is 13 minutes per pound. This 15-pound turkey should take about 3 hours to cook. To make sure the turkey is fully cooked through, check its temperature with a meat thermometer in three places—the breast, the outer thigh, and the inside thigh—to be sure it registers at least 165°F. If any place is under that temperature, put the turkey back in the oven for 20 minutes more. Shield the breast meat with aluminum foil, if needed, to keep it from overcooking.

Once you determine that the turkey is cooked, remove it from the oven and let it rest in the roasting pan for 10 minutes before transferring to a cutting board. Tent the turkey with aluminum foil and let it rest for at least 30 minutes more. This gives time for the juices to be reabsorbed into the muscle tissue so the meat is firm, making the turkey easier to slice and juicier.

Before you carve, spoon out all of the stuffing and transfer to a heated serving dish. You can keep the stuffing in the turned-off oven while you carve the turkey.

ONE FINAL NOTE: Once you sit down at the table and finish your meal, the leftover meat needs to be refrigerated within 2 hours of cooking. Leftover stuffing and meat can be mixed together with gravy to make a wonderful casserole the next day.

TURKEY POTPIE
WITH BUTTERMILK BISCUITS

Serves 6 TO 8

————◆◆————

A potpie is comfort food at its finest, and here we use turkey rather than the more common chicken. If you have leftover roast turkey (see recipe on page 64) and turkey stock made from the carcass, you're more than a step ahead. If not, we give you a quick way to make not only a fragrant stock but also wonderfully tender turkey. The real flavor key to a good old-fashioned turkey potpie is the stock, so we encourage you to use homemade or the best you can buy. Keep the turkey in chunks for more succulent bites.

Making a potpie takes a few steps: making the stock and cooking the meat, combining the potpie ingredients, and making the biscuits that crown the pie halfway through baking. But the end product is well worth it! Make this turkey potpie for Sunday night dinner or to take to a church supper, and you're guaranteed clean plates all around.

POTPIE

3 carrots, cut into ½-inch pieces (about 1¼ cups)

4 tablespoons (½ stick) unsalted butter

1 onion, finely diced (1 cup)

1 tablespoon finely chopped fresh sage

1 tablespoon finely chopped fresh tarragon

¼ cup unbleached all-purpose flour

2 cups turkey or chicken stock, preferably homemade (recipe follows)

1 tablespoon sherry or Madeira

¾ cup heavy cream

Salt and freshly ground black pepper

3 cups cooked turkey meat, cut into 1½-inch chunks (recipe follows)

¾ cup frozen peas, defrosted

Preheat the oven to 350°F.

MAKE THE POTPIE: Bring a small saucepan of water to a boil over high heat. Add the carrots and boil until just tender, about 5 minutes. Drain and set aside. In an 8-quart stockpot, melt the butter over medium heat. Add the onion and sauté until translucent, about 8 minutes. Add the sage and tarragon and cook, stirring occasionally with a wooden spoon, until fragrant, about 2 minutes.

Sprinkle the flour over the onion mixture and cook for another minute, stirring to incorporate. Slowly add the stock and the sherry and continue cooking over medium heat until thick and smooth, about 5 minutes. Add the cream and reduce the heat to maintain a low simmer. Season with salt and pepper.

Evenly spread the turkey, peas, and carrots into an 8 × 10-inch rectangular dish. Pour the onion mixture over the top and stir gently so that the turkey and vegetables are coated. Bake for 35 minutes, until the mixture is bubbling hot. Remove from the oven.

Top the potpie with the biscuit dough rounds (see page 69), evenly covering the surface. Raise the oven temperature to 425°F and bake for 15 to 20 minutes more.

(Continued)

BUTTERMILK BISCUITS

2 cups unbleached
all-purpose flour, plus more
for dusting

1 tablespoon baking powder

1 teaspoon sugar

¾ teaspoon salt

6 tablespoons (¾ stick)
unsalted butter, chilled

¾ cup buttermilk

MAKE THE BISCUITS: In the bowl of a stand mixer fitted with the paddle attachment, mix together the flour, baking powder, sugar, and salt on medium speed. Add the cold butter, piece by piece, and mix until the butter is the size of small peas. Slowly pour in the buttermilk and mix until everything just comes together.

Turn the dough out onto a lightly floured surface and fold it over two or three times. Shape it into a rectangle about ¾ inch thick and cut out rounds (you should get 6 to 8), using a 2½-inch cookie cutter or inverted water glass.

QUICK TURKEY STOCK

Makes 4 CUPS STOCK AND 2 CUPS DICED TURKEY

2 turkey thighs

1 turkey breast

1 medium onion,
unpeeled, quartered

1 medium carrot,
cut into large chunks

1 medium stalk celery with
leaves, cut into large chunks

4 sprigs fresh flat-leaf parsley

2 sprigs fresh
rosemary or sage

1 bay leaf

¼ teaspoon whole
black peppercorns

Place the turkey pieces in a large stockpot along with the onion, carrot, celery, parsley, rosemary, bay leaf, and peppercorns. Add water to cover by 2 inches. Cover and simmer for 1 hour. Remove the turkey from the stock, let cool, and cut into 1½-inch chunks. Pour the stock through a mesh strainer set over a bowl; discard the solids and reserve the stock.

TURKEY BURGERS
WITH BASIL MAYO

Serves 4 TO 6

———◆◆———

For hard-core burger lovers, it may be a tough sell to serve turkey burgers instead of red meat. Yet this juicy, flavorful burger could change hearts and minds. As a bonus to its more nuanced and complicated—in a good way—taste, it has less fat than a traditional beef burger. It can handle the usual toppings of sliced tomato and onion, but we prefer the delicacy and depth of sliced avocado. Serving it with basil mayonnaise gives it a rich, luscious quality, with or without the bun.

Easily adaptable to many of the same cooking methods as the beef burger, this turkey burger cooks up quickly and is delicious grilled or cooked on the stovetop. Serve it with corn on the cob and sliced tomatoes at a cookout, and no one will miss that other burger.

BASIL MAYO

¼ cup sour cream

¼ cup mayonnaise

¼ cup thinly sliced fresh basil

Zest of 1 lemon

BURGERS

¼ cup whole milk plain yogurt

1 carrot, shredded (¼ cup)

2 tablespoons finely diced onion

2 teaspoons Dijon mustard

1 clove garlic, minced

½ teaspoon dried tarragon

1 teaspoon kosher salt

¼ teaspoon freshly ground black pepper

1½ pounds ground turkey

1 teaspoon vegetable oil

4 to 6 hamburger buns (optional)

Butter, for the buns (optional)

1 ripe avocado, thinly sliced (optional)

MAKE THE BASIL MAYO: In a small bowl, mix the sour cream and mayonnaise. Stir in the basil and lemon zest. Set aside while you prepare the burgers.

MAKE THE BURGERS: In a medium bowl, use a fork to gently combine the yogurt, carrot, onion, mustard, garlic, tarragon, salt, and pepper, then add the turkey and combine all the ingredients by hand or with a wooden spoon, handling the mixture as little as possible. Divide the meat into 4 to 6 portions and gently press each one into a patty about 1 inch thick.

In a grill pan or large skillet, heat the oil over medium heat until it shimmers. (If cooking on a grill, prepare the grill as you would for cooking a burger.) Add the patties and cook on one side for about 3 minutes. Flip and cook until browned on the other side, about 3 minutes. Toast and butter the hamburger buns (if using). Transfer the burgers to the buns and top with a dollop of basil mayonnaise and some avocado, if desired.

HUNTERS' PORK POCKET PIES

Makes EIGHT 5-INCH HALF-MOON PIES

I*n the Haskell Free Library and Opera House in Derby Line, Vermont (population: 663), a skinny black line across the reading room's hardwood floor marks the international border with Canada. With such a close neighbor, it's not surprising that nearly a quarter of Vermont's population is of French Canadian ancestry, like Eliot Orton's wife, Julie. She recalls a hearty meat pie called* tourtière *that was served as a special treat, especially after church service on Christmas Eve.*

Julie makes an authentic tourtière—*just meat, no vegetables—yet assures us that everyone has his or her own version. Some are made with pork, others with a combination of pork and beef with vegetables. Here, we add a few spices and turn our recipe into a pocket pie, the ideal lunch for hunters spending a long day perched in a deer blind, or for a family picnic at a soccer game.*

Although this does not take much time, it is a fairly involved process, so we suggest you make several batches and keep them in your freezer, ready for times when you are on the go. Reheat frozen pies in a preheated 350°F oven for 45 minutes.

DOUGH

2 cups unbleached
all-purpose flour

1 teaspoon table salt

1 cup (2 sticks)
unsalted butter,
cut into ½-inch pieces

1 egg yolk

4 to 5 tablespoons ice water

MAKE THE DOUGH: In a food processor fitted with the steel blade, pulse the flour and table salt together. Drop in the butter one piece at a time, pulsing after each addition, until it is fully incorporated and the mixture is like coarse cornmeal or sand. With the motor running, add the egg yolk, then add the ice water, 1 tablespoon at a time, until the dough pulls away from the sides of the bowl and begins to come together. Pat the dough into a flat disc, wrap it in plastic wrap, and refrigerate for 30 minutes.

(Continued)

Looking down on Weston, 1900. The pastures are now grown into woods.

SMALL FAMILY FARMS

2 tablespoons olive oil or
unsalted butter

1½ pounds ground pork

2 large onions, finely chopped
(2 cups)

1 clove garlic, minced
(½ teaspoon)

½ teaspoon celery seeds

½ cup chicken stock

½ teaspoon table salt

1 teaspoon freshly ground
black pepper

¼ teaspoon dried sage

¼ teaspoon ground allspice

Flour, for dusting

Whole milk or 1 egg yolk,
beaten, for brushing

Coarse salt, for sprinkling

MAKE THE FILLING: In a large skillet, heat the oil over medium heat. Add the pork and cook, stirring with a wooden spoon, until the meat loses its red color. Add the onion and garlic and cook, stirring occasionally, for 2 minutes. Add the celery seeds, chicken stock, table salt, pepper, and sage. Cover the skillet and bring the mixture to a boil, then reduce the heat to maintain a simmer. Cook, stirring occasionally, for 35 to 40 minutes, or until all the liquid has evaporated. Remove the skillet from the heat and set aside to cool.

Line two sheet pans with parchment paper.

On a lightly floured surface, divide the dough in half to make it easier to work with. One half at a time, roll out the dough to about ⅛ inch thick. Use an inverted bowl to measure a 5-inch circle (if your bowl's a little bigger or smaller, it doesn't matter), tracing the circle with a paring knife in the dough. Repeat with the remaining dough until all the dough has been used up. This may require that you combine dough pieces and reroll, keeping the surface floured. Try not to overhandle the dough or it may become tough.

Place ¼ cup of the filling onto half of a dough circle, wet the edges of the dough with water, fold over, and seal with the tines of a fork. Slash three small vents in the top of pocket and place it on the prepared baking sheet. Repeat to fill all the dough circles. Refrigerate the pockets for 30 minutes (or freeze uncooked; when frozen, place in plastic bags until ready to bake).

Preheat the oven to 375°F.

Brush the tops of the pockets with milk or yolk and sprinkle coarse salt over the tops. Bake for 20 minutes, rotating the baking sheets halfway through the cooking time, until golden. Remove from the oven and let cool slightly before serving.

THE SMOKEHOUSE

There was a time when every Vermont farm had its own smokehouse in which to cure and smoke pork, and every farmhouse made its own sausage. Bacon was an absolute staple. At The Vermont Country Store, bacon and sausage are made by Vermont Smoke and Cure, a small family farm that still cares about the old ways. More artisan butcheries are opening around the state, selling the neighboring farms' grass-fed pork in roasts and sausages and maple-smoked bacon. We are huge fans of the magic that happens when smoke meets pig and just about anything else. Perhaps a primal memory sparks when we eat foods smoked long and low over glowing embers, some remnant of our ancient ancestors' fires.

PORK TENDERLOIN
WITH BRAISED CABBAGE

Serves 4

———— ◆ ————

Pork chops served with braised cabbage and apples are classic New England fare, hearty with sweet under-tones. You can adapt this recipe for chops, if you prefer, yet we find tenderloin to be easy and a bit more elegant to serve. Start the recipe early, as the pork marinates for a while. Red or green cabbage, gently sautéed with apple and red pepper flakes for a little kick, makes a colorful bed for the pork.

MARINATED PORK

1 (1½-pound) pork tenderloin

¼ cup olive oil

1 clove garlic, minced

1 tablespoon Dijon mustard

1 tablespoon
prepared horseradish

1 tablespoon chopped
fresh rosemary

1 tablespoon chopped
fresh thyme

1 teaspoon salt

BRAISED CABBAGE AND APPLES

2 tablespoons unsalted butter

1 tablespoon olive oil

1 clove garlic, smashed

1 small red onion, thinly sliced

2 pounds red or green
cabbage, thinly sliced (8 cups)

1 Cortland apple, cored and
cut into ½-inch slices

½ cup apple cider or
chicken stock

¼ teaspoon red pepper flakes

¼ teaspoon caraway seeds

1 teaspoon salt

½ teaspoon freshly ground
black pepper

1½ tablespoons
apple cider vinegar

MAKE THE MARINATED PORK: Trim the silver skin off the pork tender-loin. In a small bowl, combine the oil, garlic, mustard, horseradish, rosemary, thyme, and salt. Whisk together and pour into a large resealable plastic bag. Add the pork tenderloin and marinate in the refrigerator for at least 2 to 3 hours and up to 12 hours.

Preheat the oven to 350°F.

Heat a large nonstick skillet over medium-high heat. Remove the pork from the marinade and shake off any excess. Sear each side for 2 to 3 minutes, until browned. Transfer to a medium flameproof baking pan and place in the oven. Bake for 35 minutes, or until the meat reaches an internal temperature of 145°F.

MAKE THE BRAISED CABBAGE AND APPLES: While the pork is bak-ing, in a heavy 12-inch skillet, melt the butter with the oil over medium heat. Add the garlic and onion and sauté until soft, about 10 minutes. Add the cabbage, apple, cider, red pepper flakes to taste, caraway seeds, salt, and black pepper. Stirring occasionally, cook until the cabbage is tender, about 15 min-utes. Just before serving, add the vinegar and simmer until the liquid has evaporated. Keep the skillet on the stovetop to reheat when the pork is ready to serve.

Transfer the tenderloin to a cutting board and tent with aluminum foil. Let rest for 5 to 10 minutes before slicing.

PAN SAUCE

½ cup chicken stock

2 teaspoons butter

MAKE THE PAN SAUCE: While the pork is resting, place the baking pan from the baked pork on the stovetop over medium heat. Add the chicken stock and scrape all the browned pieces from the bottom of the pan. Boil down for 2 to 3 minutes and remove from the heat. Add the butter and stir until melted.

Arrange some braised cabbage and apple on each plate, top with fanned slices of pork, and pour some pan sauce over the top.

↬ THE WORLD'S BIGGEST PIG

The Bryant House Restaurant at the Weston store buys its grass-fed beef from the Morse family at Ephraim Mountain Farm up the road in North Springfield, Vermont. Steve and Esta Morse are hardworking folks who care deeply about the products they create. To show you what kind of people they are, they've taken in dozens of foster children and adopted six—to date.

Several years ago, Steve was given a pregnant black Yorkshire pig. One hot summer day, the pig delivered a dozen healthy piglets. But then the pig became very sick, and the vet told the family she would not make it through the night. Esta and some of her girls tended the pig all night, putting cold blankets on her to help control her fever. In the morning, the reason for her illness became clear: The pig gave birth to another piglet—a twenty-pound stillborn, so the story goes. For several weeks, Esta and her daughters nursed the mother back to health.

Several months later, Steve told the family at the dinner table it was time for the pig to go to the butcher. After much protest, the daughters decided they would give part of their allowance from doing chores to help pay for feed so they could keep the pig on the farm. Today the pig weighs close to one thousand pounds. Steve calls her the biggest pig on earth, and we don't disagree!

—ELIOT ORTON

SMALL FAMILY FARMS

GRANDMA HAMILTON'S SAUSAGE

Makes 6 PATTIES

❖

*I*n our first attempt to make sausage, we did it the way Mildred and her mother would have, using a six-pound pork butt (also known as Boston butt or picnic shoulder) with five pounds lean pork butt and one pound pork fat. We ran it through the meat grinder twice, seasoned it, and stuffed it into links. While it made the most delicious sausage, especially grilled, we've adapted the recipe to use preground pork to make it simpler for home cooks. We still think this tastes mighty fine, and encourage you to give it a try.

For serious sausage makers, you can stuff it into casings for link sausage using a special mixer attachment. Easily grilled or pan seared, link sausages make a hearty dinner with a side of potatoes and applesauce. We think patties work just as well for most dishes, with spicy seasoning that zings up a pizza or pasta sauce.

---

1 pound ground pork

2 teaspoons minced garlic

½ to 1 teaspoon
red pepper flakes

1½ tablespoons whole
fennel seeds

½ teaspoon ground coriander

1½ teaspoons salt

3 tablespoons red or
white wine

1 teaspoon vegetable oil

In a large bowl, combine all the ingredients except the vegetable oil and mix with your hands just to incorporate. Cover tightly with plastic wrap and refrigerate for at least 2 hours or up to 2 days to meld the flavors.

Form the sausage meat into patties (or keep it loose if adding it to other dishes such as pizza or sauce). In a large skillet, heat the oil over medium heat. Add the patties and cook until crispy on both sides, about 3 minutes. The patties (and especially stuffed link sausages, if you went that route) are also excellent grilled.

SAUSAGE KNOWLEDGE

Tucked into Mildred's notebook was a small scrap of paper with a "recipe" for her grandmother's sausage: "Meat, spices, fat." Back then on a family farm, people just knew how much meat to use, what proportions were right, which spices would enhance. They understood how to use up all parts of a slaughtered animal, including the intestines; they learned how to grind the meat, flavor it, and use it as is or stuff it into links. (Mildred would never bother with the links, Lyman remembers, but just used the ground sausage to make pasta sauce or for breakfasts.) With knowledge passed down by doing, who needed recipes?

SMALL FAMILY FARMS

MILDRED'S MAPLE-GLAZED HAM
WITH MAPLE MUSTARD

Makes ONE 8-POUND (BONE-IN) SMOKED HAM; *Serves* 12

T*he Orton family would often serve ham for Easter dinner when everyone gathered, because no one cooked a ham like Mildred. She would start with a fresh ham, straight from a local farm, but we suggest you start with a bone-in smoked ham, more easily found in the supermarket. Fresh hams require a brine; smoked ham can go directly into the oven.*

A glance at this recipe may lead you to believe it's too simple to be worthy. Sometimes we feel the simplest things are the best—and trust us, it's worthy. Coated with a mixture of sweet maple syrup and spicy mustard, the ham sits over a pan of hot water. As it cooks, the syrup drips into the water; the water evaporates, infusing the ham with moist flavor. With a sweet, spicy, and salty trifecta, when served with our homemade mustard, it is Ham Perfection.

1 (8-pound) bone-in smoked ham

½ cup whole cloves

2 cups pure maple syrup

½ cup Maple Mustard (recipe follows) or Dijon mustard, plus more for serving

Preheat the oven to 300°F.

Trim any gristle from the ham, keeping the skin and fat on. Bring a kettle of water to a boil. Set a roasting rack in a deep roasting pan. Pour the boiling water into the pan so it comes to just below the rack, about 1 inch up the sides of the pan. Place the ham, fat side up, on the rack, making sure the water does not touch the ham. Insert an ovenproof meat thermometer into the ham at a slight angle or through the end of the ham so the tip is in the center of the thickest part of the ham and does not touch bone or fat.

Bake for 45 minutes. Remove the ham from the oven and peel back and remove the skin, keeping the fat intact. Score the fat, cutting ¼-inch-deep strips on an angle to create a decorative crosshatch. At the corners of each crosshatch, press a whole clove into the ham.

In a small bowl, stir together the maple syrup and mustard. With a pastry brush, rub the ham with half the mustard mixture. Return the ham to the oven and bake for 30 minutes more. Remove from the oven and coat with the remaining mustard mixture. Return the ham to the oven and bake for 15 minutes more, or until the thermometer reads 135°F. Remove from the oven, tent with aluminum foil, and let stand for 10 minutes before transferring to a carving platter. Serve with Maple Mustard.

MAPLE MUSTARD

Makes 1 CUP

¼ cup black mustard seeds

6 tablespoons dry mustard

⅔ cup apple cider vinegar

2 teaspoons salt

¼ cup vegetable oil

2 tablespoons
dark brown sugar

2 tablespoons honey

This quick spicy mustard makes a wonderful condiment for baked ham and a superior spread for sandwiches of all kinds. We particularly like the zing it gives to all it touches.

Combine all the ingredients in a pint-size jar, cover, and shake vigorously. Refrigerate until ready to use.

∽ LET THEM EAT HAM!

Back in 1946, when The Vermont Country Store opened its doors, traveling the winding, rutted dirt roads to Weston was hardly a picnic, especially in cars with no air-conditioning, no power steering, and early suspension that made for rough going. Mildred insisted travelers be treated like family and served lunch after the trying journey, as there was no place in town to eat once customers finally did arrive, unless they made a meal from cheese samples in the Store.

She began baking cob-smoked hams and whole-grain bread in her wood-fired oven at home. Each morning, Mildred would deliver a basket across the Village Green to the simple lunch counter Vrest put together in the back of the Store. Vrest sliced cheese off the 35-pound wheel of Vermont Cheddar and Mildred put it all together—bread slathered with fresh dairy butter from her family farm, a thick slice of cheese, and a big chunk of juicy baked ham—and offered up sandwiches and home-brewed iced tea to the hungry customers. Whenever her brothers could make it from the farm up the mountain to Weston, bowls of fresh Wilcox ice cream appeared on the chalkboard menu.

Hungry patrons yearning for Mildred's ham sandwiches quickly began to outnumber seats at the lunch counter. As the Store grew, the menu grew, and in 1959, Vrest and Mildred bought the Bryant House from friends next door to the Store and opened the restaurant customers enjoy today.

When you order a ham and cheese sandwich and an ice cream sundae at Mildred's Dairy Bar or the Bryant House Restaurant, think of the woman who spent years baking hams to feed customers, never letting on the secret she revealed at age ninety-eight: "I was always allergic to ham!"

The first lunch counter at the back of the Store.

Mildred serving at Old Home Day in the 1950s.

Edgar Wilcox, like many small family farmers today,
kept bees on the Wilcox farm in the 1920s.

CHAPTER 4

STREAMS *and* FIELDS

A HUNDRED-PLUS YEARS AGO, TREES COVERED only about 20 percent of Vermont, as timber was cleared for settlement. That ratio slowly reversed, and now our remaining fields work hard, providing plentiful grazing land for contented sheep and grass-fed herds. Vermont wouldn't be the same state without the cattle, goats, and sheep scattered across pastoral vistas—which, thanks to a ban on billboards that's nearly a half century old, remain unspoiled—or without our many lakes, and the cold, clear streams flowing from the mountains that hide trout in their eddies.

FISH, BEEF, *and* LAMB

Vermont Grass-Fed Flocks and Herds

SHEEP AND WOOL

AS ALL-PERVASIVE AS DAIRY IS TO VERMONT TO-day, Merino sheep raised for their fine wool dominated the state from 1812, when that war significantly increased demand for wool, until the mid-1800s, when railroads could bring in wool from the west at lower prices and the sheep industry began to decline. Sheep made Vermont a major player in the Civil War, as the state provided wool for uniforms. But Vermont's small farms couldn't compete with the opening of the western plains and Australia to sheep production, and so the niche our farmers had enjoyed throughout the nineteenth century shrank like wool in a dryer and the pastureland once cleared for and by the sheep reverted to forest.

Mildred's mother, Maria Wilcox (left), and a friend
with the sheep on the family farm in 1928.

THE VERMONT UNIFORM

SINCE SHEEP WERE THE LARGEST LIVESTOCK crop in nineteenth-century Vermont, it's no surprise that the wool plaid shirt became the staple attire. Vrest Orton, a marketing genius, always made sure that someone in every photo he took of the Store was wearing a red wool shirt, as it telegraphed "Vermont" and "country" in a colorful shorthand.

Vrest with his plaid wool shirt, undoubtedly red, in a 1952 photograph.

FIVE REASONS TO SWITCH TO GRASS-FED BEEF

OUR FRIENDS AT THE EPHRAIM FARM, WHO PRO-vide all the beef for the Bryant House Restaurant and Mildred's Dairy Bar, list five reasons to make sure your beef is grass-fed. We summarize here:

Healthier for you and your family: Pasture-raised beef is lower in total fat than regular beef and is rich in omega-3 fatty acids.

Tastes better: You aren't consuming a lot of antibiotics and hormones. You'll taste the difference.

Environmentally responsible: Unlike most livestock, pasture-raised cattle don't live in huge feedlots where waste seeps into the groundwater and finds its way to our rivers, polluting the water. Also, the corn and grains used to feed grain-fed cattle have often been sprayed with herbicides and pesticides that harm our environment.

Humane treatment: In order to get cattle as big and fat as fast as possible, and to make as much money as possible, big ranchers use grain, hormones, and antibiotics liberally to move Mother Nature along. Feedlots stress the animals, and respect for the animals is not a priority.

Safer meat: Why? Because the cattle are eating a diet suited for their bodies, as Mother Nature intended.

GREAT ENOUGH *for* US

Lake Champlain, the 125-mile lake known as "New England's western coast," was declared the sixth Great Lake by President Clinton for a mere eighteen days before he bowed to pressure and demoted it. We still think it's a pretty great lake, and between it, our many smaller lakes, and our world-famous trout rivers, fishing season empties offices almost as much as hunting season.

PAN-SEARED CORNMEAL-CRUSTED WHOLE TROUT

Serves 4

———◆———

*I*t might be hard to find fresh trout out of season in the stores, but in the spring we have a short window when trout is abundant in the local streams. The taste is nothing like saltwater seafood: It's meaty and earthy, yet delicate and delectable. Cook it with the bones; once cooked, carefully slice it open through the back and, starting at one end, peel off the whole spine. It will stay intact and come out cleanly.

Preparing a whole trout is simple, and this recipe leaves a crisp crust around the fish. We like to fancy it up by serving it on a bed of steamed or sautéed dandelion greens, with a good squeeze of lemon, to revel in the abundance of lively spring flavors.

½ cup cornmeal

½ cup unbleached all-purpose flour

1 teaspoon salt

½ teaspoon freshly ground black pepper

2 (8-ounce) whole trout, or 4 trout fillets, cleaned

2 tablespoons unsalted butter

2 tablespoons olive oil

Steamed greens, for serving

2 lemons, for garnish

In a large flat baking dish, stir together the cornmeal, flour, salt, and pepper with a fork. Be sure the trout is completely dry by blotting it with paper towels, then press the sides of the fish into the cornmeal mixture to coat. If using the whole fish, coat just the outside and season the inside well with additional salt and pepper.

In a large skillet, melt the butter with the oil over medium heat. Place the trout in the pan and cook for 4 minutes each side for whole trout, or 2 to 3 minutes each side for fillets.

Line a platter with steamed greens, lay out the trout on top, and bring to the table with lemons alongside for squeezing over the fish.

NOTE: Be sure the whole trout are very clean and that all the blood along the inside backbone is removed under running water.

If the trout are fresh, the skin is delicious to eat. When eating a whole fish, you can easily eat the meat while all the bones stay intact if you don't want to attempt the deboning described above. If eating fillets, you can remove the string of bones starting at the neck area and pulling back toward the tail. It is easier to remove the bones after the fish are cooked.

FISH TRUCKS

Not all that long ago, fresh fish and seafood from the ocean arrived in Vermont on fish trucks that made their rounds to customers' houses. Nowadays, they park in convenient places and let customers come to them. Our personal favorite is a fish truck parked at a local gas station that also sells guns. Gas, guns, and lobster—talk about a one-stop shop!

✑ SALMON PEA WIGGLE, OUR FAVORITE COMFORT FOOD

While Mildred's lamb stew was a triumph of New England farm cooking, her signature dish could have been Salmon Pea Wiggle. Of humble origins, simple and wholesome, this overlooked classic reflects everything splendid about our grandmother.

Originally made with fresh salmon and peas, and traditionally served on July 4th in New England, the dish morphed into a comfort food with canned salmon and often frozen peas creamed and served on toast. Many children of Mildred's era, who came of age during the Depression, also came to loathe this hallmark of supper on a budget. Yet as kids we savored it with gusto, even the occasional salmon vertebrae one finds in canned salmon, with its delicate, morbidly satisfying crunch.

My grandmother made Salmon Pea Wiggle for us often, and to this day I look warmly upon those childhood luncheons: tin dinner trays, goblets of whole milk, Mildred's epic home-baked wheat toast, softened to perfection beneath a bed of lightly salted, steaming, creamed goodness, punctuated by the crisp snap of fragrant green peas from our garden. As Mildred grew quite old, it was my turn. I would sauté salmon and chopped onions, heat the mix with a sauce made of milk, flour, and butter, and add peas, serving it over toast. I made it for her quite a few times, and she still loved it—even after ninety-eight years!

–CABOT ORTON

Cabot enjoys his favorite comfort food at his grandmother's house.

FRIDAY NIGHT CLAM AND COD CHOWDER

Serves 8

———◆◆———

*O*riginal chowder recipes were mostly water-based fish soups, sometimes flavored with wine, and featured vegetables like onions, potatoes, and carrots. The fish varied, and many included some sort of bread product such as crackers or croutons to add bulk.

Chowder versions with milk and cream grew out of regions where dairy was in abundance, such as Vermont and other parts of New England, which is why we prefer this rich and warming one-pot clam chowder. We use chunks of carrots, celery, and potatoes along with cod, to give it visual interest and added flavor. Whenever possible, use fresh clams, but this recipe is so delicious, no one would ever know if you substituted frozen clams, easily found in most supermarkets.

---

6 pounds cherrystone clams, rinsed and scrubbed, or 1 (16-ounce) container frozen or fresh shucked clams, thawed (if frozen) and coarsely chopped

1 pound fresh cod fillets

2 (8-ounce) bottles clam juice

2 tablespoons unsalted butter

4 slices bacon (4 ounces), cut into ½-inch pieces

1 large onion, coarsely chopped

2 cloves garlic, coarsely chopped

6 carrots, cut into small coins

4 stalks celery, coarsely chopped

2 pounds Yukon Gold potatoes, unpeeled, cut into ½-inch pieces

1 tablespoon fresh thyme

1 bay leaf

1 cup heavy cream

Sea salt and freshly ground black pepper

Chopped fresh chives, for garnish

Vermont Common Crackers, for serving

Preheat the oven to 350°F.

If using fresh clams, place the clams and the cod in a single layer on a rimmed baking sheet and bake for 12 to 15 minutes, until the clams open. Remove from the oven and transfer to a large bowl along with any liquid that collected during the cooking process. Let the clams cool slightly, then pull the meat from the shells. Discard the shells and chop the meat into bite-size pieces. Refrigerate the clam meat and the cod while you prepare the stock. (If you are using pre-shucked clams, bake the cod alone on a lightly oiled rimmed baking sheet for 10 to 12 minutes.)

Strain the liquid from cooking the clams and cod through a fine-mesh sieve set over a large bowl. Add the clam juice and enough water to measure 6 cups. Set the broth aside.

In a heavy 8-quart stockpot, melt the butter over medium heat. Add the bacon and cook, stirring occasionally, until the fat has rendered and the bacon begins to brown, about 8 minutes. Add the onion and garlic and continue to stir until the onion is translucent, about 10 minutes. Add the carrots and celery and cook for 5 minutes. Add the clam broth, potatoes, thyme, and bay leaf. Return to medium heat and simmer until the potatoes are tender, 20 to 25 minutes. Stir in the heavy cream and gently reheat.

Discard the bay leaf and stir in the cooked clam meat and cod. Taste and season with salt and pepper. Let sit for 10 minutes for the flavors to meld. When ready to serve, divide the chowder among bowls and garnish with chopped chives and Vermont Common Crackers.

YANKEE COD CAKES

Serves 6

—◆◆—

Cod has been the favored New England fish for centuries and is available here year-round. This classic Yankee-style cod cake is sweet and savory, easy to prepare, and wonderful served with a dab of chutney (see page 210) or maple-tomato salsa (see page 198). You can even make your own tartar sauce by adding piccalilli (see page 214) to mayonnaise. These cakes will quickly become a favorite for all ages, and a great way to stretch out a pound of cod to feed a family. With the crunch of celery and bread crumbs, it's like a crab cake, but with a nice subtle cod flavor and without the expense of the crab.

1 medium russet potato, peeled and cut into 1-inch cubes

1 tablespoon unsalted butter

1 pound fresh cod fillet

1 large egg

2 tablespoons mayonnaise

1 teaspoon Worcestershire sauce

1 teaspoon Tabasco or other hot sauce

2 tablespoons finely chopped fresh flat-leaf parsley

1 stalk celery, finely chopped

4 scallions, white parts and 1 inch of green, finely chopped

Salt and freshly ground black pepper

2 cups panko bread crumbs

2 to 6 tablespoons vegetable or olive oil

Watercress or microgreens, for garnish

Bring a saucepan of water to a boil. Add the cubed potato and cook until soft, about 10 minutes. Drain, add the butter, and mash. Set aside to cool.

Place the cod in a large skillet and add water to cover. Simmer over medium-low heat until just cooked through, about 7 minutes. Drain and let cool, then break into large flakes.

In a large bowl, beat the egg. Add ½ cup of the mashed potato (reserve the rest for another use), stir well, then add the mayonnaise, Worcestershire, Tabasco, parsley, celery, and scallions. Gently fold in the flaked cod and season with salt and pepper.

Put the panko bread crumbs in a small shallow bowl. Form the cod mixture into 6 large patties, about ¾ cup per patty. Press both sides of each patty into the bread crumbs and set aside on a plate. Refrigerate until ready to cook, at least 1 hour and up to 6 hours.

In a large skillet, heat 2 tablespoons of the oil over medium heat. Add the cod cakes in a single layer, working in batches if necessary, and cook for 2 to 3 minutes per side. Add more oil to the pan as needed. Serve hot, or keep warm in a preheated 275°F oven for up to 1 hour. Plate and serve with a garnish of watercress or microgreens.

Looking across milldam on West River at the Old Grist Mill, Weston.

❧ IN COD WE TRUST

Near the penny candy in the Weston store, a huge salted cod has been hanging for sixty years. If you'd never laid eyes on salt cod, you'd wonder who on earth would eat such a thing. Of course, you don't eat it as is—you soak the cod for days and go from there. Properly cooked salt cod—a staple not only in New England but in many countries—is heavenly.

Salting then drying cod—whether sun-dried on rocks or on racks—is a tradition of preserving that dates back hundreds of years. Walk into a New England home as recently as a half century ago and you were likely to see salt cod, or *baccalà*, as it's known in Italian, hanging from kitchen ceilings just like it hangs in the Store. We're told that in the summer months, its smell was hardly divine, but the one in our store is totally dry, long past any reviving.

Notice the dried cod hanging from the Store rafters in this 1947 photograph. That cod's still hanging today.

SMOKED TROUT SALAD
WITH HORSERADISH DRESSING

Serves 4

————— ◆◆ —————

Heart-shaped watercress with mixed greens, topped by smoked trout and a creamy horseradish dressing, creates the perfect appetizer salad for dinner. Or serve it as a simple luncheon salad, alongside sliced tomatoes and steamed string beans lightly coated in a vinaigrette.

2 tablespoons prepared
horseradish

½ cup crème fraîche

¼ cup chopped fresh dill

¼ cup chopped fresh chives

Salt and freshly ground
black pepper

1 head butterhead lettuce,
torn into bite-size pieces

1 bunch watercress or
arugula, washed and stemmed

1 cup mesclun mixed greens,
washed and dried

2 tablespoons olive oil

Juice of ½ lemon
(1½ tablespoons)

8 ounces smoked trout fillet

4 scallions, white parts
and a portion of the green,
thinly sliced

1 tablespoon capers

In a small glass bowl, combine the horseradish, crème fraîche, dill, chives, and salt and pepper to taste. Set the dressing aside.

In a salad bowl, lightly toss together the lettuce, watercress, mesclun, olive oil, and lemon juice. Divide the salad evenly among four individual salad plates. With fingers or a knife, coarsely crumble the smoked trout over the greens, about 2 ounces per serving. Spoon 2 tablespoons of the horseradish dressing over each salad and top with scallions and capers. Refrigerate any leftover dressing for up to 1 week.

SMOKED HERRING *for* THE FEW *Who* DARE

Because Vermont is landlocked, in the old days much of our saltwater fish came to us dried, smoked, or pickled. Smoked herring still holds a place in many of our customers' hearts, so of course we sell it at the Store, direct from Nova Scotia, laid out in a covered glass container on the counter, where customers can lift and smell. Only the most acquired-taste devotees dare try or buy. It's rugged. It also makes a great substitute for anchovies.

—LYMAN ORTON

ORTON FAMILY MEAT LOAF

Makes 1 LARGE LOAF; *Serves* 6

Everyone loves a good meat loaf, and most of us have a family recipe that uses either ground beef or a combination of ground beef, pork, and veal. Feel free to adapt the below to your preference. Grass-fed organic beef would be the Orton family choice, since Vermonters tend to support local family farms.

The secret ingredient in this hearty meat loaf is the bacon, which infuses the ground beef with flavor. Then there are the prunes. Trust us, you'll barely know they're there, but they'll add moisture, texture, and just a touch of natural sweetness (still, you can leave them out if you prefer). If you have Vermont Common Crackers on hand, try them as a substitute for the bread crumbs.

MEAT LOAF

1 cup bread crumbs, or 12 Vermont Common Crackers, pulverized in a food processor

½ cup whole milk

1 tablespoon unsalted butter

2 cloves garlic, minced (1 teaspoon)

½ onion, cut into ½-inch pieces (about ½ cup)

2 stalks celery, cut into ½-inch pieces (about 1 cup)

2 carrots, cut into ½-inch pieces (about 1 cup)

2 pounds freshly ground beef chuck

2 large eggs

½ cup chopped fresh flat-leaf parsley

1 teaspoon coarse sea salt

½ teaspoon freshly ground black pepper

½ cup pitted prunes (optional), finely chopped

4 thick slices bacon (4 ounces), frozen, then finely chopped

Preheat the oven to 350°F.

MAKE THE MEAT LOAF: In a large bowl, combine the bread crumbs and the milk and let sit for 5 minutes. In a medium skillet, melt the butter over medium heat. Add the garlic, onion, celery, and carrots and cook until softened, about 5 minutes. Transfer to the bowl with the bread crumbs and stir to combine.

Add the beef and the eggs, stir to combine, then add the parsley, salt, pepper, prunes (if using), and bacon. Gently mix with your hands or a wooden spoon until all is well blended. Do not overwork.

Transfer the meat mixture to a large loaf pan (or two smaller ones) or form a freestyle meat loaf in an ovenproof dish. (We actually prefer the freestyle method, as it gives more crunchy crust goodness.)

COW *Pace*

When I was a kid, my brother Jeremy and I played a car game called I Spy Cows. We made it up, of course. The first one to see a herd had to call it out and then count how many cows were in the field. We begged our parents to slow the car down so we could get an accurate count. I think our biggest fights happened on car trips when we accused each other of double-counting cows. When I cycle past a herd now, I realize how much I value a pace—and a place—where you can count the cows.

—LYMAN ORTON

SAUCE

1 cup sweet chili sauce
(preferably Heinz)

½ cup chopped sweet pickles
or piccalilli (see page 214)

MAKE THE SAUCE: In a small bowl, combine the chili sauce and chopped sweet pickles. Make one long indentation along the top of the meat loaf and fill it with the chili sauce, coating the top with any remaining sauce. (This will marinate and add flavor to the meat, rather than simply bake on the top.)

Bake for 40 to 45 minutes, or until the internal temperature is 160°F. Remove from the oven and let cool slightly before serving.

THE BRYANT HOUSE RESTAURANT

By 1960, the eating area in the Store was getting way too crowded. When the house next door, owned by John and Maude Bryant, came up for sale, Vrest bought it and the Bryant House Restaurant opened that year. The restaurant serves classic New England specialties like maple Johnnycake, pot roast, Indian pudding, chicken potpie, New England clam chowder, and meatloaf.

Vrest furnished The Bryant House with extraordinary finds, including a Victorian-era Tufts soda fountain of ebony and marble with spigots, flavor containers of German silver, and a splendid mahogany tavern salvaged from a New York speakeasy.

The tavern's story bears telling. When Vrest couldn't find an elegant barroom for sale, he heard of a man in Albany who had, in a warehouse, a solid mahogany bar with brass rails, a back-bar with mirrors, and handsome mahogany wall paneling. When Vrest asked how many feet of panels there were, the old man didn't know. Vrest bought the whole lot, moved it to Weston, and when workmen finished installing it, there were only two inches left over!

MARINATED GRILLED FLANK STEAK

Serves 4

———◆◆———

With its robust flavor, tender texture, and pleasant bit of good chew, flank hits all the steak notes while being relatively inexpensive. It's thin enough to cook in minutes, but thick enough to get a nice, rosy medium-rare center, and takes well to marinating. And it's easy to slice and serve, important if you're feeding a crowd.

A one- to four-hour sit in the marinade will allow the salt of the soy sauce to penetrate and tenderize the meat; don't marinate for longer than that, or the lemon juice will make it mushy. Make sure to pat the steak dry after marinating to let the sugar encourage a crust to form. Grilling is the way to go here (and we grill all winter despite the snow), although you can also sear the steak in an ovenproof skillet on both sides and then stick it in a preheated 450°F oven for eight minutes to finish.

---

1 flank steak (about 2 pounds)

1 red onion, chopped (about 1 cup)

3 cloves garlic, minced (about 1 tablespoon)

½ cup light rum

¼ cup olive oil

¼ cup soy sauce

Juice of 2 lemons

1 cup chopped fresh cilantro

1 tablespoon light brown sugar

1 teaspoon grated fresh ginger

1 teaspoon anchovy paste

½ teaspoon red pepper flakes

With a sharp knife, lightly score both sides of the steak at 1½-inch intervals to allow the marinade to flavor the meat more deeply. Combine the remaining ingredients in a medium bowl and stir until the sugar has dissolved. Transfer ¼ cup of the marinade to a small bowl and set aside. Place the remaining marinade in a gallon-size resealable plastic bag and add the steak. Press the air out of the bag, seal, and refrigerate for at least 1 hour and up to 4 hours.

Remove the steak from the marinade a half hour before grilling and pat it dry with paper towels to prevent flare-ups and to make sure it grills rather than steams. Discard the marinade in the bag.

Meanwhile, light the charcoal in a grill; after the coals die down, push all the coals to one side of the grill. If using gas, heat the grill for 15 minutes with all burners on high, then turn off all but one of the burners. Sear the steak on both sides over the high-heat side of the grill, about 2 minutes per side, then move it to the low-heat side of the grill and cook for 2 minutes more per side for medium-rare (130°F). Let stand, tented with foil, for 5 minutes to redistribute the juices before thinly slicing against the grain on an angle. Drizzle with the reserved marinade before serving.

PEPPER-CRUSTED BEEF TENDERLOIN
WITH PORT WINE AND MUSHROOM SAUCE

Serves 8

◆

Beef tenderloin in any iteration is a treat. This preparation, with a rich, winey sauce deepened by the earthiness of a blend of two mushrooms, makes an elegant dinner worthy of any celebration. If you have the time, salt the meat well in advance. Water is drawn out of the meat and then gets reabsorbed with the salt, intensifying the flavor, tenderizing the meat, and leaving the meat's exterior slightly dry, which aids browning. Dry brining overnight in the refrigerator both amps up flavor and juiciness and creates a beautiful, crispy crust.

Serve with Yorkshire pudding or oven-roasted potatoes, both of which will love the sauce, and steamed green beans with a squeeze of lemon.

BEEF TENDERLOIN

1 (2-pound) center-cut beef tenderloin, tied every 3 inches

2 teaspoons coarse sea salt

2 tablespoons whole black peppercorns

2 tablespoons extra-virgin olive oil

MAKE THE BEEF TENDERLOIN: Sprinkle the tenderloin all over with the coarse salt. Place the beef on a rack set over a rimmed baking sheet. Refrigerate, uncovered, for at least 24 hours and up to 36 hours. An hour before roasting, remove the beef from the refrigerator; wipe any salt off the baking sheet.

Preheat the oven to 400°F.

Coarsely crack the peppercorns in a mortar with a pestle or in a resealable plastic bag with a mallet. Rub the beef with 1 tablespoon of the olive oil and coat all over with the cracked pepper, pressing to adhere.

Heat the remaining 1 tablespoon olive oil in a large skillet over medium-high heat until it shimmers. Add the beef and brown it on all sides, about 8 minutes. Transfer the beef back to the rack set over the baking sheet; set the skillet aside, unwashed. Roast the meat until a thermometer inserted into the thickest part reads 120°F, about 30 minutes for medium-rare.

(Continued)

A MOO-VING EXPERIENCE

The days when cows outnumbered people in Vermont are long gone—we now have more than twice the number of people as cows—but the perception lives on. The Strolling of the Heifers, a parade that celebrates our farmers, local food, and iconic cows, draws tens of thousands of people to Brattleboro each June.

PORT WINE AND MUSHROOM SAUCE

1 ounce dried
porcini mushrooms

1 cup hot water (from the tap)

2 tablespoons unsalted butter

2 medium shallots,
finely chopped (¼ cup)

10 ounces cremini or baby
bella mushrooms, sliced
(about 2 cups)

1 cup port wine

1 cup heavy-bodied red wine
(such as Zinfandel)

3 cups Easy Homemade Beef
Stock (recipe follows)
or chicken stock

1 cup fresh or frozen
cranberries

2 fresh rosemary sprigs

2 fresh thyme sprigs,
plus ¼ cup chopped fresh
thyme for garnish

½ teaspoon table salt

MAKE THE PORT WINE AND MUSHROOM SAUCE: Rinse the dried porcini mushrooms to remove any dirt and soak in the hot water until reconstituted, about 30 minutes. Strain through an unbleached paper towel into a small bowl, reserving the strained liquid. Coarsely chop the porcini.

In the skillet you used to cook the beef, melt 1 tablespoon of the butter over medium heat. Add the shallots and cook until translucent, about 3 minutes. Add the chopped porcini mushrooms and the sliced creminis and cook until the creminis release their liquid and the liquid cooks off, about 8 minutes. Add the port, scraping up any browned bits in the pan. Add the red wine, reserved mushroom soaking liquid, beef stock, cranberries, rosemary sprigs, and thyme sprigs. Bring to a boil and cook until the sauce has reduced by about half to about 2 cups. Off the heat, remove any herb sprigs and whisk in the remaining 1 tablespoon butter; add the table salt and taste for seasoning. For an ultra-mooth sauce, whir with an immersion blender directly in the pan. Keep warm until serving.

Remove the tenderloin from the oven and transfer to a cutting board. Tent with aluminum foil and let rest for 15 minutes.

Carve the beef into ¼-inch slices. Serve with the port wine and mushroom sauce and garnish with the chopped thyme.

EASY HOMEMADE BEEF STOCK

Makes 3 TO 4 CUPS

¼ cup vegetable oil

4 to 5 pounds meaty beef
marrow bones (shank or neck)

Salt and freshly ground black
pepper

1 large onion, thickly sliced

1 large carrot, cut into 1-inch
chunks

1 stalk celery, cut into 1-inch
chunks

If you take the time to make your own beef stock, you will never go back to store-bought again. Here we offer the simplest possible recipe that takes almost no time to put to the boil—the hardest part is remembering to do it ahead of time. If you end up with extra stock, it will keep for a week in the fridge, or freeze it for later use. (If you don't have time to make beef stock, substitute 2 cups of chicken stock, which works better than store-bought beef stock.)

Heat the oil in a large stockpot over high heat. Sprinkle the bones with salt and pepper. Add the bones, onion, carrot, and celery to the pot and cook until deeply browned all over, turning often, about 20 minutes. Add 4 quarts water and bring to a boil. Reduce the heat to medium-low and simmer for about 3 hours, until the liquid has reduced to 3 to 4 cups. Strain, discarding the solids. If you have time, refrigerate the stock uncovered until the fat solidifies; remove the fat cap and rewarm the stock when ready to use. If you don't have time to refrigerate the stock, spoon off and discard all the fat before using.

VERMONT SHEPHERD'S PIE

Serves 4 TO 6

The ultimate comfort dish, shepherd's pie is easy to make ahead, loved by kids and adults, and satisfyingly filling. As many versions of shepherd's pie exist as there are layers of an onion, and variations are found in almost every cuisine around the world. In Vermont and traditionally, shepherd's pie is made from lamb (when beef is used, it's called cottage pie), so our version is made from ground lamb; if you prefer to use beef, the result is just as delicious.

This recipe makes a chunky, tender stew under a layer of mashed potatoes, made extra creamy with hot milk, cream, and butter. It's easier to make in stages. Start with boiling and mashing the potatoes, making sure they are smooth and creamy enough to form decorative peaks.

POTATOES

1½ pounds russet potatoes (about 4), peeled and quartered

1 tablespoon sea salt

½ cup whole milk

¼ cup half-and-half

4 tablespoons (½ stick) unsalted butter

½ teaspoon kosher salt

¼ teaspoon freshly ground black pepper

1 egg yolk

MAKE THE POTATOES: Place the potatoes in a medium saucepan and add cold water to cover. Bring to a boil over high heat, then add the sea salt and decrease the heat to maintain a simmer. Cook until tender and easily crushed with a fork or soft enough to pierce with a knife, 25 to 30 minutes.

Drain the potatoes in a colander. Wipe out the pan with a paper towel to remove any residue left from the potatoes and pour in the milk and half-and-half. Add the butter and heat over low heat until the butter has melted, about 1 minute. If you have a ricer, rice the potatoes into the warm liquid in the pan; if not, return the potatoes to the saucepan and mash until smooth. Season with kosher salt and pepper and stir in the egg yolk until well combined and very smooth.

(Continued)

MEAT FILLING

2 tablespoons canola or olive oil

1 yellow onion, coarsely chopped (1 cup)

2 carrots, diced (1 cup)

2 cloves garlic, smashed and minced (1 teaspoon)

1 pound ground lamb

1 teaspoon kosher salt

½ teaspoon freshly ground black pepper

2 tablespoons unbleached all-purpose flour

1 tablespoon tomato paste

1 cup chicken stock

1 tablespoon Worcestershire sauce

2 teaspoons chopped fresh rosemary leaves, or 1 scant teaspoon dried

1 teaspoon chopped fresh thyme leaves, or ½ scant teaspoon dried

1 cup fresh or frozen peas or corn kernels

½ teaspoon paprika

MAKE THE MEAT FILLING: Heat the cooking oil in a large sauté pan over medium-high heat. Add the onion and carrots and sauté just until they begin to soften, about 3 minutes. Add the garlic, lamb, salt, and pepper and cook until the lamb is browned and cooked through, about 5 minutes. Sprinkle the meat with the flour and toss to coat, then continue to cook for another minute. Add the tomato paste, chicken stock, Worcestershire, rosemary, and thyme and stir to combine. Bring to a boil, reduce the heat to low, cover, and simmer for 10 to 12 minutes, or until the sauce has thickened slightly.

Preheat the oven to 425°F.

Spread the lamb mixture evenly in an 8 × 8-inch glass baking dish. Add a layer of peas (still frozen, if using frozen), and with a large serving spoon or rubber spatula, spread the mashed potatoes over the top, starting around the edges to create a seal to prevent the mixture from bubbling up, until the top is fully covered. With the back of the spoon or spatula, twist the potatoes to form little peaks, as if you were decorating a cake. Sprinkle with paprika and bake for 20 minutes, or just until the potatoes begin to brown. Transfer to a wire rack to cool for at least 10 minutes before serving.

BRAISED LAMB SHANKS
WITH MASHED POTATOES WITH CHIVES

Serves 6

━━━ ◆◆ ━━━

In the colder months, which around here means a good portion of the year, we crave rich, deeply flavored, fall-off-the-bone-tender meats, and whenever we can find lamb shanks, we turn to this recipe to deliver. Lamb shanks are a relatively inexpensive cut that returns tenfold. This time-tested recipe never fails to please, whether at Sunday night family dinners or Saturday night dinner parties. We serve the shanks over mashed potatoes with chives, the recipe for which follows. As long as you have something to soak up the luscious sauce, you can't go wrong.

4 tablespoons olive oil

2 large onions, sliced

2 large shallots, sliced (½ cup)

2 cloves garlic, finely minced
(1 teaspoon)

2 tablespoons chopped
fresh rosemary,
or 2 teaspoons dried,
plus a few sprigs for garnish

1 cup unbleached
all-purpose flour

½ teaspoon salt

¼ teaspoon freshly ground
black pepper

6 (¾- to 1-pound)
lamb shanks

2½ cups dry red wine

2½ cups Easy Homemade
Beef Stock (page 100)
or chicken stock

4 teaspoons tomato paste

2 bay leaves

¼ cup chopped fresh
flat-leaf parsley

Mashed Potatoes with Chives
(recipe follows)

In a large cast-iron Dutch oven, heat 2 tablespoons of the olive oil over low to medium heat. Add the onions and cook until golden brown, about 15 minutes, stirring to keep them from burning. Add the shallots and garlic and cook, stirring occasionally, for 10 minutes more, until softened. With a slotted spoon, transfer to a small bowl and sprinkle with the rosemary. Set aside; set the Dutch oven aside, unwashed.

In a large bowl, combine the flour, salt, and pepper. Coat the lamb shanks with the seasoned flour. In the same Dutch oven you used to cook the shallots, heat the remaining 2 tablespoons olive oil over medium-high heat. Working in batches, add the lamb shanks to the pot in a single layer. Brown on both sides, about 10 minutes total. Using tongs, transfer the lamb shanks to plate.

Add 1 cup of the red wine to the now-empty pot and bring to a boil, stirring with a wooden spoon and scraping up any browned bits on the bottom of the pot. Add the onions, the remaining 1½ cups red wine, the beef stock, tomato paste, and bay leaves and bring to a boil, stirring until the tomato paste has dissolved. Return the lamb shanks to the pot, turning them to coat with the liquid, cover, and reduce the heat to maintain a simmer.

Simmer for 1½ hours, turning the shanks once or twice while they cook. (The recipe can be prepared to this point up to 1 day ahead. Cover and refrigerate.)

Fifteen minutes before you're ready to serve, uncover the Dutch oven, remove the bay leaves, and raise the oven heat to 450°F to brown and reduce the sauce consistency. Cook for about 15 minutes, stirring and turning the lamb shanks once or twice.

Divide the mashed potatoes among six shallow pasta bowls and top each with one lamb shank and some of the sauce. Sprinkle parsley over all.

MASHED POTATOES WITH CHIVES

Serves 6

2 pounds white potatoes, unpeeled and scrubbed

1½ teaspoons salt

1 bay leaf

4 tablespoons (½ stick) unsalted butter, melted

¼ cup ricotta

½ teaspoon freshly ground black pepper

½ cup chopped fresh chives

Place the potatoes in a large saucepan and add cold water to cover by 1 inch. Add 1 teaspoon salt and the bay leaf. Bring to a boil, then reduce the heat and simmer gently until the potatoes are easily pierced with a paring knife, about 45 minutes. Reserving ½ cup of the cooking water, drain the potatoes. Discard the bay leaf. Return the potatoes to the pan and let stand, uncovered, for about 5 minutes, until dry.

Meanwhile, whisk together the butter and ricotta in a medium bowl until smooth. Add ¼ cup of the reserved potato cooking water, the pepper, the remaining ½ teaspoon salt, and the chives.

With a wooden spoon or spatula, smash the potatoes in the pan just until the skins are broken. Gently fold in the butter mixture, adding more cooking water a tablespoon at a time if necessary to leave the potatoes looser than you ultimately want (the potatoes will thicken with standing). Taste and adjust the seasoning with salt and pepper. Serve immediately.

MAPLE-MUSTARD GRILLED RACK OF LAMB

Serves 4

———— ◆◆ ————

A rack of lamb is one of the most elegant cuts of lamb, but is so easy to grill that it shouldn't intimidate the home cook. Grilling the lamb intensifies the rich flavor of the meat and results in a crusty exterior with a meltingly tender interior. And it looks spectacular coming off the grill.

We got this recipe from Eliot Orton, who usually doubles the recipe when guests come, as two ribs each are rarely enough for hearty omnivores. (Make sure to count the ribs on the rack to ensure everyone gets at least two.) Eliot makes his own charcoal; when you grill this on a wood charcoal fire, you get a smoky, sweet treat. "It caramelizes and gets a super-yummy, sticky mess all over the lamb," Eliot notes. What more can we say?

1 (4-pound) rack of lamb

1 tablespoon olive oil

1 teaspoon kosher salt

½ teaspoon freshly ground black pepper

¼ cup Colman's mustard powder

1 cup pure maple syrup

2 tablespoons dark brown sugar

¼ cup finely chopped fresh thyme leaves

Take the rack of lamb out of the refrigerator an hour before you intend to grill it. Trim off the excess fat. Rub the lamb with the olive oil and season with the salt and pepper. Let sit, loosely covered with plastic wrap, until room temperature.

Meanwhile, in a small bowl, combine the mustard powder, maple syrup, and brown sugar and mix thoroughly. If you have a mortar and pestle, mash the thyme leaves a bit to extract flavor (the broad side of a chef's knife works for this, too), then add the thyme to the mixture.

Prepare and light a charcoal grill, grouping the coals to one side to create a two-temperature grilling area. (If using a gas grill, heat the grill with all burners on high for 15 minutes, then turn off one or two to create the same effect. Consider placing a pierced foil packet of hickory wood chips on the grill to impart a smoky flavor.)

Place the lamb on the hottest part of the grill, meat side up, baste with the marinade, and cook for 3 minutes; flip, baste, and cook on the other side for 3 minutes. Be watchful, as lamb tends to flare up. Move the lamb to the low-heat side of the grill, with the meaty portion closest to the high-heat side, cover, and continue to cook, basting and turning often, for 15 minutes or so for rare (120°F), 20 minutes for medium-rare (130° to 135°F). Don't cook lamb past the medium point, as it will lose much of its natural flavor and tenderness, and remember that lamb will continue to cook as it rests.

Remove the lamb from the grill and transfer to a large serving platter. Let it rest for 10 minutes to redistribute juices throughout the meat. Slice into individual ribs or two-rib servings.

CHAPTER 5

WILDS *and* WOODS

THE WOODS ROBERT FROST WROTE ABOUT while living here *are* lovely, dark, and deep— and definitely back, covering four-fifths of the state. Our rich tapestry of forest vegetation invites wildlife in abundance: deer, quail, rabbit, wild turkey. Hence the wild, the foraged, and the hunted are an integral part of Vermont cuisine. If you see folks in spring bent over in the woods, chances are they're plucking prized morels, ramps, or fiddlehead ferns from secret spots. In summer, we pick wild berries; in autumn, wild apples are a hiker's reward. In fall, the hunter dreams of filling a freezer for dinners to last until the next hunting season.

MUSHROOMS, QUAIL, DUCK, RABBIT, VENISON, *and* BERRIES

Vermont Maple Syrup

DIY MAPLE SYRUP

LONG AGO, WHEN YOUNG AND AMBITIOUS, OUR parents thought it might be fun to tap the backyard maple trees and make syrup. For a month our dad, Lyman, trudged through the snow to witness a dozen sap buckets fill with glacial progress. Finally, our mother set out to boil the hard-won proceeds on her 1973 General Electric kitchen stove, despite suspicion that grievous toil lay ahead. After fourteen solid hours of sluggish boiling, the house was a steam bath, wallpaper began to curl, the electric meter betrayed a mortifying leap in wattage. On the counter rested a warm mason jar of lovely amber syrup, testament to optimism in the face of adversity. Our mother insists the pancakes that weekend were the finest ever eaten, and in family legend they remain so, undisputed to this day. Life can be sweet; maple makes it more so.

—CABOT ORTON

A 1950s *Vermont Life* photo of sugaring; for some, the method hasn't changed, with tin pails catching the maple sap.

MAPLE BY THE NUMBERS

WE BELIEVE VERMONT MAPLE SYRUP IS THE world's finest. Here are the numbers:

4	grades of maple syrup
5	weeks in a year maple trees produce sap
40	gallons of sap required to produce 1 gallon of maple syrup
150	years a healthy maple tree can produce sap
1,000,000	gallons of syrup produced in Vermont in an average year
1	Vermont's state rank in U.S. maple syrup production

CHANGING GRADES FOR MAPLE SYRUP

OUR DAD, LYMAN, LIKES TO GET HIS HAIR CUT down at the local barbershop for the good value and the jabbering with the men. One of his favorite conversations is about which grade of Vermont maple syrup is best. The men in the barbershop will get to talking and everyone has a different opinion. You might even say it gets to the point of a friendly argument, spurred by the fact that the mother-daughter owner-barbers happen to sell Vermont maple syrup. Maple is likely Vermont's highest point of pride.

Part of the reason for the maple argument is that for a long time, Vermont's maple grading system has caused quite a bit of confusion. The grades we sell were defined as Grade A Fancy, Grade A Medium Amber, and Grade B. To many, that meant that Grade A Fancy was the best and Grade B was somehow inferior. Not true.

Which is why Vermont has taken the leap and is leading the country not only in maple syrup production, but in another way, too: It's the first state to adopt the International Maple Syrup Institute's grading system. Don't worry, your favorite syrup isn't going away; it's just changing names. Now all syrup will be labeled Grade A (which makes sense, since it's all equally good), with flavor descriptors like Delicate, Rich, Robust, and Strong Taste.

Under the new standards, there are four types of Grade A: Golden (the old "fancy"); Amber (the old medium and dark ambers); Dark (the old Grade B); and Very Dark (commercial grade).

No matter which grade you choose, they all take the same amount of hard work and dedication to produce. We hope this clears the air on the subject, before someone loses an ear down at the local barbershop, especially since Dad favors Fancy and his barbers like Grade B!

—ELIOT ORTON

DON'T BE FOOLED

THE DEMAND FOR MAPLE SYRUP KEEPS GROWing as more people become health conscious and realize what a travesty some supermarket "syrups" are. For instance, here's the ingredient list of one of the most popular brands of fake maple: high-fructose corn syrup, corn syrup, water, salt, cellulose gum, molasses, potassium sorbate (preservative), sodium hexametaphosphate, citric acid, caramel color, natural and artificial flavors. Here's the ingredient list of Vermont maple syrup: maple sap—forty gallons boiled down to make one gallon of pure golden sweetness.

WILD SPRING GREENS
WITH LEMON-TAHINI DRESSING

Serves 4

———◆———

Preparing a salad with wild greens and herbs is a tasty way to learn about foraging in Vermont. Dandelion greens, a wild chicory, are ubiquitous; purslane grows in everyone's gardens; and watercress can be found in local streambeds. Blend these with wild herbs such as mint, thyme, and sorrel, and then combine with early spring lettuces from the garden for a one-of-a-kind salad. The exact combination will depend entirely on what is available, the season, and your geography, but the basic idea is that when you add more wild foods to your diet, you are also feeding yourself a rich, healthy spring tonic.

Wild flavors can be a little piquant on their own, but because the leaves are so delicate, we like to use this light and lemony dressing, which softens the assertive flavors while letting the various greens shine.

LEMON-TAHINI DRESSING

Juice of 1 lemon
(3 tablespoons)

¼ cup extra-virgin olive oil

¼ cup tahini

1 tablespoon honey

1 clove garlic, smashed

Salt and freshly ground
black pepper

SALAD

6 cups mixed wild and garden
greens (such as lettuce,
arugula, mâche, radicchio,
young spinach, dandelion,
purslane, curly endive,
dandelion, and sorrel)

½ cup chopped fresh
spring herbs
(such as mint, chives, parsley)

4 scallions, white and green
parts, thinly sliced (1½ cups)

Toasted croutons, for garnish

Edible spring flowers,
for garnish

MAKE THE LEMON-TAHINI DRESSING: In a small bowl, combine the lemon juice, oil, tahini, honey, and garlic. Stir with a fork to blend. Taste and season with salt and pepper.

MAKE THE SALAD: In a large bowl of cold water or in the sink, submerge the salad greens and gently stir with your hands to shake loose any dirt (or bugs). Let the greens sit for a few minutes, then gently lift the leaves, allowing any residue to stay behind in the cold water. Spin dry in a salad spinner or shake outside (the old-fashioned way was in a pillow case), and spread in a single layer on a clean, dry kitchen towel layered with paper towels. Gently roll in a loose tube, and place in a plastic bag with the end open; let chill and crisp in the crisper drawer of the refrigerator until ready to use.

In a large salad bowl, gently toss the greens with the herbs and scallions. Add the dressing, about 1 tablespoon per serving, and toss again. Taste the greens, adding more dressing or seasoning if necessary. Divide evenly among chilled salad plates. Garnish with toasted croutons and edible flowers.

FORAGING FOR WILD EDIBLES

For some Vermonters, a hike through the woods is just that. For others, it's a way to gather foods that are nutritious, plentiful, and free. Combining slow food with slow travel just makes sense. Look what edibles you can find in our woods and fields (and this is only a partial list):

Mushrooms: chaga, morels, lobster, chanterelles, black trumpets, hedgehogs, king boletus, oyster

Dandelions

Wild leeks

Nettles

Milkweed

Garlic mustard

Fiddlehead ferns

Ramps

Watercress

Mint

Japanese knotweed

Purslane

Primrose

Daylilies

Blueberries, raspberries, and blackberries

CRISPY WILD RICE CAKES

Makes 8 SMALL PANCAKES

We like to serve these pancakes as a stand-alone dish with a dab of Ginger-Peach Chutney (see page 210), or as a side dish for smoked pheasant, chicken, or fish. The carrot, celery, and bell pepper add a nice hint of color. It's a terrific way to combine vegetables and grains, and turn a wild food into a mainstream favorite.

We mix the wild rice with nutty-flavored basmati rice, because it both gives the pancake better texture and stretches the wild rice, which can be pricey. Cook them separately, since they have different cooking times, but if you time it just right, the rices can be ready at the same time, your vegetables will be sautéed, and the dish will come together nicely.

½ cup uncooked wild rice

½ teaspoon salt,
plus more for seasoning

½ cup uncooked basmati rice

4 tablespoons olive oil

2 cloves garlic, pressed or
finely chopped (1 teaspoon)

1 carrot,
very finely chopped (½ cup)

1 stalk celery,
very finely chopped (½ cup)

½ yellow or red bell pepper,
very finely chopped (½ cup)

2 large eggs, lightly beaten

1 cup fine bread crumbs or
panko bread crumbs

Freshly ground black pepper

Rinse the wild rice in a colander under cold running water to clean. In a 2-quart saucepan, bring 2 cups water to a boil. Add the salt and stir in the wild rice. Cover, reduce the heat to low, and cook until the rice is tender and the kernels pop open, about 55 minutes.

Meanwhile, rinse the basmati rice in a colander under cold running water to clean and remove excess starch. In a separate 2-quart saucepan, bring 1¼ cups water to a boil. Add the basmati rice, reduce the heat to low, and simmer until the rice is tender and the water has been fully absorbed, about 15 minutes.

Drain both the wild rice and the basmati rice in the colander in the sink to remove any excess water. Do not rinse under cold running water—all the flavor goes down the drain!—but let cool naturally.

While the rice is cooking, in a medium skillet, heat 2 tablespoons of the oil over medium heat. Add the garlic and sauté for 30 seconds until fragrant, then add the carrot, celery, and bell pepper. Sauté until soft, about 5 minutes, stirring occasionally with a wooden spoon. Turn off the heat and set aside to cool.

Transfer the wild rice and basmati rice to a large bowl; add the beaten eggs, bread crumbs, and sautéed vegetables, setting the skillet aside, unwashed. Stir to combine and season with salt and pepper. Let the mixture sit on the counter to cool for 20 minutes. This rest is important to allow the bread crumbs to absorb the liquid. (If you are cooking the cakes later, cover the bowl with plastic wrap and refrigerate.)

Preheat the oven to 250°F.

Wipe out the skillet with a paper towel. Heat the remaining 2 tablespoons olive oil in the skillet over medium heat. Firmly fill a 2-ounce ice cream scoop or a ¼-cup measuring cup with the rice mixture and release it carefully into the skillet. Repeat with as many pancakes as will fit in the pan without crowding; you may have to do this in batches. With the back of a nonstick spatula dipped in water (to keep from sticking), press to slightly flatten the rice mixture into a pancake shape. Cook for 3 minutes per side, then transfer to a baking sheet. Keep warm in the oven while you cook the remaining cakes; you can leave the cakes in the oven until dinner is ready. Leftovers are easy to reheat in a preheated 350°F oven for 15 minutes.

SAVORY FIDDLEHEAD
OR ASPARAGUS TART

Serves 8

———◆———

fter a long winter, a short and fickle spring teases Vermonters, and we take heart in spring miracles that restore hope and spirits, like fiddlehead ferns foraged in our woods. Only available for a few weeks in the spring, fiddleheads are curled little wonders packed with protein and iron that serve up a woodsy crunch.

Tempered by a thin, crisp crust, this tart counters the earthy flavor of fiddleheads with the smooth tang of fresh ricotta spiked with lemon zest to bring out a light spring flavor. If you can't find fiddleheads, this recipe can be easily adapted with fresh asparagus, either steamed or roasted.

Flour, for dusting

1 sheet frozen puff pastry dough

1½ cups fresh fiddleheads (½ pound), or ½ pound asparagus

4 tablespoons olive oil

1 large shallot, thinly sliced (about ¼ cup)

1 medium yellow onion, peeled and thinly sliced (1 cup)

2 cloves garlic, smashed and minced (1 teaspoon)

Salt and freshly ground black pepper

2 cups ricotta cheese

½ cup grated Cheddar cheese

2 large eggs

2 tablespoons chopped fresh chives

Zest of 1 lemon

On a lightly floured surface, roll out the pastry dough to an inch larger than the fluted tart pan you wish to use. Place the dough in the pan and trim off the edges with the back of a spoon or a rolling pin. Refrigerate until ready to use.

Bring a saucepan of water to a boil. Rinse the fiddleheads to remove any grit and place them in a steam basket. Set the steamer basket in the saucepan of boiling water and steam the fiddleheads for 8 to 10 minutes, or until they are crisp-tender. Transfer them with a slotted spoon to a bowl of ice water to stop the cooking, then transfer to paper towels to drain. (If you don't have a steamer, drop directly into boiling salted water.)

In a medium skillet, heat the olive oil over low heat. Add the shallot and onion and cook, stirring occasionally with a wooden spoon, until soft, about 15 minutes. Add the garlic, stir, and cook until fragrant, about 30 seconds. Season lightly with salt and pepper.

Preheat the oven to 375°F.

In a large bowl, blend together the ricotta, Cheddar, eggs, chives, and lemon zest. Remove the tart crust from the refrigerator. Spread the cheese mixture evenly over the crust, top with the browned onions and finally with the fiddleheads. (If you are using asparagus instead, try to leave the spears whole, which will make for an attractive presentation.)

Bake for 40 minutes, until the pastry is golden. Remove from the oven and let cool on a rack for 5 minutes before slicing and serving.

VERMONT GLAZED QUAIL
WITH CRANBERRY STUFFING

Serves 4

◆◆◆

*L*ocally hatched native birds provide hunting early in the season. Ruffled grouse, partridge, quail, and woodcocks are the most widely available upland game in Vermont. Skillful hunters can find game birds wherever brushy forest stands provide nesting cover, protection from predators, and food in the form of berries and buds.

For those of us who don't hunt, we can find cultivated wild poultry, such as quail, grown in captivity and sold ready to serve, often with bones removed. Quail make a wonderful holiday dish and play well with winter root vegetable side dishes like turnips and carrots. While Cornish game hen won't give you the same delicate meat, it can be substituted for quail if you can't find a source. Adjust the cooking procedure and time accordingly, giving them more time in the oven, forty-five minutes to one hour.

---

4 boneless quail

Salt and freshly ground black pepper

3 tablespoons olive oil

2 tablespoons unsalted butter

2 shallots, minced (¼ cup)

¼ cup coarsely chopped portobello or wild mushrooms

1 teaspoon fresh sage, or ½ teaspoon dried

1 teaspoon fresh thyme, or ½ teaspoon dried

3 cups cornmeal bread crumbs, cut into ½-inch cubes, or cornmeal stuffing mix

½ cup fresh cranberries, or ⅛ cup dried cranberries softened in boiling water

½ cup chicken stock

½ cup boiled cider or Marsala wine

Preheat the oven to 350°F.

In a medium bowl, season the quail thoroughly with salt and pepper.

In a large skillet, heat 2 tablespoons of the oil and the butter over medium heat. Add the shallots and sauté until soft, about 5 minutes. Add the mushrooms, sage, and thyme and sauté for 5 minutes more, until all are gently cooked. Transfer to a bowl (setting aside the unwashed skillet) and stir in the bread crumbs or stuffing and cranberries (drained from their soaking water, if using dried); add the chicken stock and toss to combine.

Place the quail on a cutting board or platter, and with your hands or a spoon, fill the cavity with the stuffing until loosely filled. Do not overstuff, as the stuffing will expand as it cooks. Tie together the legs with kitchen twine. (Or you can be fancy and make a slit just under the wing on one side, then slip the leg bone through to secure.) Repeat for each of the birds.

In the skillet you used to cook the shallots, heat the remaining 1 tablespoon oil over medium heat until shimmering. Sauté the birds for less than a minute on each side, turning them to brown all sides. The birds will puff up nicely, like a small balloon, when ready.

Transfer the birds to a baking dish. Pour the boiled cider (or Marsala wine) into the skillet to deglaze, scraping up all the browned bits on the bottom of the pan with a wooden spoon. Pour the glaze over the birds, then bake for 15 minutes. Serve warm.

ROAST DUCK
WITH WILD PLUM SAUCE

Serves 4

———◆◆———

*L*ike grandchildren, fruit trees are an investment in the future, and we prize our heirloom fruits for their flavor and durability. Not all fruit grows in Vermont, but luckily we succeed at many types of apples, plums, pears, and occasionally cherries and peaches. This recipe, which features a basic roast duck—with luck, one harvested by a hunter friend in the fall—that is crisp and moist, pairs with a sweet, syrupy plum sauce. It makes up to a quart of rose-colored sauce, so you make a batch and then serve it with all types of poultry: chicken, quail, or turkey, too. Make it with wild fruit, heirloom plums from a local market, or cultivated plums you find in the store.

1 (5-pound) duck,
wing tips removed

8 cups chicken stock

1 tablespoon plus
1 teaspoon coarse salt

½ teaspoon freshly ground
black pepper

2 cups Wild Plum Sauce
(recipe follows),
plus more for serving

1 pound mixed shallots
and onions, quartered

1 pound mixed plums,
such as red, yellow,
and pluots, halved and pitted

Remove the giblets from the duck, and pat the inside and the outside dry with a paper towel. With a fork, lightly prick the skin all over without piercing the meat to allow the fat to drain off while the duck cooks.

In a large stockpot, bring the chicken stock to a boil with 1 tablespoon of the coarse salt. Gently slide in the duck and bring the stock back to a boil. If there isn't enough stock to cover the duck, add boiling water to cover. If the duck floats to the top, place a plate on top to keep it immersed. Once the stock returns to a boil, reduce the heat to maintain a simmer and cook for 30 minutes to render some of the duck's fat.

Preheat the oven to 450°F.

Turn off the heat and skim enough duck fat from the top of the stock to pour a film on the bottom of a large roasting pan. This will keep the duck from sticking while it cooks. Remove the duck from the stock, holding it over the pot to drain, and transfer to the roasting pan; pat the skin dry with paper towels and sprinkle with salt and the pepper. If you have time, allow the duck to sit at room temperature for 30 minutes to dry.

Roast the duck for 30 minutes. Remove from the oven, spoon any drippings from the pan over the duck to crisp the skin, and baste with 1 cup of the plum sauce. Place the mixed shallots and onions and the plums around the duck and roast for 30 minutes more. Baste again with the duck fat and the remaining 1 cup of the plum sauce. Test with a meat thermometer; when done, the temperature should register between 130° and 140°F. Remove from the oven and tent with aluminum foil. Let rest for 15 minutes before serving.

WILD PLUM SAUCE

Makes 4 CUPS

1 quart (2½ pounds)
purple plums

2 cinnamon sticks

1 tablespoon whole cloves

½ cup apple cider vinegar

2½ cups sugar

In a saucepan, combine the plums and 1½ cups water and bring to a boil. Reduce the heat to maintain a simmer and cook until the plums start to split, about 5 minutes. With a slotted spoon, transfer the plums to a colander or a food mill, leaving the water in the saucepan, and squeeze to remove the skins and pits. Cut a small piece of cheesecloth and wrap the cinnamon and cloves inside, tying the top with a piece of kitchen twine. Add the vinegar, sugar, and spice bag to the water in the saucepan and add the plum pulp. Cook briskly over medium-high heat until thick, 12 to 15 minutes. Serve fresh with the roast duck, and use to baste the duck while it cooks. Store any remaining sauce in the refrigerator for a week or freeze.

The CRANEBERRY

If you're near a cranberry bog in the spring, look closely at the small pink blossoms on the bush. Do you see the head and bill of a sandhill crane? The Pilgrims did, and thus named the fruit "craneberry." Of course, far before the Pilgrims landed, the Native Americans were using cranberries as a food, to dye fabrics, and for their healing properties. And far after the Pilgrims, American whalers and mariners took vitamin C–packed cranberries to sea.

RABBIT BRAISED IN HARD CIDER

Serves 4

———◆———

At our local farmers' markets, we often find a stall or two selling meats from small family farms, the offerings scribbled on a chalkboard and crossed off as the vendor runs out. Occasionally, we'll find rabbit, a real treat for its depth of flavor and tenderness, especially when braised with mushrooms, pancetta, and herbs. Here we use Vermont Citizen hard cider—developed as a dry hard cider for wine drinkers—as a braising liquid, and boost the slight apple flavor with a cut-up apple and a touch of Calvados. Served over pappardelle or potatoes to soak up the silky sauce, this braise is subtle yet hearty, and makes even those who have never tasted rabbit close to euphoric. If you can't find rabbit, we've made this with chicken, and it is equally sublime.

2 cups unbleached
all-purpose flour

2 teaspoons salt,
plus more for seasoning

1 teaspoon freshly ground
black pepper,
plus more for seasoning

1 (2- to 3-pound) rabbit,
cut into serving pieces

2 tablespoons vegetable oil

2 tablespoons unsalted butter

½ cup diced pancetta,
or 2 slices bacon, chopped

1 yellow onion, halved and
thinly sliced crosswise

2 sprigs fresh thyme

2 tablespoons Calvados
or brandy

2 cups dry hard cider

1 cup chicken stock

Strip of thinly pared lemon rind

1 large clove garlic, chopped
(about 1 teaspoon)

2 cups cremini mushrooms
(about 6 ounces), quartered

1 crisp cooking apple (such
as Granny Smith), peeled,
quartered, and cored

¼ cup crème fraîche
or heavy cream

In a shallow bowl, combine the flour, salt, and pepper. Dredge all the rabbit pieces in the seasoned flour, shaking off the excess. Set aside.

Heat the vegetable oil in a large Dutch oven over medium-high heat. Add the rabbit and cook until nicely browned on all sides, 2 to 3 minutes per side. Transfer to a plate.

Pour off all but 1 tablespoon of the fat from the pot. Add 1 tablespoon of the butter, the pancetta, and the onion and reduce the heat to medium-low. Cook until the onions are very soft and golden, 10 to 12 minutes. Return the rabbit to the pot, along with the thyme sprigs and a generous sprinkling of salt and pepper. Cook for 2 minutes, then pour the Calvados over the rabbit. Off the heat, ignite the Calvados with a long match. When the flames die down, add the hard cider, chicken stock, and lemon rind. Bring to a boil, then reduce the heat to low, cover, and simmer until the rabbit is tender, about 1 hour and 15 minutes.

Preheat the oven to 425°F.

Melt the remaining 1 tablespoon butter in a skillet. Add the garlic and cook until fragrant, about 30 seconds, then add the mushrooms. Cook over medium-high heat, taking care that the garlic doesn't burn, until the mushrooms are brown. Add the softened mushrooms and the apple to the rabbit and return the Dutch oven to the oven to bake, uncovered, until the liquid has reduced by half, about 15 minutes. Spoon the sauce over the rabbit as it cooks to keep it basted. Remove from the oven, and just before serving, add the crème fraîche and gently stir until blended.

BRAISED SHORT RIBS
WITH WILD MUSHROOMS AND FENNEL

Serves 4 TO 6

◆◆

Wild mushrooms are everywhere after a good rainfall, and in Vermont we are likely to find morels in the spring and chanterelles in the late summer and early fall. If you are not interested in foraging, substitute with the next-best thing: shiitake and oyster mushrooms, which are grown on logs.

We especially like the way this dish blends the earthy flavors of mushrooms with fennel and a hint of orange to create a light, aromatic dish. Cooked in three easy steps, it's the perfect way to eat well with an economical and flavorful, yet often overlooked, cut of beef. And your kitchen will smell delicious as it's cooking.

8 bone-in beef short ribs

Salt and freshly ground black pepper

6 tablespoons olive oil

1 large or 2 small fennel bulbs

1 large sweet yellow onion

2 cups coarsely chopped wild mushrooms or a mixture of shiitake and oyster

½ cup anisette or Pernod (licorice liqueur)

2 cups chicken stock

Peel from 1 orange

Preheat the oven to 350°F.

Season the ribs with salt and pepper and let sit at room temperature for 30 minutes.

Heat 2 tablespoons of the oil in a large Dutch oven over medium-high heat. Add the ribs and brown on all sides, about 2 minutes per side. Transfer the ribs to a large bowl. Do not wash the pot.

Trim the fennel, reserving some of the nice fronds for garnish later. Chop the fennel and onion into 1-inch pieces. Add 2 tablespoons of the oil to the Dutch oven and heat over medium-high heat. Add the fennel and onion and cook, stirring continuously, until browned and soften, about 5 minutes. Remove the vegetables from the pot with a slotted spoon and add to the bowl with the ribs.

Heat the remaining 2 tablespoons oil over medium-high heat. Add the mushrooms and cook, stirring occasionally, for 3 minutes, until browned and soft. Add the anisette and cook down for 2 to 3 minutes. Return the short ribs, fennel, and onion to the pot, stirring to combine. Add the chicken stock and the orange peel. Cover and braise over medium heat for 2 hours. Remove and discard the orange peel. Serve, garnishing each serving with the reserved fennel fronds.

AWARD-WINNING VENISON
AND APPLE CHILI

Serves 6 TO 8

—◆◆◆—

Apples lend an unexpected and pleasant surprise to this satisfying venison chili, rounding out the flavors and countering the heat of the fresh jalapeños. Perfect for a leaf-burning party or a cozy winter night around the fireplace, all it needs is a crusty loaf of bread and a leafy green salad to make a hearty, soul-nourishing meal. And, as with all chili, it is even better the next day.

2 tablespoons olive oil

2½ pounds venison stew meat or ground venison

2 large yellow onions, diced (2 cups)

2 jalapeños, seeded and finely diced

6 sweet tart cooking apples (such as Cortland or McIntosh)

¼ cup ground cumin

1 tablespoon chili powder

6 cloves garlic, smashed and minced

1 teaspoon coarse salt

¼ teaspoon freshly ground black pepper

1 (6-ounce) can tomato paste

1 (28-ounce) can whole tomatoes

1 cup red wine

2 cups Easy Homemade Beef Stock (page 100) or chicken stock

Grated Cheddar cheese, for serving

Chopped red onions, for serving

In a heavy-bottomed stockpot, heat the oil over medium heat until shimmering. Add the venison meat and cook until brown on all sides, about 8 minutes total. With a slotted spoon, transfer the venison to a small bowl.

Add the onions and jalapeños to the pot and cook over medium heat for 5 minutes, until soft. While the onions cook, peel and core the apples and cut them into ½-inch cubes; you should have about 6½ cups. Return the venison to the pot, along with the apples, cumin, chili powder, and garlic. Cook for 5 minutes more and season with salt and pepper.

Stir in the tomato paste and whole tomatoes, breaking up the tomatoes with your hands or a wooden spoon as you add them. Add the juice from the tomatoes, the red wine, and the beef stock and bring to a simmer. Cook over low heat for about 2 hours. Taste, adjust the seasonings, and serve topped with Cheddar and onions.

HUNTERS' VENISON STEW

Serves 4 TO 6

❖

*S*low roasting results in tender meat, which is exactly what makes this venison so delicious. Based on a classic *beef bourguignonne, this stew accentuates the venison with sweet dates, cumin, and a marinade of sweet port. Juniper berries can be found in most supermarkets in the spice aisle and are especially good with any wild game. Beef can easily be substituted for venison in this recipe; select a lean cut or chuck steak.*

Plan ahead, since this recipe calls for overnight marinating and will be in the oven for a couple of hours. Don't be daunted by the long list of ingredients, as it all comes together easily and is the perfect dish to bring along for a weekend in the country to simmer on a woodstove and fill the house with an irresistible aroma. It goes without saying that stew is best served with a heaping mound of buttery mashed potatoes and a Cabernet Sauvignon.

MARINATED VENISON

6 juniper berries

½ teaspoon whole cloves

1 teaspoon allspice berries

1 teaspoon
whole black peppercorns

1 teaspoon coarse sea salt

1 teaspoon dried cumin
seeds, dry roasted

1½ pounds venison shoulder
or stew meat,
cut into 2-inch cubes

1 cup dry red wine
(such as Cabernet Sauvignon)

½ cup sweet port or Madeira

MAKE THE MARINATED VENISON: With a mortar and pestle, grind the juniper berries, cloves, allspice, peppercorns, salt, and cumin.

Place the venison in a large bowl and rub the spice mix over all the pieces with your fingers. Pour the wine and sweet port over the meat to cover, toss to coat, cover the bowl with plastic wrap, and refrigerate overnight or for up to 2 days.

Preheat the oven to 350°F.

Place a colander over a large bowl. Drain the venison in the colander and pat the meat dry, reserving the marinade in the bowl.

(Continued)

STEW

3 slices bacon,
cut into 1-inch pieces

4 cloves garlic,
smashed and minced

2 large onions, quartered

4 large carrots,
halved and then quartered

1 (6-ounce) can tomato paste

1 cup dry red wine
(such as Cabernet Sauvignon)

1¾ cups Easy Homemade
Beef Stock (page 100)
or chicken stock

2 bay leaves

1 (2-inch) strip orange rind

½ cup dates,
pitted and halved

MAKE THE STEW: Heat a large Dutch oven or stew pot over medium-high heat. Add the bacon and cook, stirring with a wooden spoon, 3 to 4 minutes, until just crisp. Add the garlic, onions, and carrots and cook until the vegetables are lightly browned, about 10 minutes. With a slotted spoon, transfer the vegetables and bacon to a medium bowl and set aside.

Add the venison to the Dutch oven and brown well on all sides, about 5 minutes, being careful not to overcrowd the pot (work in batches, if necessary). Pour the reserved marinade into the pot and bring to a boil, scraping up the browned bits on the bottom with a wooden spoon. Add the vegetables to the meat, along with the tomato paste, wine, stock, bay leaves, and orange rind. Cover and bake for 1 hour.

Remove the pot from the oven and stir in the dates; return the pot to the oven and bake, uncovered, for 45 minutes more. Serve immediately, or let cool, refrigerate, and reheat later. As with all stews, this tastes even better the next day.

↬ THE SEARCH FOR THE CHAGA MUSHROOM

Vermont's rolling hills are covered in wild and edible foods, some of which are surprising. The chaga mushroom—said to be the greatest storehouse of medicinal healing properties of any single mushroom or herb in the world—grows in abundance on birch trees here! Considered the "king of the mushrooms," the chaga is commonly found in Siberia and Eurasian countries and has been used for medicinal purposes since the sixteenth century.

I had hiked countless hours, looking at hundreds of birch trees searching for the fungus, with no chaga in sight. Another approach was necessary. So I studied as much information as I could, looked at countless pictures, and even envisioned finding chaga growing in the forest.

I then set back out to find and harvest some of this incredible mushroom. After walking for miles, on the verge of giving up, I was suddenly overcome with a powerful urge to stop and look to my right. There, deep in the forest and high up on a hill, was a massive yellow birch tree. I ran, crashing through the brush, to discover a beautiful growth of chaga mushroom on the back side of this birch. I had found her and she had found me!

—GARDNER ORTON

Ella and Leo Orton
appreciating nature—and nurture!

⌒ HUNTING TALES

I recall waking up at four a.m., the earliest anyone has ever woken up in the entire history of the world, and stumbling out of the house half asleep. No noise, no birds, dead-still quiet. The old pickup truck—a 1969 Chevy with a 3-speed on the shift—breaks the silence. We arrive at a special place, park, wait for it to get light enough to see, and walk out on forest roads into the woods.

We spent a lot of time as kids "hunting," or rather walking, standing, being quiet, and observing. To me, that's what hunting's all about: slowing down, letting your senses take in what's around you. It's akin to meditation. We never saw a deer. I think now that

was on purpose, as we were too young to grasp the significance of taking an animal.

Five years ago, I took up hunting again. I actually call it walking a gun around the woods. I like deer meat, but not enough to buy a freezer chest. But it's a chance to spend time on our land, listening to the wind.

I take Leo and Ella out at dusk in the summertime in the field behind our house. I have them sit on a wall and just look. Their ability to pay attention is remarkable. It's about teaching stewardship, and I'm happy to say they already have an intense appreciation of the animals and birds all around us.

—ELIOT ORTON

ELDERBERRY SHRUB

Makes ABOUT 2 CUPS

◆◆◆

*R*ecipes for shrubs vary greatly and date as far back as pre-Colonial times. They are simple to make by combining equal parts berries, vinegar, and sugar, then leaving the mixture alone to ferment.

Generally, shrubs are poured over ice or served with a bit of sparkling water. By themselves, they are not alcoholic, but are often added to rum, brandy, or vodka to make a delicious cocktail. For a Shirley shrub, start with 1 part shrub to 6 parts sparkling water, and adjust to taste.

We especially like this elderberry shrub, since elderberry is an old-time remedy for congestion and sore throats, which makes it an excellent tonic for the body at the same time. Elderberries are in many ways little grapes, with a similar aroma, bloom on the skin, and color; they even have little seeds inside. If you don't have elderberries, try this shrub with other berries, such as blueberries, raspberries, blackberries, currants, gooseberries, or a combination. It's key to find apple cider vinegar with the "mother," which is important for fermentation (look in health food stores or the organic section of the supermarket), rather than the pasteurized vinegar commonly available.

---

2 cups elderberries

1 cup sugar

2 cups apple cider vinegar with the "mother"

Harvest the elderberries when they are deep purple and fully ripe. Place them in a small bowl and lightly crush using a whisk or potato masher. Stir in sugar, cover, and allow the berries to macerate overnight at room temperature. Transfer to a 1-quart mason jar and add the vinegar. Shake to combine everything. Cover the jar top with cheesecloth and secure with a rubber band or twine. Label and set aside in a cool, dark place for 1 week.

Give the mixture a good shake or stir and pour through a colander or fine-mesh strainer set over a bowl in the sink. Discard the berries in the colander and bottle the shrub in sterilized jars (see page 194) or fancy bottles, with nonmetallic lids, preferably plastic caps. Store in a cool, dark place for up to 1 year.

BLACKBERRY CORDIAL

Makes **ABOUT 4 CUPS**

This old-time favorite recipe produces a warm, rich liqueur that will remind you of a tawny port. Serve chilled or at room temperature, sipped from a cordial glass. Select ripe wild blackberries, and use this recipe as a general guide, adapting to fit the amount of berries you pick. If you have two cups of berries, for instance, cut the sugar in half, and add just enough brandy to suit your taste.

4 cups fresh blackberries

2 cups sugar,
plus more as needed

About 4 cups brandy

Place the blackberries in a preserving kettle or stockpot and add 2 cups water, or just enough water to keep them from burning. Let them stew slowly over low heat until soft. Strain through cheesecloth or a jelly bag, letting it drip, and then gently press out all the remaining juice.

Measure out the liquid, and for every 4 cups, stir in 2 cups sugar. Return the mixture to the stockpot and boil for 30 minutes to dissolve the sugar and concentrate the juice. Add brandy, adjusting the amount to your taste preference. Let cool and bottle. Seal with hot wax or a lid and store in a cool pantry for up to a year.

✃ FROST AND VREST

When we head into the woods, no matter the season, verses by Robert Frost pop into mind. "Two roads diverged in a yellow wood…" "Nature's first green is gold…" "Whose woods these are I think I know…"

When Robert Frost lived down the road in Shaftsbury, Vermont, he and our grandfather struck up a friendship that lasted a quarter century. The two saw many seasons together, with long afternoons spent in deep conversation. Or rather, as Vrest wrote in his book *Vermont Afternoons with Robert Frost*, "Those were afternoons I did not spend…I saved them up."

One letter from Frost to Vrest begins, "Sometime in the fall when the flood of summer people has subsided, you and I will be left still clinging to the rocks of Vermont." As we climb those rocks and explore those woods, we think of our grandfather and the poet, sitting on the porch, endlessly talking.

—CABOT ORTON

Vrest and poet Robert Frost on Frost's front porch, 1930.

CHAPTER 6

The
GRISTMILL

BY THE DAM ACROSS THE WEST RIVER JUST BE-
yond the Village Green in Weston sits the Old
Grist Mill, worthy of note because, in a small but
significant way, it played a part in the way we think about
nutrition today. Built in 1785 and, at the time The Vermont Country Store opened, run by Vrest's father, Gardner Lyman Orton, it specialized in cold-stone-grinding
whole grains, which The Vermont Country Store sold as
flours and cereals—the first to do so through the mail.

Mildred, convinced she could replace refined white flour
in her cooking, took these flours home to develop recipes.
The result was *Cooking with Wholegrains*, published by the
famous New York publishing house Farrar, Straus and Company in 1947, the first whole-grain cookbook in the country,
and our inspiration for the following.

BREADS *and* WHOLE GRAINS

THE RECIPE FOR A WHOLE-GRAINS PIONEER

Mildred Ellen Orton and Vrest Orton,
in front of the wood-fueled stove she used to test recipes.

A DISCIPLE OF ADELLE DAVIS AND A STAUNCH believer in the nutritional superiority of whole grains, our grandmother developed recipes using grains from the old gristmill across the Village Green, testing them on the woodstove in her house.

"For the longest while, I couldn't quite get the temperatures right for the book because it was all by feel," our grandmother told us one day. "I couldn't rely on a thermometer with a woodstove—but you can't quite write, 'This is a one-log recipe and this is a two-log recipe,' now can you?"

In 1947, she compiled these recipes into *Cooking with Wholegrains*, which was sold nationally. Realizing that cooks interested in healthy tried-and-true recipes abound in today's world, Farrar, Straus and Giroux republished the cookbook in 2010.

Mildred Ellen Orton was a pioneer proponent of using whole grains and eating healthy, natural food. Maybe that's why she lived to be ninety-nine years old!

—GARDNER ORTON

THE ONE-ARMED MILLER

VREST ORTON WAS KNOWN TO HARANGUE ABOUT all sorts of things in short editorials sprinkled through *The Voice of the Mountains*, as he started calling the Store's catalog in 1952. One of his favorite pet peeves: how "anemic" refined white flour took the place of healthy whole grains. After he spearheaded the restoration of the Old Grist Mill, his father, Gardner Lyman Orton (known as G.L.), ran it. Throwing belts over the water-powered spinning wooden drive wheels is tough with two arms, but due to a trolley car accident, G.L. had only one. The Store started selling whole grains, and Mildred took up the cause in her groundbreaking cookbook, to which Vrest wrote a scathing introduction lambasting the giant food companies for producing insipid, nutritionless white flour that was gaining in popularity at the time, and singing the virtues of stone-ground whole grains.

AN IMPRESSIVE REVIEW

AFTER THE PREEMINENT AMERICAN FOOD WRITER M. F. K. Fisher received *Cooking with Wholegrains*, she wrote back, "I like the wholegrain cookbook very much…Give…Mrs. O…my sincere congratulations and thanks…I expect a friend who is in love with baking, and will turn him loose with the samp and other flours, and the Orton cookbook."

BREAD LOVE

A WOODEN SIGN LEANING ON THE BRICK SHELF above the stone oven of Jedediah Mayer, baker and owner of Rupert Rising Breads in West Rupert, reads: *Bake bread with your eyes open, eat it with your heart open and your eyes closed.*

(ABOVE) Gardner Lyman Orton at the Old Grist Mill.
(RIGHT) Gardner Lyman Orton on the porch of the Old Grist Mill.

WHEN COMMON CRACKERS DEBUTED IN VERmont in 1828, they were the first commercially made crackers in America. This simple, round, dry biscuit made of flour, water, shortening, and salt became a staple of Vermont farm families, who would buy a forty-gallon wooden barrel full every fall to stock the pantry. They have little flavor—which is, strangely, what makes them so popular. Each cracker, split open with a thumbnail, was used not only as a base for cheese but for breading when crushed, an ingredient in mock mince pie, a filler for meat loaf and turkey stuffing, as well as in every Vermonter's iconic Sunday night supper: crackers crumbled into a bowl of milk served with a hunk of Cheddar.

Common Crackers were originally made by horse-powered machinery—not machinery with horsepower, but actually a huge inclined treadmill on which a horse walked, turning a shaft connected to gears and a flywheel for a belt. Before the electric motor was invented (simultaneously, by two Vermonters living across the mountain from each other), farm animals supplied the power for all kinds of machinery. Farm dogs walked a smaller inclined treadmill to run the farm's washing machine, tool sharpener, and often even a small mill.

For a time the common crackers were made in St. Johnsbury and were called St. Johnsbury Crackers, and then, when production was moved to Montpelier, they were called—you guessed it—Montpelier Crackers. In 1970, the Cross Company making the crackers went bankrupt, and I heard its machinery was going on sale at auction. I bid on it and the oven and other equipment and won. A man named Bob Mills introduced himself to me at the auction as the cracker baker and before the bidding was over, I hired him.

Today, my sons run the bakery business, producing these historic crackers and the very popular

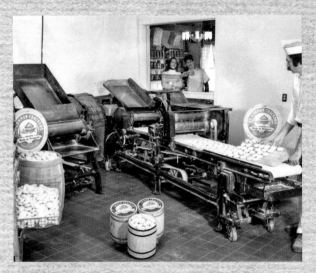

Baking Common Crackers in the 1980s.

Orton Brothers Cookie Buttons. When you visit us at the Store and sample the jams, salsas, and special spreads we sell, you'll be spooning treats on half a Vermont Common Cracker, a product with an almost two-century history.

–LYMAN ORTON

WHAT DID JULIA CHILD THINK WAS "ABSOLUTELY MARVELOUS"?

JULIA CHILD USED TO ORDER VERMONT COMMON Crackers from us and praised their virtues thus:

> They're absolutely marvelous with fish chowders, but I like them best split in half, brushed with butter and baked in a 375-degree oven for just a few minutes until browned. Vermont Common Crackers are so versatile— they can be crumbled and mixed into stuffings or they can top a scalloped-oyster casserole. Of course they're lovely when sprinkled with some grated Vermont Cheddar cheese.

Farm dogs in Vermont worked.
Vrest Orton and brothers Lyman and Paul with their dog, named Guess, circa 1901.

BUCKWHEAT CREPES
WITH SPICY APPLESAUCE

Makes TWENTY-FOUR 8-INCH CREPES

—◆—

*M*ildred's griddlecakes (see page 12) inspired us to explore using whole-grain flours for other pancake-type recipes, like tiny blini straight from her recipe (excellent as appetizers, topped with smoked salmon, crème fraiche, and a sprig of dill) and these crepes. The nutty goodness and firm texture of the buckwheat holds any filling, yet is still delicate and delicious. Crepes are fairly quick to make, and this recipe makes a big batch that you can keep in the refrigerator to fill throughout the week with a variety of savory or sweet ingredients. Or layer them individually with waxed paper and freeze. If you don't have a crepe pan, use a shallow 9-inch nonstick skillet with slanted sides.

½ cup whole wheat flour

½ cup buckwheat flour

½ cup unbleached all-purpose flour

1 teaspoon salt

4 large eggs

1 cup whole milk

4 tablespoons (½ stick) unsalted butter, melted

Canola or other vegetable oil, for the skillet

In a large bowl, combine the whole wheat flour, buckwheat flour, all-purpose flour, and salt. Add the eggs and mix with a whisk to combine. Gradually pour in the milk and 1¼ cups water, whisking vigorously to prevent lumps. Add the butter and continue to whisk until smooth. Cover and refrigerate for at least 1 hour. Before cooking, give it another quick whisk to blend again. (You can also make this in a blender or in the bowl of a stand mixer fitted with the whisk attachment.)

Lightly oil an 8-inch crepe pan and place over medium heat. When the pan is warm, lift it from the heat and wait 3 seconds, then pour in ¼ cup of the crepe batter while tilting the pan so the batter coats the bottom evenly. Return to the heat. Cook until lightly browned underneath, about 2 minutes. Turn the crepe with a thin spatula and cook the other side for about 1 minute. Transfer to a plate, cover with a plate or clean kitchen towel to keep warm, and repeat until you have used all the batter.

You can either fill the crepes while warm, or let them cool completely, then wrap in plastic and store in the refrigerator for up to 5 days. Reheating in a dry skillet over medium-low heat gives them a nice crisp exterior.

To fill the crepes, spread about 3 tablespoons of your filling of choice over the crepe, then fold it in half and plate. Or roll it into a tube, slice it in half, and plate.

(Continued)

SPICY APPLESAUCE

Makes 4 CUPS

½ cup sugar

Juice of ½ lemon

½ teaspoon ground cinnamon

¼ teaspoon
freshly grated nutmeg

¼ teaspoon ground ginger

⅛ teaspoon ground cloves

8 medium cooking apples
(such as Cortland
or McIntosh) (2 pounds),
cored and thinly sliced

Applesauce is so easy to make that there is no reason to buy it from the grocery store. Simply simmer sliced apples with a little water or apple cider until soft. Keep the skins on for added flavor and color. The type of apple will determine the cooking time: A firm Cortland will take slightly longer to cook than a soft McIntosh. The sauce can be passed through a food mill to make a smooth sauce, or served slightly chunky.

In a small saucepan, bring 1 cup water to a boil. Add the sugar, lemon juice, cinnamon, nutmeg, ginger, and cloves. With a wooden spoon, stir until the sugar has dissolved. Reduce the heat to low and simmer for 5 minutes to release the flavor from the spices.

Add the apples and cover. Cook over medium-low heat, stirring often, until the apples are tender, about 10 minutes. Don't overcook the apples, as they will continue to cook off the heat.

For a smoother sauce, mash the apples with a fork or run them through a food mill to puree. Serve warm or refrigerate and serve cold.

TOASTER COLLECTION

A favorite collection at the Weston store is a display of vintage toasters showcased behind a glass wall, the gleaming polished chrome highlighting intricately etched designs. Stand here for a few minutes and you're bound to hear, "Oh, my grandmother had that very toaster!"

GERMAN COCOA RYE BREAD

Makes 2 SMALL ROUND LOAVES

❖

It's hard to actually taste the cocoa in this dark, dense bread, but the resulting loaf is ideal for slathering with mayo and layering with pickles and melted Cheddar cheese. It's also the perfect appetizer serving platter when sliced thinly and cut into squares: Try it toasted with cream cheese, smoked salmon, and a dab of horseradish.

This recipe has been passed down through several generations, and is the type of bread that is hard to find anywhere except your own kitchen. The recipe does not follow traditional methods for combining the bread ingredients, which makes it easy to assemble and fast to prepare in one bowl.

2 (¼-ounce) packets active dry yeast (1 tablespoon plus 1½ teaspoons)

2 cups warm water

⅓ cup molasses

1 tablespoon unsalted butter, melted, plus soft butter for serving

¼ cup unsweetened cocoa powder

1 tablespoon caraway seeds

1 tablespoon salt

2 cups rye flour

3 to 4 cups unbleached all-purpose flour

1 teaspoon vegetable oil

About 1 tablespoon cornmeal, for sprinkling

In a large bowl, dissolve the yeast in the warm water for 5 minutes, then gently stir in the molasses and the melted butter. Add the cocoa powder, caraway seeds, salt, and rye flour. Stir to combine, then begin to add the all-purpose flour 1 cup at a time, stirring with a wooden spoon (or the paddle attachment, if you are using a stand mixer). Add just enough flour so that the dough comes together to form a ball.

Turn out the dough onto a lightly floured surface and knead for 10 minutes, adding more flour as needed. Test the dough for doneness by pressing two fingers into it; if it bounces back, it is ready for rising.

Lightly oil a bowl (you can use the same one, washed out) with ½ teaspoon of the oil and place the dough in the bowl; flip the dough to coat both sides with oil. Cover with plastic wrap and set aside in a warm place until doubled in size.

Divide the dough into two portions and shape each into an oblong or round loaf. Cover with a clean kitchen towel and let rise a second time, about 45 minutes.

Preheat the oven to 375°F. Grease a baking sheet with the remaining ½ teaspoon oil.

Place the loaves on the prepared baking sheet, slash the tops with a knife or baking blade, and sprinkle with cornmeal. Bake for 35 to 40 minutes. Remove from the oven and let cool on a rack before serving with a tub of soft butter.

NOTE: Day-old bread makes wonderful crisps. Thinly slice the bread, then cut it into cracker-size pieces. Brush with olive oil and sprinkle with kosher salt. Place on a rimmed baking sheet and bake in a preheated 350°F oven for 10 minutes.

COFFEE CAN BROWN BREAD

Makes 2 CANS; *Serves* 10

Brown bread was once a New England dinner staple, served with baked beans and frankfurters. Most of us grew up with the store-bought version, without any thought about the possibility of making our own. So we tracked down this recipe and found that it not only is simple to make, but is far superior in flavor, not to mention far healthier than most canned brown breads since it uses all-natural ingredients.

For this recipe, you'll need two 11- to 13-ounce coffee cans (empty tomato cans and large metal soup cans work well) in which you'll bake the brown bread. Be sure to clean the cans and remove their labels, and leave the bottoms on the cans.

1 tablespoon unsalted butter, at room temperature, plus more for serving

2 cups whole milk

¾ cup unsulphured molasses

¼ cup packed light brown sugar

1 teaspoon coarse (kosher or sea) salt

1¼ cups whole wheat flour

1 cup unbleached all-purpose flour

1 cup rye flour

⅓ cup cornmeal

2 teaspoons baking soda

1 teaspoon baking powder

1 cup golden raisins

Preheat the oven to 350°F. Coat the inside of two 11- to 13-ounce coffee cans with butter. Cut two 6-inch squares of aluminum foil and butter one side of each square.

In a small saucepan, stir together the milk, molasses, brown sugar, and salt and cook over low heat until the sugar has dissolved and the mixture is warm but not yet boiling. Remove from the heat.

In a large bowl, whisk together the whole wheat flour, all-purpose flour, rye flour, cornmeal, baking soda, and baking powder until combined. Gently pour in the milk mixture, stirring until the batter is well combined and smooth. Fold in the raisins.

Fill a large 8-quart pasta pot halfway with water and bring to a boil. Remove from the heat. Pour the batter evenly into both coffee cans. Cover the top of each can with the greased foil, butter side down, and secure tightly with kitchen twine. Place the coffee cans upright in the hot water in the pot, making sure the water comes up the sides but does not cover the top. (Remove water if there is too much.)

Place the whole pot in the oven and bake for 1½ hours. Test for doneness by inserting a skewer through the foil into the center of each loaf—it should come out clean. Transfer to a wire rack and let cool for 10 minutes. Remove the foil and run a thin knife around the edges of the cans. Remove the bottom of the can and push the bread out from the bottom (if you can remove the bread without cutting into the can, you can save the can to use next time). Slice and serve with soft butter.

FARMHOUSE WHOLE WHEAT HONEY BREAD

Makes TWO 4 × 8-INCH LOAVES OR 1 LARGE LOAF

———◆◆———

This just could be the only sandwich bread recipe you will ever need. Made in the traditional way, it is a flavorful, everyday sandwich bread, and once dried, becomes excellent for bread crumbs. If the release of kneading bread dough doesn't tempt you to revive the tradition of baking fresh bread often, the aroma that fills your house when the bread is baking will.

If this is your first time making bread, a small kitchen thermometer will help to find the correct temperature for the liquid. The ideal temperature for liquid to activate dry yeast is 105° to 115°F—too hot or too cold will destroy the yeast and the bread will not rise. You can also use it to check the loaves for doneness, which ensures a lovely full loaf with good texture.

2½ cups buttermilk

1 (¼-ounce) packet active dry yeast (2¼ teaspoons)

2 tablespoons honey

5½ cups fine-ground whole wheat flour

1½ cups unbleached white bread flour, plus more for the pans

1 tablespoon kosher salt

1 large egg

3 tablespoons unsalted butter, at room temperature

1 tablespoon vegetable oil, plus more for the pans

In a small saucepan, heat the buttermilk until warm to the touch, but not hot (stick a finger in or use a thermometer—see headnote—to check). Pour the buttermilk into a large bowl. Sprinkle with the yeast and stir in the honey (which gives the yeast something to eat) and allow the yeast to bloom for 10 minutes. Don't wait much longer, as everything should be mixed together while still warm.

In a separate large bowl, stir together the whole wheat flour, 1 cup of the bread flour, and the salt. Slowly stir the flour mixture into the buttermilk mixture, 1 cup at a time. This can be done in a stand mixer fitted with the paddle attachment, or using a thick-handled wooden spoon, mixing the dough in a circular fashion. Once the dough starts to come together, add the egg, mixing to combine, and then the butter.

Once the dough is less sticky and coming together in a ball, remove it from the bowl and set it on a lightly floured countertop or cutting board. Knead the dough until it is smooth and elastic. This activates the gluten in the bread, and the more it is kneaded, the better the texture will be in the final bread. Knead until it forms a cohesive ball—when you press two fingers into it, the impressions should fill back in immediately. This may take up to 10 minutes. (You can also knead dough in a stand mixer fitted with the dough hook.)

Clean the bowl in which you made the dough, dry it, and pour in the oil. Place the dough in the bowl and flip it to coat both sides lightly with the oil.

(Continued)

Cover with plastic wrap and set aside in a warm place until doubled in size, about 1 hour. At the end of the hour, punch down the dough to take out the air, and divide it in half to make two loaves. Lightly oil and flour two loaf pans. Press each piece into a rectangle the length of the pan, and roll it to fit into the pan, flip to cover both sides lightly with oil.

Set the dough in the pans and cover with plastic wrap again. Set the dough aside to rise for 45 minutes to 1 hour.

Preheat the oven to 375°F.

Once the loaves have doubled in volume, dust the tops with flour. Bake for 40 to 50 minutes, rotating the loaves halfway through baking, to an internal temperature of 205° to 210°F. Remove the loaves from the pans and let cool on a wire rack.

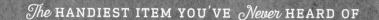

The HANDIEST ITEM YOU'VE *Never* HEARD OF

Wood Toast Lifter

This handy little device surprised us last year by selling in the hundreds. Because, I guess, there's nothing like it. Everyone who has an electric toaster needs one. It's simply a pair of wood tongs, 6" long, so you can reach down inside the toaster and pull out toast without getting burned or electrocuted. #6565. $.65* each. *Ship. wt. ¼ lb. Del. costs, p. 30.*

A half century ago, a retired fellow in Massachusetts figured out that if you took two tongue depressors and affixed them to each other at one end, you'd get a handy wooden tool to get toast out of the toaster safely. In 1966, the catalog started selling the Wood Toast Lifter, and it took off. Now it's a tad fancier (no tongue depressors), with a magnet on one side to stick to your toaster. But it still sells today because, as the original copy says, "there's nothing like it."

Lumberjack Granola (p. 153)

LUMBERJACK GRANOLA

Makes 24 CUPS

Homemade granola is a delicious way to bring a variety of grains and nuts into your diet and has many other uses beyond the breakfast table. We like it best with homemade yogurt (see page 11), but we also pack it for snacks, and it can be made into granola bars for on-the-go energy. Leave it chunky, or grind it a bit in the food processor for a smoother blend. Stored in the freezer in resealable plastic bags, granola will keep for months. Here's our basic recipe, but feel free to add different nuts, grains, and fruits as you prefer.

8 cups old-fashioned rolled oats

1 cup hulled sunflower seeds

1 cup hulled pumpkin seeds

2 cups walnuts

2 cups almonds

2 cups pecans

1 tablespoon coarse sea salt

1 cup maple syrup

1 cup canola or olive oil

1 cup golden raisins

1 cup dried cranberries

1 cup shredded coconut

Preheat the oven to 325°F.

In a large stainless-steel bowl, combine the oats, sunflower and pumpkin seeds, walnuts, almonds, and pecans. Stir with a large wooden spoon (or clean hands) to combine.

Transfer about 4 cups of the oats, seeds, and nuts mixture to a food processor fitted with the steel blade and pulse to coarsely chop, but do not make the pieces too small. (This is just to slightly reduce the size of the chunks to bite-size, and you can skip this step if you prefer really chunky granola.) Transfer the chopped oat mixture to a second large stainless-steel bowl. Repeat until you have coarsely chopped the whole batch—again, not too fine.

Toss the chopped oat mixture with the salt. Pour the maple syrup and the oil over the top and stir with a wooden spoon or clean hands to completely combine the liquids with the oat mixture. It will look just slightly moist.

Spread the granola evenly over two shallow roasting pans or rimmed baking sheets in a single layer, about 1 inch deep. (You may need to do this in two batches.) Bake, stirring every 15 minutes or so to keep the granola from burning and turning the pans to bake evenly. Toast to a golden brown, about 45 minutes. Remove from the pan and transfer back to one of the large bowls. Toss while still warm with the raisins, cranberries, and coconut. Let cool before packing into large mason jars to keep up to 2 months.

NEW ENGLAND PESTO SPIRAL ROLLS

Makes 24 ROLLS

— ◆◆ —

We found a recipe for *New England Herb Butter Bread Squares* in *Great–Aunt Delia's handwritten family cookbook. We've kept the ingredients more or less the same, but we've simplified the original recipe, which called for scalded milk and a filling of butter, egg, and a medley of chopped herbs.*

Since most cooks know how to make a sweet basil pesto, we focused on this familiar herb and supplemented the butter with olive oil. Finishing with Maldon salt, a flaky sea salt, gives the rolls that extra note of flavor that takes this recipe over the top. Serve as a satisfying side for soup, or line a basket with napkins and heap high with these delectable spirals for a potluck gathering.

ROLLS

4 tablespoons (½ stick)
unsalted butter

1 (¼-ounce) packet active dry
yeast (2¼ teaspoons)

1 teaspoon sugar

1½ cups warm water
(105° to 115°F)

1 teaspoon sea salt

3 cups unbleached
all-purpose flour,
plus more as needed

1½ cups whole wheat flour

1½ teaspoons vegetable oil,
for greasing

MAKE THE DOUGH FOR THE ROLLS: In a small saucepan, melt the butter and set aside to cool to lukewarm. In a large bowl, combine the yeast, sugar, and warm water, stirring slightly. Let stand until the mixture looks foamy, about 10 minutes.

Stir the melted butter and the salt into the yeast mixture. In a medium bowl, whisk together the all-purpose and whole wheat flours. With a wooden spoon, gradually stir the flour into the butter and yeast mixture, 1 cup at a time, until it makes a stiff dough. Turn out onto a lightly floured work surface and knead, adding more flour as required, until the dough is smooth and elastic, about 10 minutes. Gather the dough into a ball, and test it by poking two fingers into the dough; if the impressions bounce back immediately, the dough is ready to rise.

Lightly oil a large bowl with the vegetable oil. Place the dough in the bowl and turn it to coat the dough with the oil on both sides. Cover the bowl with plastic wrap and let stand in a warm place until the dough has doubled in volume, about 1 hour.

(Continued)

PESTO BUTTER

½ cup walnuts

4 cloves garlic, smashed

4 cups fresh basil leaves

1 cup (2 sticks)
unsalted butter,
at room temperature

¼ cup olive oil

½ cup grated
Parmesan cheese

½ teaspoon sea salt

¼ teaspoon freshly ground
black pepper

1½ teaspoons vegetable oil,
for greasing

Olive oil,
for brushing on the rolls

1 teaspoon flaky sea salt,
such as Maldon

MAKE THE PESTO BUTTER: While the dough is rising, in a small skillet, toast the walnuts over medium heat, stirring constantly until lightly browned and fragrant, about 5 minutes. Place the garlic, basil, and walnuts in a food processor fitted with the steel blade. Pulse until finely blended, slowly adding the butter and olive oil, then the cheese, salt, and pepper. Pulse until smooth, about 1 minute.

Turn out the dough onto a lightly floured work surface. Divide the dough in half. Working with one section at a time, roll the dough into a 12 × 18-inch rectangle, ½ inch thick. Evenly spread half the pesto butter to the edges of the dough. Starting at one long end, roll up the dough into a tight cylinder and pinch the seams closed. Using a sharp knife, cut the roll into 1-inch-thick rounds. Repeat with the remaining dough and pesto butter.

Lightly oil two 12-cup muffin tins with the vegetable oil, and place each round in an individual cup, cut side up. Cover with a damp kitchen towel and let the pans stand in a warm place until the rolls look puffy, about 30 minutes.

Preheat the oven to 375°F and position a rack in the center.

Brush the rolls with olive oil and sprinkle the tops with Maldon salt. Bake until golden brown, about 20 minutes. Remove from the oven and let the rolls cool for a few minutes before popping them out of the pans.

✌ MAKE YOUR OWN: BREAD CRUMBS

You know how just one bite of really good, crusty homemade or bakery bread spoils you forever when it comes to plastic-bagged sliced loaves? The same is true of bread crumbs. Make your own and you'll never go back to the sawdust they sell in cans again.

Making your own bread crumbs is exceedingly easy. Throw any day-old ends, bits, and crusts—mixing different kinds makes for more complex crumbs—into a resealable plastic bag and keep it in the freezer. When you have critical mass, take the bread out and grate it using your food processor's grating disc. This gives you more of a panko-type bread crumb. (Panko, the Japanese version of bread crumbs, is made from grated crustless bread, resulting in airy, large flakes that absorb less oil and provide both crunch and flavor.) You can grate the bread by hand if you have the patience and muscle. If you want finer bread crumbs, use the steel blade and pulse in the processor until the crumbs are the texture you want. Bread crumbs can be stored in a resealable plastic bag in the freezer for up to 6 months.

SAVORY CHEESE AND HERB BREAD

Makes 1 LARGE LOAF

This easy herb bread recipe brings the scent of the garden into your kitchen. The golden bread infused with herby green flecks is heavenly when sliced for a grilled cheese sandwich or thinly spread with herbed butter. You can substitute cottage cheese for the Cheddar, which will yield a soft, moist interior.

1 (¼-ounce) packet active dry yeast (2¼ teaspoons)

1 teaspoon sugar

1½ cups warm water (105° to 115°F)

4 cups unbleached all-purpose flour, plus more as needed

1 cup shredded Cheddar cheese or cottage cheese

¼ cup finely chopped fresh mixed herbs (such as parsley, sage, rosemary, thyme)

3 tablespoons extra-virgin olive oil

2 teaspoons sea salt

½ teaspoon freshly ground black pepper

1 tablespoon vegetable oil, for greasing

In a large bowl, sprinkle the yeast and sugar over the warm water. Let stand until the mixture looks foamy, about 10 minutes. Stir to dissolve the yeast. Stir in 1 cup of the flour, the cheese, herbs, olive oil, salt, and pepper. Gradually stir in enough of the remaining flour to make a stiff dough. Turn out onto a lightly floured work surface and knead, adding more flour as required, until the dough is smooth and elastic, about 10 minutes. Gather the dough into a ball.

Lightly oil a large bowl. Place the dough in the bowl and turn it to coat the dough with the oil. Cover the bowl with a damp kitchen towel and let it stand in a warm place until the dough has doubled in volume, about 1½ hours.

Punch down the dough and turn it out onto a lightly floured work surface. Lightly oil a large loaf pan and shape the dough to fit inside. Turn the dough over to coat both sides with oil and cover again with the damp kitchen towel. Let stand in a warm place until doubled in volume, about 45 minutes.

Preheat the oven to 375°F and position a rack in the center.

Bake for 45 minutes, or until the bread sounds hollow on the bottom when tapped. Transfer to a wire rack to cool.

IRISH SODA BREAD
WITH CURRANTS AND CARAWAY

Makes 1 ROUND LOAF

————— ◆ —————

Want to have a fresh-baked loaf of bread on the table in thirty minutes? This Irish soda bread is simple, almost ridiculously quick to make, and versatile. It's a top-notch weeknight quick bread to serve with soups or stews, and leftovers make great croutons for salads.

The secret behind any good Irish soda bread is buttermilk (see page 4 for how to make your own), which activates the baking soda to allow the bread to rise in a hot oven. To keep a good texture, this bread requires that you mix the ingredients by hand—literally! Unlike yeast breads, soda bread will toughen if kneaded, so mix only just enough to blend the dry with the wet ingredients. This basic recipe showcases currants and caraway seeds. See the next page for variations, because once you've mastered the recipe, the possibilities abound for the humble soda bread.

2 cups unbleached all-purpose flour, plus more for dusting

2 cups stone-ground whole wheat flour

1 teaspoon salt

1 teaspoon baking soda

¼ cup dried currants or raisins

1½ teaspoons caraway seeds

2 cups buttermilk, plus 2 tablespoons for brushing

2 teaspoons cornmeal

1 large egg, lightly beaten

Preheat the oven to 450°F.

In a large bowl, mix together the all-purpose and whole wheat flours with the salt and the baking soda. Add the currants and the caraway seeds. Make a well in the center and pour in the 2 cups buttermilk all at once. Using your hands, stir in a full circle starting in the center of the bowl and working toward the outside until all the flour has been incorporated. The dough should be soft but not too wet and sticky. When it all comes together—a matter of seconds—turn it out onto a well-floured surface. Wash and dry your hands, then flour your hands.

Roll the dough around gently for a second, just enough to tidy it up, then flip the dough over. Pat the dough into a round loaf, about 1½ inches thick. Sprinkle 1 teaspoon of the cornmeal onto the center of a baking sheet and place the dough on the cornmeal. In a small bowl, whisk together the egg and 2 tablespoons buttermilk and brush the mixture over the top of the loaf, which will give it a tasty brown crust, then sprinkle with the remaining 1 teaspoon cornmeal.

With a sharp knife, score the top of the dough with a deep X and let the cut go all the way down the sides of the bread. This allows air to escape while the bread bakes and is essential, so don't be timid!

Bake for 8 to 10 minutes, then reduce the oven temperature to 400°F and bake for 18 to 20 minutes more, turning the pan halfway through so both sides cook evenly. Test the bread by removing it from the oven and tapping the bottom: If it sounds hollow, it is done. Let cool on a wire rack before slicing.

VARIATIONS

Add to the dry ingredients before mixing with the liquid:

CHEDDAR CHEESE WITH HERBS: Add 2 tablespoons chopped fresh herbs, such as thyme, rosemary, sage, chives, or parsley. Add 1 cup grated Cheddar cheese. Sprinkle ¼ cup grated Cheddar on top of the loaf before baking.

ROSEMARY AND OLIVE: Add 1½ tablespoons chopped fresh rosemary and 2 tablespoons chopped pitted black olives.

BASIL AND SUN-DRIED TOMATO: Add 2 tablespoons finely chopped fresh basil and 2 tablespoons chopped sun-dried tomatoes.

From **A CLIPPING** *in*
MILDRED ORTON'S RECIPE NOTEBOOK

"Perhaps in your household the advent of a bread pudding for dessert is greeted with wails of protest and derision. It is for your benefit, then, that I have written this article, which aims to show how a bread pudding can be toothsome enough to satisfy the most exacting family.

Mildred Ellen Orton, in her 90s.

"The first and greatest fault to be found with the ordinary bread pudding is the amount of bread used. To many cooks, a bread pudding is exactly what its name implies, a pudding of bread and very little else, stiff, tasteless, more like a poultice than a delicate dessert.

"For a family of five, a bread pudding should contain just one large slice of bread, a pint of milk, two eggs, one cup of granulated sugar, and a piece of butter the size of a walnut. If butter happens to be very moderate in price, this quantity may be more generous..."

COUSCOUS, LENTIL, AND ARUGULA SALAD

Serves 4 TO 6

◆◆

*O*nce you get the hang of combining grains and greens in a salad bowl, the mix will quickly become part of your repertoire. The healthy, satisfying combination can be adapted to suit your tastes and what you have on hand. Substitute quinoa for the couscous, or change it up with the seasons. For winter, try combining wild rice with the lentils and add dried cranberries and toasted walnuts. A refreshing splash of summer, the lemony vinaigrette dressing is especially good for bringing out the tart notes in arugula.

1 cup dry green lentils

½ teaspoon sea salt

1½ cups vegetable or chicken stock

1 cup couscous

½ cup Lemon Vinaigrette (recipe follows)

4 cups fresh arugula, washed and dried

6 scallions, white and tender green parts, thinly sliced (½ cup)

1 cup halved cherry tomatoes

1 medium cucumber, peeled, seeded, and cut into ½-inch cubes (1½ cups)

½ cup crumbled feta cheese

Place the lentils in a medium saucepan and add enough water to cover them by 1 inch. Simmer over medium heat until tender, about 15 minutes. Drain any excess water and let cool.

Meanwhile, in a separate medium saucepan, combine the salt and the stock and bring to a boil. Add the couscous, bring to a boil, then cover, take off the heat, and let stand until all the liquid has been absorbed, about 10 minutes. Fluff the couscous with a fork.

In a large salad bowl, combine the lentils and the couscous and toss with half the Lemon Vinaigrette. Let cool at room temperature or refrigerate until ready to serve.

Just before serving, coarsely chop the arugula and combine it with the lentils and couscous, along with the scallions, cherry tomatoes, and cucumber. Crumble the feta cheese over the top and add more dressing as desired.

LEMON VINAIGRETTE

Makes 1 CUP

½ cup extra-virgin olive oil

¼ cup fresh lemon juice (from about 2 lemons)

¼ cup red wine vinegar

1 tablespoon Dijon mustard

2 cloves garlic, smashed and minced

Salt and freshly ground black pepper

Combine all the ingredients in a mason jar with a lid. Shake to blend until emulsified. Set aside until the salad is prepared.

Vrest Orton struck up a three-plus-decades-long correspondence with a
customer—not just any customer, but the famed cookbook author M. F. K. Fisher.
In 1949, her salutation was "Dear Mr. Orton"; by 1980, it was "Dear Vrest" and
signed "Mary Frances." We love the excerpt from one letter below—and the way
she dated her letters!

```
          13935 Sonoma Highway
          Glen Ellen
          CA 95442

          8.ix.80
          Dear Vrest:

          How very nice it is of you send me the two books, so generous-
          ly inscribed! I do thank you.

          They came today, and I look forward to reading VERMONT AFTERNOONS
          tonight. I admire Frost very much. As for Mrs. Orton's book, it
          has long been a classic to me, znd I must have given a dozen
          copies to Deserving Friends...and of course lost a  few more
          to the dedicated book-thieves in our midst. (My husband Dillwyn
          Parrish maintained that one firm pproof of a book's lasting
          value is how many times it is quietly stolen from the shelf.
          I count Mrs. Orton's WHOLEGRAINS, in there. Another one is
          THE ENORMOUS ROOM, e.e.cumming's strange little gem. Another,
          oddly enough, is the pocket Larousse French-English dictionary.y)..
          even the noblest gentleman can't resist slipping them quietly
          in his pocket...)

          Did you sell the vintage cars?

          Do you remember sending me a lot of real estate information
          when I was thinking seriously about stying for a couple of
          years in Vermont, in the late 40s? I sent some of it lately
          to Stephen Green's daughter Stephanie, in Brattleboro...
          a real proof that Time passes, if we need that reminder!
          She found the prices and so on  unbelievable...

          All my good wishes, and again my thanks for the two books....


          Mary Frances

          MFKFisher
          to
          Vrest Orton
          Weston
          VT
```

QUINOA SALAD
WITH PAN-GRILLED RADICCHIO

Serves 8

———◆———

Everyone appreciates a make-ahead salad that is not only tasty but also colorful and healthy. Julie Orton makes this often for family and friends, as it's best made early in the day and left to chill for dinner—perfect for a busy mom.

Smoked paprika livens up the salad dressing, which is made in a small mason jar, easy to shake and store in the fridge or on the countertop. Dry-roasting the quinoa until it's a nutty brown adds the same kind of intensity of flavor as toasting nuts does, and elevates the flavor of the whole salad. Julie's recipe uses canned black beans for convenience; if you have time or leftovers, use two cups homemade black beans instead.

DRESSING

½ cup apple cider vinegar

½ cup olive or canola oil

2 tablespoons Dijon mustard

2 tablespoons
pure maple syrup

1 teaspoon dried thyme

1 teaspoon smoked paprika

1 clove garlic, minced

½ teaspoon salt

¼ teaspoon freshly ground
black pepper

SALAD

3 cups uncooked quinoa

1 tablespoon olive oil

2 red bell peppers,
seeded and chopped into
½-inch pieces

1 medium head radicchio,
shredded (about 2 cups)

2 cups grated Cheddar
cheese

1 (15.5-ounce) can black
beans, drained and rinsed

MAKE THE DRESSING: In a pint-size mason jar, combine the vinegar, oil, mustard, maple syrup, thyme, paprika, garlic, salt, and black pepper. Shake vigorously until emulsified. Set aside until ready to serve.

MAKE THE SALAD: In a medium saucepan, toast the quinoa over medium-high heat, stirring often, for 5 to 7 minutes, or until golden brown and nutty smelling. Add 3 cups water and bring to a boil, then reduce the heat to low and simmer for 10 to 12 minutes, until there is no water left. Remove from the heat, fluff with a fork, and cover.

In a large nonstick skillet, heat the oil over medium-high heat. Add the bell pepper and cook until it's blistered, then add the radicchio and cook until it's wilted and starting to blacken.

In a large salad bowl, mix the warm quinoa with about ¼ cup of the dressing. Add the shredded cheese and beans and mix. Stir in the peppers and radicchio. Taste, and toss with additional dressing, if desired. (A little goes a long way, so make sure to toss and taste. You will have leftover dressing for another salad.)

CHAPTER 7

POTLUCKS *and* CROWD-PLEASERS

THE CHARM OF THE VERMONT COUNTRY STORE starts with the potbellied stove and checkerboard, where the old men of the village used to gather to play a game or three of chess. In villages all over Vermont today, a trip to the country store is still part of the fabric of daily life.

Perhaps because our towns and villages are so small and isolated by their landscape, a strong sense of community defines Vermont. Like elsewhere in America, traditions celebrating community abound, and food always plays a major role. Seen through the prism of Vermont, that means state fairs, picnics, farmers' markets, church suppers, potluck dinners, celebrations—and the country store.

DISHES *and* DESSERTS *for* GATHERINGS *and* CELEBRATIONS

{ *Vermont Community:* FAIRS *and* FESTIVITIES }

A PERFECT COUNTRY FAIR

MOST PEOPLE DRIVING FROM WESTON TO MANchester zip right past the charming little village of Peru, Vermont (population: 363), and miss its triangular green, classic New England church, minuscule post office, and venerable country store. But there's one day every September when it's impossible to miss Peru—during the annual Peru Fair, now more than three decades old.

Preparations begin with the overnight roasting of a country pig, to be savored the next day with tangy barbecue sauce, maple baked beans, corn on the cob, ice cream, and fruit pie. The whole town is cordoned off, the streets lined with booths featuring local crafts and foods. Entertainment abounds: clog dancing, hayrides, wandering fiddlers, puppet shows, and live bluegrass. Treats from local kitchens—caramel apples, kettle corn, cookies, cobblers, cakes, and pies—offer a prodigious challenge to those trying to save room for the noon barbecue.

What outside visitors may not catch is that the fair is really an annual excuse for residents of Peru and neighboring towns to "run into" one another. It's a daylong social mixer, where folks start in the morning at one end of town and spend all afternoon working toward the other. While kids flit from one attraction to the next, their parents get down to the serious business of engaging in community.

—CABOT ORTON

OLD HOME DAY

IN WESTON, ROCKINGHAM, AND OTHER VILLAGES around Vermont and New England, one midsummer Saturday after the first cut of hay is designated Old Home Day. The tradition began in the early 1900s to lure people who used to live in town but had moved away after the Civil War to come back and see what they'd been missing.

The highlight of the day is a parade, and some towns go all out with wild costumes and decorated floats. Sheldon's parade winds through the village with pomp and pageantry: music and creaky wagons, flivvers, bikes, ponies, and marching chickens. In Plymouth, home of Calvin Coolidge, there are wagon rides, sheepshearing, traditional craft demonstrations, historic children's games—and, of course, a reenactment of Cool Cal's "Homestead Inaugural." Belvidere brings back the egg toss, the frying pan toss, the hammer throw. The mountain town of Jamaica caps its day with a square dance at the Jamaica Town Hall; Rockingham with fireworks.

Our Old Home Day in Weston is fairly low-key. Food is in abundance, all done by potluck. Then comes the parade—no marching chickens, but rather adults and kids on bikes decorated with crepe paper and flags, riding around and around the Green, and decorated floats following the same path. When The Vermont Country Store celebrated its fiftieth anniversary in 1996, we piggybacked on Old Home Day with quite a party. Riding an old Schwinn bike, I proudly led the parade.

—LYMAN ORTON

(RIGHT) Mildred rides the Association
(Village Green trustees) float
at Old Home Day in the 1950s.

(BELOW) Lyman leads the parade at
Old Home Day in 1996, celebrating
The Vermont Country Store's
fiftieth anniversary.

❧ SUMMER PICNICS WITH MILDRED

Our grandmother was a genuine picnic enthusiast. For summer drives along un-paved roads, she would often plan to stop by a field for lunch. Out came the plaid blanket and wicker basket. For lunch: chicken sandwiches with lettuce and butter on home-baked wheat bread, a slab of Vermont Cheddar cheese, Common Crackers, pickled fiddleheads, oatmeal cookies, and a thermos of Wilcox's milk.

   We still have Mildred's picnic basket and thermos, keepsakes of a happy time when our father and uncle were boys. The basket and thermos were still in use by the time we brothers were old enough to picnic, and our grandparents could make a two-hour drive to Rutland seem as exotic and perilous as a safari to Rangoon. The highlight was always wholesome food in the tall grass of a Vermont hay meadow, somewhere along Route 100, on a July afternoon. This was simple and good, and thinking back, few things brought more contentment than being together under clear summer skies, a grateful family well fed.

—CABOT ORTON

(LEFT) A picnic with the Wilcox clan, circa 1920.

(BELOW) A late 1940s side-of-the-road picnic with Mildred serving milk to Lyman, Jeremy, and their friends; you can just see Mildred's thermos.

SUMMER ROASTED CAPONATA DIP

Serves 12

The secret to this piquant roasted spread is the assortment of summer vegetables, roasted to bring out their deep flavors, blended with fresh summer herbs and the sweet and sour accent of the vinegar. Heap the caponata on lettuce leaves or spread it on crackers, pita, or toasted bread, alongside a platter of assorted cheeses. It also doubles as a great vegetarian sandwich spread or a side with grilled fish.

1 medium eggplant, peeled and cut into ¾-inch cubes (3½ cups)

4 small zucchini, cut into ½-inch chunks (3 cups)

2 fennel bulbs, tops removed, bulbs coarsely cut into bite-size pieces (3½ cups)

6 scallions or 1 red onion, chopped (¾ cup)

1 large red bell pepper, seeded and sliced (1 cup)

1 teaspoon salt

½ teaspoon freshly ground black pepper

3 cloves garlic, minced (1½ teaspoons)

½ cup olive oil

¼ cup balsamic vinegar

¼ cup brown rice vinegar

2 tablespoons chopped pitted black olives

1 small can tomato paste (¼ cup)

2 tablespoons capers

¼ cup chopped mixed fresh summer herbs (such as basil, lovage, thyme, parsley, sage, and oregano)

Preheat the oven to 400°F.

Place the eggplant, zucchini, fennel, scallions, and bell pepper in a large roasting pan. (There should be about 12 cups vegetables.) Toss with the salt, black pepper, and garlic. Drizzle with the olive oil and toss to fully coat. Roast for 45 minutes, tossing occasionally to evenly cook all the vegetables.

In a small bowl, whisk together the vinegars, olives, tomato paste, capers, and fresh herbs. Remove the vegetables from the oven and evenly pour the vinegar and olive mixture over them, turning with a wooden spoon or spatula to coat.

Return the vegetables to the oven and bake until tender and slightly golden on the edges, 30 minutes or so more. Remove from the oven and let cool. Refrigerate until ready to serve. Serve in a bowl with bruschetta or toasted pita triangles alongside.

GOOD *Wholesome* "SMALL BEER" (1845)

"Take two ounces of hops, and boil them, 3 or 4 hours, in 3 or 4 pailfuls of water; and then scald 2 quarts of molasses in the liquor, and turn it off into a clean half-barrel, boiling hot, then fill it up with the cold water; before it is quite full, put in your yeast to work it. The next day you will have agreeable, wholesome, small beer that will not fill you with wind, as that which is brewed from malt or bran; and it will keep good till it is all drank out."

—*Vermont Food as We Like It*,
COMPILED BY THELMA SPAULDING COLBURN,
MODERN PRINTING CO. (BARRE, VERMONT), 1949

MACARONI AND CHEESE
WITH BACON TOPPING

Serves 8

◆◆

Everyone has his or her favorite recipe for macaroni and cheese, but it all starts with good ol' white noodles (whole wheat may be healthier, but somehow is never quite as comforting), butter, cream, and cheese. We've seen recipes with as many as five cheeses, delicious but complicated. Here we concentrate on one cheese, not surprisingly Vermont Cheddar, lighten it up a bit, and add a colorful touch or two. Don't worry, there's still a goodly amount of cream and cheese here, too, along with the smoky, porky, crunchy bits in the topping, so you'll get your mac-and-cheese fix.

We find this recipe is a hit even for those who are not macaroni and cheese lovers, because it is less heavy than the mac and cheese we loved as kids. We like to think it's a more grown-up version. We use shells instead of the traditional elbows to hold the sauce, but feel free to use any shaped pasta. Serve hot as a side dish or cold as a salad for a picnic.

2 tablespoons unsalted butter, plus more for the baking dish

1 (16-ounce) box medium-sized pasta

1 onion, coarsely chopped (¾ cup)

½ teaspoon salt

¼ teaspoon freshly grated nutmeg

¼ teaspoon freshly ground black pepper

3 cups heavy cream

2 cups grated Cheddar cheese

4 fresh tomatoes, chopped, with their juices (about 2 cups)

1 teaspoon Dijon mustard

1 tablespoon chopped fresh thyme

4 thick slices bacon, frozen, cut into small pieces

1 cup fine bread crumbs or panko bread crumbs

Preheat the oven to 350°F. Butter a 13 × 9-inch baking dish or ovenproof casserole.

Cook the pasta according to the package directions. Drain, rinse with cold water to stop the cooking, and set aside.

In a large saucepan, melt the butter over medium heat. Add the onion and the salt and sauté until soft, about 5 minutes. Add the nutmeg, pepper, and cream, stirring to blend. Bring the mixture to a simmer over medium heat, then, off the heat, add the cheese, tomatoes, mustard, and thyme. Stir to thoroughly combine.

In a skillet, sauté the bacon and bread crumbs until crisp and brown, turning with a wooden spoon or spatula to cook evenly and prevent burning. Combine the cooked pasta with the cheese sauce, toss to thoroughly coat, and pour into the prepared baking dish. Top with the bread crumb mixture, spreading it evenly. Bake for 30 minutes, until the edges are bubbling.

MAPLE AND MOLASSES BAKED BEANS

Serves 6 AS MAIN COURSE, 12 AS SIDE DISH

——— •• ———

These aren't your mother's baked beans! Our recipe is the perfect blend of sweet and spicy, with real bacon instead of pork fat, molasses instead of sugar, and a bit of Tabasco to give it a kick. Soaking beans then cooking them takes a bit of time, so plan on starting the soaking early in the day or the night before. Baked beans can be kept in the refrigerator for a week, or frozen and reheated.

Once a staple in every kitchen, the cast-iron Dutch oven is especially useful when it comes to one-pot meals or these baked beans. Another advantage? You can cook, store, serve, and easily carry anything you cook in a Dutch oven to a potluck or the table for a family-style dinner. Of course, if you have traditional individual bean pots, use them for the final bake, adjusting the cooking time down to about forty minutes.

1 pound dried navy beans

1 tablespoon plus
½ teaspoon salt

2 cloves garlic,
minced (1 teaspoon)

2 medium onions,
chopped (2 cups)

2 bay leaves

½ pound thick-cut bacon
(6 slices),
cut into bite-size pieces

1 cup packed
dark brown sugar

1 cup dark
unsulphured molasses

½ cup apple cider vinegar

¼ cup country-style Dijon
mustard (regular mustard
will do, too)

1 tablespoon Tabasco sauce

Freshly ground black pepper

Place the beans in a 6-quart stockpot and add boiling water to cover by 2 inches. Add 1 tablespoon of the salt, stir, and leave to soak for 2 hours or overnight. Drain in a colander, then return the beans to the wiped-out stockpot, add water to cover by 2 inches and the remaining ½ teaspoon salt. Add ½ teaspoon of the garlic, 1 cup of the onion, and the bay leaves. Simmer over low heat, slightly covered, for up to 1 hour, or until the beans are tender but not falling apart and the water has been mostly absorbed. Remove from the heat. Place a colander over a medium bowl. Drain the beans, reserving any liquid in the bowl. Remove the bay leaves.

Preheat the oven to 325°F and position a rack in the center.

In a cast-iron Dutch oven or large pot, cook the bacon over medium-low heat until most of the fat has rendered but the bacon is not yet crisp, about 15 minutes.

Add the remaining 1 cup chopped onion and ½ teaspoon garlic and sauté until soft, about 5 minutes. Add the brown sugar, molasses, vinegar, mustard, and Tabasco. Stir in the cooked beans, a good grinding of pepper, and just enough of the reserved bean liquid, up to 1 cup, to make a slightly soupy mixture.

Cover and bake for 1 hour, or until the beans are thick and look dark and glazed. Check at the 45-minute mark to see if they need more liquid, and stir in ½ cup of the bean liquid or water, if needed. Taste and adjust the seasonings. After an hour, taste, and if the beans aren't completely soft, return them to the oven and bake for up to 30 minutes more, until soft. Remove from the oven and keep covered until ready to serve.

ROASTED VEGETABLE LASAGNA

Serves 12

—◆—

Ever notice how lasagna is the first dish to disappear at a potluck? Our version is no exception. Roasting the vegetables makes the flavors alive and vibrant, and their earthy taste is not overpowered by too much sauce. If you have fresh herbs, by all means use them instead of dried.

If for you it's not lasagna unless there's sausage, cook up some ground sweet or spicy sausage (see page 77) and add it before the second layer of noodles. Either way, this makes a luscious lasagna that is sure to be the hit of any party.

ROASTED VEGETABLES

2 red bell peppers, seeded and cut into ½-inch pieces (2½ cups)

1 eggplant, ends trimmed, cut into ½-inch pieces (3½ cups)

2 red onions, halved and cut into ½-inch pieces (2 cups)

2 large portobello mushrooms, cut into ½-inch pieces (2½ cups)

4 tablespoons olive oil

2 teaspoons salt

½ teaspoon freshly ground black pepper

½ cup red or white wine

2 tablespoons tomato paste

MAKE THE ROASTED VEGETABLES: Preheat the oven to 450°F.

Line two rimmed baking sheets with aluminum foil. Divide the bell peppers, eggplant, onions, and mushrooms between the two pans. Drizzle 2 tablespoons of the oil over each baking sheet and toss to coat the vegetables. Spread the vegetables apart and sprinkle with the salt and pepper. Roast for 20 minutes. Remove the baking sheets from the oven.

In a small bowl or measuring cup, whisk together the wine and tomato paste. Divide the mixture evenly between the baking sheets. Use a wooden spoon or spatula to mix and flip over the vegetables to coat. Roast for 10 to 15 minutes more, until the vegetables are dark and caramelized. Remove from the oven and set aside.

---

1 pound dry lasagna noodles

1 pound whole milk mozzarella

8 ounces ricotta cheese

2 large eggs

1½ teaspoons
dried oregano, or ¼ cup
minced fresh oregano

1 teaspoon dried basil,
or 1 cup finely chopped
fresh basil

1 (28-ounce) can
crushed tomatoes

1 cup grated
Parmesan cheese

½ teaspoon red pepper flakes

½ teaspoon salt

MAKE THE LASAGNA: Reduce the oven temperature to 350°F.

Bring an 8-quart stockpot of water to a boil. Add the lasagna noodles and cook to al dente according to the package instructions. Drain and rinse with cold water. Lay the noodles out on a clean kitchen towel or on paper towels in a single layer.

Shred the mozzarella into a small bowl. In a medium bowl, whisk together the ricotta with the eggs and herbs. Set up a workstation by placing the tomato sauce, the noodles, the roasted vegetables, and the cheeses on the counter in that order.

Spread 1 cup of the tomato sauce evenly over a 9½ × 12½ × 3-inch baking dish. Place a layer of noodles over the sauce and top with 2 cups of the roasted vegetables, spreading them evenly. Add dabs of ricotta to cover, then sprinkle with mozzarella, and top with a cup of the tomato sauce. Add another layer of noodles, roasted vegetables, ricotta, mozzarella, and tomato sauce. Sprinkle the top with Parmesan, the red paper flakes, and the salt.

Bake for 45 minutes, until bubbling. Let rest for 10 minutes before cutting. Serve hot.

SETTING *the* TABLE: TRADITIONAL MOUNTAIN WEAVE

Woven into each Mountain Weave tablecloth that we sell in the Store is a rich history of self-reliance and ingenuity that harkens back to the homespun fabrics hand-loomed in the mountains of Vermont 150 years ago. Except that instead of using whatever material happened to be on hand like they did then, Mountain Weave is pure U.S.A.-grown cotton, hand-woven by master weavers on looms in New England, then cut and hand-fringed by our neighbors down  the road in Dorset. This kind of homespun, great for farm kitchens and for the informal type of entertaining we do here, would have been familiar to my great-grandfather, and his grandfather, and his. Our family's been in Vermont for eight generations now, so who knows— maybe the first Orton here set his table with a cloth like this.

—GARDNER ORTON

SWISS CHARD PHYLLO PIE

Serves 16

—◆◆—

A riff on the classic spanakopita, this recipe uses fresh chard instead of spinach and cream cheese instead of feta, which softens the flavor and gives it a lighter interior. This is our go-to dish when we have an abundance of greens in the garden and someplace to go for a potluck dinner, because it is so impressive and yummy. Without a doubt, it's a good way to get young ones to eat their greens, because who can resist layers and layers of buttery phyllo dough? For a nice presentation, bring it to the table or potluck in its baking dish, and then, just before serving, cut it into 2½-inch squares. Serve warm or cold. Feel free to substitute spinach for the chard, or use spinach mixed with kale and chard.

---

8 ounces frozen phyllo dough

2 tablespoons olive oil

1 large red onion, chopped (1 cup)

2 pounds Swiss chard, stems removed, leaves coarsely chopped (about 10 cups)

3 large eggs

8 ounces cream cheese

¼ teaspoon freshly grated nutmeg

1 teaspoon salt

½ teaspoon freshly ground black pepper

4 ounces (1 stick) unsalted butter

1½ cups grated Parmesan cheese

Defrost the phyllo according to the package instructions, either at room temperature for 2 hours or in the refrigerator overnight.

Preheat the oven to 375°F.

In a large skillet, heat the olive oil over medium heat. Add the onion and sauté until soft and golden, about 10 minutes. Add the Swiss chard, one handful at a time, until the pan accommodates all of the greens. Cover, reduce the heat to low, and simmer until reduced in bulk, about 5 minutes. Turn off the heat.

In a large bowl, mix the eggs and cream cheese together, adding the nutmeg, salt, and pepper. Pour this over the cooked greens and onions and stir to combine.

In a small saucepan, melt the butter. With a pastry brush, coat the inside of a 9½ × 12½ × 3-inch baking dish or baking pan. (Baking in a metal pan will yield an especially crispy crust.) Lay one piece of phyllo dough down in the pan, brush lightly with melted butter, sprinkle with a rounded tablespoon of the Parmesan, and repeat for ten layers (or until you have used half the package of phyllo).

Pour in the filling, spreading it to the edges with a spoon or spatula. Top with a layer of phyllo dough, brush lightly with melted butter, sprinkle with a rounded tablespoon of the Parmesan, and repeat for ten layers, or until the package is done. Brush the top with the remaining melted butter. Bake for 45 minutes, until crisp and golden.

✑ BUILDING A CHEESE BOARD

In Vermont, we're blessed to have award-winning artisans making cheese all over the state, near enough for us to visit. But you can experience a similar thrill walking into a great cheese shop, like the one at The Vermont Country Store, inhaling the milky, toasty, caramelized fragrance of cheese and taking in colors ranging from soft white to rich gold in a variety of shapes. And you can re-create a slice of that experience by presenting a fine cheese board at your next gathering, whether it's at home or at a picnic or potluck.

Arranging a cheese board is easy. Select no more than five cheeses, featuring a range of cow, sheep, and goat cheeses with an assortment of textures, flavors, and aromas. To savor the subtleties, set up with young, soft ripened cheese first and build toward a stronger aged or blue cheese. Vermont Common Crackers or other unsalted plain crackers are just the thing to serve, along with sweet dabs of fig chutney or jam to offset the salty nature of aged cheese and highlight the nutty, caramelized notes. Be sure to take the cheese out of the refrigerator at least a half hour before serving to bring out the delicate notes.

OLD-FASHIONED JELLY ROLL

Makes 1 JELLY ROLL; *Serves* 12

It's easy to impress guests when you make an old-fashioned jelly roll, because it appears to be quite a feat to roll a thick cake into a spiral. In reality, it isn't as hard as it looks. The key to rolling is to not overbake the cake and to deftly slide it out of the pan and onto a kitchen towel. Lining the pan with parchment paper helps.

Our traditional jelly roll is a soft, delicious sponge cake with a hint of lemon in the batter, filled with jam and dusted with confectioners' sugar. There was an era when all good cooks owned a jelly roll pan, but if you don't have one in your cupboard, a rimmed baking sheet will do.

---

1 tablespoon unsalted butter or nonstick cooking spray, for the pan

1 cup unbleached all-purpose flour, plus more for dusting

¼ teaspoon salt

5 large eggs, separated

Zest and juice of 1 lemon (2 teaspoons zest and 2 tablespoons juice)

1 cup granulated sugar

1¼ cups jam of choice

¼ cup confectioners' sugar

Preheat the oven to 350°F. Lightly grease a 15 × 10 × 1 jelly roll pan with butter or nonstick spray. (**NOTE:** These pans come in different sizes, so adapt to what you have. Line it with a large piece of parchment or waxed paper, grease the top, and lightly flour it, shaking off excess flour.

In a small bowl, stir together the flour and salt. Set aside.

In another small bowl, beat together the egg yolks, lemon zest, and lemon juice until thick and lemon colored, about 5 minutes. Gradually add ½ cup of the granulated sugar to the egg yolks while beating continuously until incorporated. In the bowl of a stand mixer fitted with the whisk attachment, beat the egg whites until foamy; gradually add the remaining ½ cup granulated sugar and continue to beat until stiff peaks form and the whites are glossy.

With a wire whisk or plastic spatula, fold the egg yolk mixture into the beaten egg whites, then gently fold in the flour mixture until all is combined. Pour the batter into the prepared pan.

Bake for about 10 minutes, or until lightly browned. Keep an eye on it so it does not get overly browned, which makes rolling it up difficult. Remove from the oven and, while warm, run a knife around the edges of the cake and invert onto a clean kitchen towel dusted with a few tablespoons of confectioners' sugar.

Remove the parchment or waxed paper from the cake. Carefully roll up the cake in the towel, starting at one short end, and set aside with the seam down to cool completely.

When cool, carefully unroll the cake, remove the towel, and spread the cake with the jam, leaving a ½-inch border around the cake. Roll the cake up again, and place it seam side down on a serving dish. Dust with more confectioners' sugar before serving.

GINGERSNAP PUMPKIN CHEESECAKE

Serves 16

——◆——

This makes one very large, irresistible cheesecake that is perfect for a special occasion. The tawny pumpkin topped with sweetened sour cream looks festive, the filling is rich and smooth, and the crunch of the gingersnap cookie crust adds the texture and flavor boost that brings it all home. Here we use the Orton Brothers Snappy Ginger Cookie Buttons, which are all natural, low in calories and sugar, and big in flavor, but regular boxed gingersnaps will do. It's best to make this cake in the morning or the day before, so it can chill before serving.

CRUST

2 (6-ounce) boxes Snappy
Ginger Cookie Buttons,
or 12 ounces gingersnaps

¼ cup sugar

6 tablespoons (¾ stick)
unsalted butter, melted

FILLING

3 (8-ounce) packages cream
cheese, at room temperature

1½ cups sugar

1 teaspoon ground cinnamon

½ teaspoon ground cloves

5 large eggs

1 (15-ounce) can pumpkin
puree (*not* pumpkin pie filling)

¼ cup heavy cream

2 teaspoons
pure vanilla extract

2 tablespoons dark rum

TOPPING

2 cups sour cream

1 tablespoon sugar

1 teaspoon pure vanilla extract

½ teaspoon ground cinnamon

½ teaspoon
freshly grated nutmeg

MAKE THE CRUST: Preheat the oven to 325°F and position a rack in the center.

In a food processor fitted with the steel blade, process the cookies into small crumbs. Add the sugar and pulse just to combine. Slowly pour in the melted butter and process until the crumbs are moistened. Press the mixture evenly over the bottom of a 10-inch springform pan. Bake for 10 minutes. Remove from the oven and let cool while you prepare the filling. Keep the oven on.

MAKE THE FILLING: In the bowl of a stand mixer fitted with the paddle attachment, beat the cream cheese, sugar, cinnamon, and cloves until blended and smooth. Stop the mixer and scrape down the sides of the bowl and the paddle with a rubber spatula as necessary. With the mixer running, beat in the eggs one at a time. Add the pumpkin, cream, vanilla, and rum and beat to combine.

Pour the cream cheese filling into the crust. Bake for 1 hour and 45 minutes. Remove the cheesecake from the oven and let cool for 15 minutes in the pan on a wire rack. Raise the oven temperature to 450°F.

MAKE THE TOPPING: Whisk together the sour cream, sugar, vanilla, cinnamon, and nutmeg in a small bowl.

Spread the sour cream topping evenly over the cheesecake and return it to the oven for 10 minutes. Remove from the oven and again let cool on a wire rack for 30 minutes to 1 hour, then refrigerate for several hours, or up to overnight.

When ready to serve, run a sharp knife between the cake and the side of the pan, then release and remove the springform ring, leaving the cake on the bottom part. Set on a decorative cake plate and serve.

FOURTH OF JULY
STRAWBERRY SHORTCAKE

Makes 8 LARGE BISCUITS

Sweet strawberries, ethereal whipped cream, and light, fluffy cream biscuits combine to form the ultimate summer dessert. Leftover biscuits do freeze easily (reheat them directly from the freezer)—but we can pretty much guarantee you won't have leftovers!

1 quart fresh strawberries, washed, hulled, and halved

¼ cup plus 2 teaspoons plus 3 tablespoons granulated sugar

2 cups unbleached all-purpose flour or pastry flour, plus more for dusting

1 teaspoon salt

1 tablespoon baking powder

4 cups heavy cream, chilled

1 tablespoon unsalted butter, melted

2 tablespoons turbinado sugar

1½ teaspoons pure vanilla extract

1 teaspoon grated lemon zest

In a medium bowl, mash 1 cup of the strawberries with a potato masher or a fork to release their juices. Add the rest of the strawberries and sprinkle with ¼ cup of the granulated sugar. Set aside to macerate at room temperature for several hours, or refrigerate for up to a day.

Preheat the oven to 425°F. Line a baking sheet with parchment paper.

In a large bowl, sift together the flour, salt, baking powder, and 2 teaspoons of the sugar. Stir in about 1¼ cups of the heavy cream, just enough to moisten the dough thoroughly. You should be able to gather the dough together, squeeze it gently, and have it hang together without dry bits falling off. Add more cream, little by little, if necessary. If you have leftover cream, stick it back in the fridge.

Turn the dough out onto a lightly floured counter or cutting board and very gently pat it into an 8-inch circle about ¾ inch thick. Use a sharp 2¼-inch biscuit cutter (or the edge of a drinking glass) to cut rounds. Brush the tops with melted butter and place the biscuits on the prepared baking sheet.

Evenly sprinkle the tops with turbinado sugar and bake for 15 to 18 minutes. If you have any melted butter left over, brush it on the biscuits when they come out of the oven.

Meanwhile, in the bowl of a stand mixer fitted with the whisk attachment, combine the remaining 2½ cups heavy cream, the vanilla, the remaining 3 tablespoons granulated sugar, and the lemon zest. Whip on high speed just until the cream forms soft peaks.

Split the oven-warm biscuits in half and place them on dessert plates. Onto one half of each biscuit, spoon some whipped cream, strawberries, and more whipped cream, then top with the other half. Keep the bowl of whipped cream and strawberries nearby, to add more as you eat!

OLD-FASHIONED ICE CREAM CUSTARD:
STRAWBERRY AND MAPLE-WALNUT

Some of the Wilcox ice cream flavors you see on the board of Mildred's Dairy Bar at the Weston store have been made by Mildred's family for more than eight decades. If you visit, perhaps you'll find some originals—orange pineapple, strawberry-rhubarb, and maple were three of the oldest flavors—and be able to experience "the crescendo of flavor" (as Howard Wilcox puts it) born of dairy-fresh ingredients and decades of New England know-how.

But why wait to visit? Here we re-create two of the classic Wilcox flavors, crescendo of flavors and all. We've adapted the custard recipe to reflect modern ice cream makers, although truth be told, we sometimes like to make ice cream the old-fashioned way with a hand-cranked machine packed with ice and salt. It requires a lot of patience and a modicum of strength, but there's something about working hard that makes the final reward even sweeter.

The basic custard recipe here is made into a delightful strawberry ice cream or a maple-walnut ice cream with a sweet and nutty flavor as old as the hills. But don't feel limited! Add your favorite fruit, chocolate chips, or crushed cookies to make your own flavor. At Mildred's, they add the Chocolate-Covered Bridge Mix sold at the Store for a sumptuous concoction called Vermont Covered Bridges Ice Cream. We've tagged on our favorite quick hot chocolate sauce, because, well, why not?

2 egg yolks

1 cup whole milk

2 cups heavy cream

½ cup sugar

Pinch of salt

In a large bowl, whisk together the egg yolks and set aside.

In a 3-quart saucepan, whisk together the milk, cream, sugar, and salt over medium heat. Once it starts to simmer, remove from the heat, let cool for 3 minutes, then gradually add the yolks, whisking between each addition. Pour the mixture back into the pan and heat it to 180°F, whisking continuously. This will only take a minute or two.

Pour the custard through a strainer into a bowl. Stir in flavorings of your choice and pour the chilled custard into the container. Place a piece of plastic wrap directly on top of the custard to prevent a skin from forming. Refrigerate the custard until well chilled, several hours or up to overnight.

Pour the chilled custard into the container of an ice cream maker and churn according to the manufacturer's instructions. Transfer the ice cream to a storage container and freeze for at least 1 hour, or until ready to serve.

(Continued)

STRAWBERRY ICE CREAM

1 pint fresh strawberries, hulled and sliced

½ cup sugar

1 tablespoon fresh lemon juice

In a medium bowl, mash together the strawberries, sugar, and lemon juice. Let sit while making the custard. Before churning the chilled custard, stir in the strawberries, then proceed as directed.

MAPLE-WALNUT ICE CREAM

⅓ cup pure maple syrup

¾ cup chopped walnuts

Before churning the chilled custard, stir in the maple syrup, then proceed as directed. Add the walnuts 5 minutes before the ice cream is finished churning.

Eliot, Cabot, Lyman, and Gardner enjoy "creamees," or soft ice cream, at Mildred's Dairy Bar.

BEST EASY BITTERSWEET CHOCOLATE SAUCE

Makes ½ CUP

⅓ cup heavy cream

3 tablespoons unsweetened cocoa powder (preferably Dutch process)

4 ounces semisweet chocolate, finely chopped

½ teaspoon pure vanilla extract

Pour the cream into a small saucepan and bring to a simmer over medium heat. Whisk in the cocoa powder until smooth and remove from the heat. Add the chocolate and let stand until the chocolate has melted, then whisk until smooth. Whisk in the vanilla. Serve warm.

❧ THE WAY IT WAS–THE EARLY DAYS OF ICE CREAM

E. E. Wilcox drives the milk truck, 1925.

Wilcox ice cream was originally made the way all ice cream was: A hand crank turned the cream, while ice and salt kept it chilled. Once the liquid turned to solid it was placed in 8-quart covered tin molds. Ice was hauled each winter from the Equinox Pond for use all year to cool the deep freeze, where the ice cream stayed until solid. It was then hand-sliced into either quarts or pints. Finally it was wrapped in parchment paper and placed into a container. Mildred's father, E.E., delivered his ice cream by horse-drawn wagon and later by a Model T converted to a milk truck by E.E. and Mildred's two older brothers, the boxes packed in ice, so customers could have it for that night's dessert.

HOME SWEET HOME
GINGERBREAD HOUSE

Makes ONE 5 × 7 × 7-INCH GINGERBREAD HOUSE

—◆◆—

Assembling the materials is the best part of making a gingerbread house, and a trip to The Vermont Country Store's candy counter makes it easy. Soon after Thanksgiving, you'll find us in the kitchen surrounded by candy—piles of red licorice whips, chocolate nonpareils, cinnamon Red Hots, gumdrops, and peppermint drops—ready to decorate the family gingerbread house.

Start your design on paper (you can find patterns on the Internet), then transfer it to a sheet of light cardboard and cut out the pieces. Following your pattern pieces, cut out the gingerbread pieces before baking.

The dough is a bit stiff and requires chilling, so it is best to do this step on your own, without young children, a few hours in advance or the night before. Once baked, the pieces need to cool before they are glued together with the royal icing. Let the glued-together house sit for a day to harden before adding the candy. Then call in the kids and take your sweet time, adding a bit of candy here and there to stretch out the fun.

GINGERBREAD

8 tablespoons (1 stick)
unsalted butter

½ cup loosely packed
dark brown sugar

½ cup dark molasses

3½ cups sifted unbleached
all-purpose flour,
plus more for dusting

1 teaspoon baking soda

1 teaspoon ground cinnamon

1 teaspoon ground ginger

¼ teaspoon ground cloves

1 teaspoon salt

MAKE THE GINGERBREAD: In the bowl of a stand mixer fitted with the whisk attachment, cream together the butter and brown sugar. Add the molasses and continue mixing until well combined.

In a large bowl, mix together the flour, baking soda, cinnamon, ginger, cloves, and salt. With the mixer on low speed, add the flour mixture, alternating with ⅓ cup water, until it all comes together into a ball.

Roll out the dough on a floured surface and work the dough with your hands until it becomes smooth. Divide the dough in half, shape each portion into a ball, and wrap them in plastic wrap. Lightly press down to flatten the dough balls just a bit, then refrigerate for a few hours, or up to overnight.

Make a pattern and trace onto oak tag or cardboard; cut out the pattern pieces (see headnote). Preheat the oven to 350°F.

Remove the dough from the refrigerator and lightly flour the counter or a marble pastry board. Roll one of the balls to a ½-inch thickness, flipping it every few rolls to prevent sticking. Arrange as many cut-out pattern pieces as possible on top of the dough, cut out the shapes with a sharp knife, and place the dough pieces on a nonstick baking sheet. Repeat with the second ball, until all the pieces have been cut out. Reserve any extra dough, wrap it back up in plastic wrap, and refrigerate in case any pieces break and need to be replaced.

Bake the gingerbread pieces for 10 to 15 minutes, until the surface is firm and light brown. Let the pieces sit for a few minutes to cool, then, with a thin spatula, carefully transfer them to a wire rack to cool completely.

MAKE THE ICING: In the bowl of a stand mixer fitted with the whisk attachment, beat the egg whites on low speed until frothy; add the confectioners' sugar and cream of tartar and beat until blended. Raise the mixer speed to high and beat until stiff peaks form, 10 to 15 minutes. Test the icing to make sure it hardens by spooning out a small portion and spreading it onto a plate or an extra piece of gingerbread. After 15 to 20 minutes, it should be stiff as glue. If it is still soft, keep beating, and add a bit more confectioners' sugar as needed. Transfer the icing to a pastry bag fitted with a plain tip or a resealable plastic bag with one corner snipped off.

TO CONSTRUCT THE GINGERBREAD HOUSE: Start with the base. Squeeze out a thin line of icing onto the bottom edges of the walls where they meet the base. Then add more icing to the edges of the walls where they come together. Gently attach each wall and press the pieces together to attach them to the base. Let these pieces set completely before adding the roof.

Glue the roof pieces to the walls and to each other at the peak. Go around and fill in the gaps between the walls and roof with extra icing to completely secure. Keep adding pieces until the house is complete, then set aside for a few hours or preferably overnight before decorating with candy. To decorate, pipe a dab of icing onto the back of a candy, then press it gently onto house or base.

189

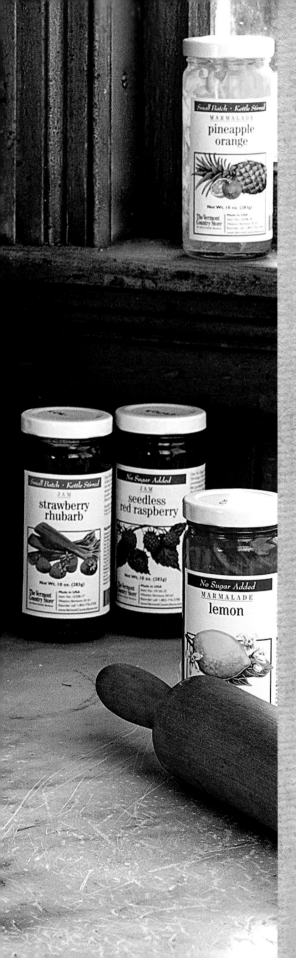

CHAPTER 8

The
PANTRY

ANY VERMONT HOUSE WORTH ITS SALT HAS A pantry filled with shelves of staples: baking necessities, of course, but also jars of dilly beans and blackberry jam put up during the summer and condiments to take the bland out of a New England diet. The Vermont Country Store samples and sells small-batch pantry items like crazy—proof that their appeal stretches beyond Vermont's borders.

A well-stocked pantry is a sign of a good cook and an always-prepared household. Making your own pantry items also cuts costs and gives you control over how much sugar goes into your jam or heat into your sauce.

CONDIMENTS, JAMS, *and* JELLIES

{The Vermont Art of Putting Food By}

A DREAM PANTRY

AS CHILDREN, WE FREQUENTLY VISITED MY grandmother Maria Wilcox, who was always baking wonderful goodies. In a big pantry in the back of the kitchen, Maria kept her cider doughnuts, maple bonbons, cookies, and, best of all, vanilla sheet cake with chocolate frosting, something my mother never baked. Grandma made cakes quickly, using her hands and fingers to measure out solid ingredients, then pouring in milk and eggs as she beat it to what felt right to her. My brother, cousins, and I had full access to those pantry shelves, and it was the first place I ran to upon arriving. Tearing around the farm, running after young livestock, or playing basketball at one end of the haymow with a hoop screwed to the barn wall easily burned off the sheet cake calories.

The family kept farmers' time, with the men up at four a.m. to milk, then returning to the kitchen for a breakfast—more like a full lunch—to fuel the rest of the morning, until dinner at midday. The evening meal was supper, with less food.

My mother, Mildred, had two sets of clothes that her aunts and mother made for her: school clothes and work clothes, just as her brothers did. (A farmer never went to town in his barn clothes for obvious reasons.) Mildred told us that helping out on the farm never felt like work, because everyone just did it; that was the life they knew. She, too, knew the pleasures of her mother's pantry.

(ABOVE) Mildred Orton swims with her brothers on the Wilcox farm, 1920.

(RIGHT) Mildred Orton, age ten.

There was lots of love and family in that life, so much connection, so many generations, such deep knowing of one another. It was so comfortable and warm being there, and I miss it still.

—LYMAN ORTON

Orton home on the Weston Green, 1949,
with seven-year-old Lyman riding his bicycle. All roads in and out of town were dirt.

WHEN VREST AND MILDRED ORTON MARRIED IN 1936, their brick house in Weston, built in 1828, had no indoor toilets, and only fireplaces, a wood-burning kitchen range, and a wood furnace in the cellar for heat. For food storage, they had a root cellar. Deep and cool year-round, it was the place they kept food for the long winters: dried beef and cod, home-canned vegetables, cheese. The floor was a bed of sand in which they laid apples, carrots, turnips, parsnips, and potatoes that would last months when covered.

Root cellars, a tradition in Vermont, were the norm on farms and in homes all across the Northeast in the eighteenth century. They were created in basements or dug into hillsides and outfitted with stone linings and wooden doors. Many folks used a platform above a covered spring, if it was close enough to the house to be convenient, to keep things cool.

Some Vermonters and others across the nation are returning to the root cellar as a way to store food they've grown or bought in bulk at the peak of ripeness, so they can eat local through the winter, without the use of energy. The best way is to build an insulated partition in the cool northeast corner of an unheated cellar with a small screened hole for ventilation. Not a bad place for wine, too.

ALWAYS PREPARED

IN WINTER HERE, SNOW, OR MORE OFTEN ICE, can fall heavily and snap the limbs of trees, sending them down onto the power lines and leaving our village in darkness, sometimes for days. Our grandmother was always prepared. We first learned how to trim the wick of a kerosene lantern in her kitchen. She taught us to always fill the bathtub when storms were coming, so there was plenty of water at hand. She kept a stocked pantry and a root cellar filled with canned goods she'd put up herself. Years ago, a terrible ice storm took out the power in Weston for six days. Just imagine whose house was the first to have light glowing in all the windows, and whose family was well fed all through the storm's aftermath.

—CABOT ORTON

VERMONT HUMOR: LIGHTBULB JOKE

HOW MANY VERMONTERS DOES IT TAKE TO CHANGE a lightbulb? Three. One to change the bulb and two to sit around discussing how they liked the old one better.

CANNING PRIMER

FOR THOSE OF YOU NEW TO PRESERVING FOODS by canning, here are the basics you'll need to know for the recipes in this chapter. Although this may seem daunting at first, it's really quite simple and becomes a cherished ritual over time. And the results—spicy, sweet, or sour—make welcomed gifts and feed both soul and palate for months.

HOW TO STERILIZE JARS AND LIDS: Always use heatproof jars, which are commonly known as mason jars. These are sold with lids containing two parts: a ring and a top with a rubber lining that will adhere to the top of the glass jar when it is sealed. Jars can be sterilized by running them through the dish-washer just before filling, or they can be scrubbed clean and placed upside down in a pot of water and boiled for 10 minutes. Keep them inverted in the hot water until just before filling. Lids should not be boiled, since the rubber may not seal properly. Place the lids and rings in a bowl and pour boiling water over them to keep warm and gently sterilized. Once the jar is opened, you can keep and reuse the ring, but will have to replace the top with the rubber seal.

HOW TO FILL THE JARS: Cover a counter or cutting board with a kitchen towel to catch any drippings. Place the sterilized jars on top. Place a wide-mouth funnel on the top of a jar and ladle the filling into the jar, leaving ¼ to ½ inch of headroom at the top. Always fill hot jars with hot filling, or they may crack when reheated. Continue for each of the jars, making sure all are evenly filled. Dip a paper towel into the hot water in which you're holding the rings and lids and wipe the rims clean. This is important for a good seal and to avoid any mold growing under the lids. Place the hot lid with the rubber seal on the jar and screw on the ring. Don't squeeze too hard, just enough to close and seal. Flip the jar upside down to start the sealing process.

HOW TO DO A HOT-WATER BATH: Fill a large stockpot with water and bring the water to a boil. Carefully lower the filled jars into the water and add more water, if needed, to cover the jars by 1 inch. Bring the water back to a boil and keep the jars submerged for the number of minutes specified in the recipe (this can be anywhere from 10 to 25 minutes and depends on the ingredients being canned). Carefully lift the jars from the hot-water bath and let them cool on the counter until you hear the lids pop. Wipe the jars clean and label them with their contents and the date. **NOTE:** Jams and jellies do not need to be hot-water bathed. Simply turn over to seal the jar and flip it back over after 10 minutes.

VERMONT CIDER JELLY IS THE ESSENCE OF OUR APPLES

Tart and intense, Vermont Cider Jelly is 100 percent apple. It's made somewhat like maple syrup, by boiling cider until the natural pectin in apples causes it to jell, producing a dark, pure essence of apple. After the fall apple harvest, the farmer presses the juice from apples, then boils it in his maple sugarhouse, with a yield of one gallon of jelly from nine gallons of apple cider. There's hardly anyone left doing this, as it's a lot of work for not much profit, but the Ortons have had it made and promoted it for years. It should be in your pantry for serving with meats and cheeses, to use in sauces and marinades as a flavor booster, to rub on a roasting pork, and to enjoy on toast and in sandwiches. Don't confuse cider jelly with the commercial apple jelly favored by children—this is an adult food with an intense flavor and tart-sweet taste.

From DELIA WILCOX'S RECIPE BOOK

- Keep ants from pantry shelves with oil of sassafras.

- Oil of sassafras sprinkled around in shelves and windowsills will rid a room of flys [sic], ants and cockroaches.

- If ants are troublesome sprinkle sugar through small pieces of sponge, leave these about pantry shelves. When full of ants put in boiling water then set again. [We can't imagine anyone nowadays who would even think of doing this!]

Removing STAINS, SEVENTY YEARS AGO

Okay, kids, don't try these at home. Or if you do, let us know if any of them work! We found stain-removing suggestions in the 1949 book *Vermont Food As We Like It*, and these three were new to us:

- Grass Stains—wash in alcohol and rinse in cold water

- Mildew—Rub with juice of raw tomato, sprinkle with salt and lay in sun. Repeat if needed, 2 or 3 times.

- Blood—Saturate with kerosene and let stand a few minutes. Wash in cold water.

VERMONT MAPLE–TOMATO SALSA

Makes 4 PINTS

————◆◆————

As New Englanders, we are wimps when it comes to hot peppers. Yet every now and again we like hot, spicy food. In this recipe we suggest using serranos, green, not-too-hot peppers that add a nice balance between the sweet of the syrup and the tang of the cilantro and cumin. If you prefer a hotter pepper, we suggest substituting with one habanero and one jalapeño, or really to taste.

Serve this vibrantly colored salsa as a snack or an appetizer with chips, a spicy condiment with crab or cod cakes (see page 92), or a topping for a crisp tortilla. This recipe makes more than you will need for one sitting, so plan to put some up for winter noshing. Be sure to heat the salsa to a simmer before packing it into sterilized mason jars.

6 ripe medium tomatoes (3 pounds), seeded and coarsely chopped

2 medium onions, finely diced (2 cups)

2 bell peppers, seeded and finely diced (2 cups)

3 green serrano peppers, seeded and minced

2 cloves garlic, minced

¼ cup chopped fresh dill

¼ cup chopped fresh cilantro

¼ cup chopped fresh flat-leaf parsley

Juice of 1 lemon (3 tablespoons)

Juice of 1 lime (1 to 2 tablespoons)

1 teaspoon sea salt

1 teaspoon ground cumin

⅓ cup pure maple syrup

2 tablespoons soy sauce

In a large bowl, combine the tomatoes, onions, bell peppers, serranos, garlic, herbs, lemon and lime juice, salt, and cumin. Pour in the maple syrup and soy sauce. Mix together well, taste, and adjust the seasoning. Refrigerate the salsa overnight so the flavors can blend. You may need to drain some of the liquid from the salsa that has accumulated overnight. At this point, the salsa can be served fresh or canned for longer storage.

HOW TO CAN IT: Bring the salsa to a simmer on the stovetop, then, using a wide-mouth funnel, pour it into sterilized 1-pint jars. Wipe the rims clean with hot water and place rubber lids and screw tops to seal. Turn upside down to vacuum seal. Process in a hot-water bath for 20 minutes. Remove, cool, and label.

HOW TO STORE IT: Fresh, the salsa will keep in an airtight container in the refrigerator for up to 1 week. Canned, it will keep for up to 1 year.

BREAD-AND-BUTTER PICKLES

Makes 12 PINTS

———◆———

*T*he most difficult thing about making pickles is deciding which recipe to use. This is our favorite for a sweet and crunchy bread-and-butter pickle. It can be adapted for other garden vegetables, such as baby zucchini or even small round lemon cucumbers. If you have them, place a washed grape leaf or two in each jar before adding the pickles—they contain an enzyme that keeps the pickles crisp. Real pickling cucumbers tend to be smaller and contain fewer seeds than a juicy, fresh eating cucumber, and are often sold by the half bushel.

24 medium pickling cucumbers (about 8 pounds), cut into ¼-inch-thick rounds

6 small yellow onions, thinly sliced (2½ cups)

1 cup pickling or kosher salt

6 cups apple cider vinegar

6 cups sugar

½ cup yellow mustard seeds

1 tablespoon celery seeds

2 fresh cayenne peppers, seeded and minced

12 fresh grape leaves, washed (optional)

Mix the cucumbers, onions, and salt in a large bowl. Add cold water to cover and let stand for 3 hours. Drain in a large colander and rinse well under cold water.

In a large stainless-steel or enameled pot, combine the vinegar, sugar, mustard seeds, celery seeds, and cayenne pepper and bring to a boil over high heat. Stir in the cucumber and onions. Cook just until the liquid reaches a simmer, but do not boil, as this will make soft pickles.

HOW TO CAN IT: Place a grape leaf or two (if using) in the bottom of each of 12 hot sterilized 1-pint mason jars, and, using a wide-mouth funnel, ladle the hot pickles into the jars. Evenly distribute the pickles and the brine, leaving ¼ inch headroom. Wipe the rims clean with hot water and place rubber lids and screw tops to seal. Turn upside down to vacuum seal. Process in a hot-water bath for 10 minutes. Remove, cool, and label.

HOW TO STORE IT: Store in a cool, dark place for at least 3 months, until crisp.

A *Super* CELLAR

The largest root cellar in Vermont is located at the now-defunct Duxbury Hospital Farm, where patients—early locavores!—worked to raise the food that supplied the hospital. Seventy by forty feet, it stored food for about 1,000 patients and a staff of 300.

WATERMELON PICKLES

Makes 3½ PINTS (7 HALF-PINT JARS)

———◆———

W atermelons and summer are synonymous. This fruity pickle is made in August, when melons are abundant, and kept in the cool pantry until Christmas, when roast beef is served. When you buy a watermelon and scoop it out in large chunks to serve to the kids and family for dessert, it always seems a shame to throw out the rinds—and now you don't have to!

When you cut the rind and peel off the green, leave a hint of the red flesh attached to make a prettier pickle. Watermelons are easier to weigh than to measure, and this recipe calculates a general ratio so you can increase or decrease the amounts based on the size of your melon. The end result is a really pretty pickle that is something a little different to serve or present as a gift from your kitchen.

---

4 pounds watermelon rind (from ½ watermelon)

5 cups sugar

4 cups apple cider vinegar

1 tablespoon whole cloves

2 teaspoons whole allspice

7 cinnamon sticks

Peel the green skin off the watermelon rind and cut the rind into small strips or cubes. Weigh the rind to make sure you have 4 pounds, or about 16 cups of cubes. In a large stainless-steel bowl, soak the rind in cold water to cover overnight.

In the morning, drain the rind and transfer it to a 4-quart stockpot. Add enough water to cover and bring to a slow simmer over medium heat. Cook until tender but not soft, 15 to 20 minutes. Drain in a colander and rinse with cold water. In the same stockpot, combine the sugar, vinegar, cloves, and allspice (to make it easier to remove the spices, wrap them in cheesecloth; otherwise, you have to spoon them out with a slotted spoon at the end). Place the watermelon rind back in the pot, bring to a simmer, and cook slowly until the rind is transparent, about 10 minutes. Don't overcook, because they will cook again in the hot-water bath. Remove and discard the spices.

HOW TO CAN IT: Place a cinnamon stick in each of 7 sterilized half-pint jars. Using a wide-mouth funnel, ladle the watermelon rind into the jars. Evenly distribute the rind and the brine, leaving ¼ inch headroom. Wipe the rims clean with hot water and place rubber lids and screw tops to seal. Turn upside down to vacuum seal. Process in a hot-water bath for 10 minutes. Remove, cool, and label.

HOW TO STORE IT: Store in a cool, dark place for at least 3 months, until crisp, before using.

RASPBERRY-PEACH JAM

Raspberries and peaches are old friends, and ripen at the same time during the summer. They are especially convivial in this jam, with chunks of sweet peaches blending nicely with the tartness of the raspberries. Spread this jam on toast on the grayest winter morning to bring back the memory of summer in a jar.

4 ripe peaches
(about 2 pounds)

2 pints fresh raspberries

Juice of 2 lemons
(6 tablespoons)

6 cups sugar

1 (3-ounce) pouch liquid
pectin

Bring a pot of water to a boil over high heat. Add the peaches and cook until the skins loosen, about 1 minute (this will take longer if the peaches are not ripe). Take care not to actually cook the peaches. Using a slotted spoon, transfer the peaches to a bowl of cold water to stop the cooking. The skins should then slip off easily. Peel and pit peaches and cut them into ½-inch cubes.

In a medium bowl, stir together the peaches, raspberries, and lemon juice. Measure out 4 cups and transfer to a large stainless-steel or enameled pot. With a wooden spoon, stir in the sugar and bring to a boil over high heat, stirring often. While the mixture is coming to a boil, open the envelope of liquid pectin and set it aside, standing it upright in a cup. When the mixture reaches a rolling boil, one that can't be stirred down, keep it at a hard boil for 1 minute, stirring continuously to prevent scorching. If you have a candy thermometer, place it in the pot and watch until it reaches 220°F.

Turn off the heat and immediately stir in the pectin. Skim off the foam on the surface of the jam with a metal spoon and continue to stir for 5 minutes, skimming as needed, to blend the pectin.

HOW TO CAN IT: Using a wide-mouth funnel, ladle the hot jam into 6 sterilized 1-pint mason jars, leaving ¼ inch headroom. Wipe the rims clean with hot water and place rubber lids and screw tops to seal. Turn upside down for 10 minutes to vacuum seal. Let cool and label.

HOW TO STORE IT: Store in a cool pantry or dark cupboard away from direct light. Best if used within the year, yet will keep longer.

CARROT-ORANGE MARMALADE

Makes 3 PINTS (6 HALF-PINT JARS)

———•◆•———

We love this sunny marmalade and the tart combination of citrus and carrots. But what's really special about this combination is that it can be made year–round. You don't have to wait until berry season, since carrots and oranges are always available in the supermarket. Half–pint jars make wonderful hostess or holiday gifts, and the natural pectin in the oranges means the ingredients are simple and require no extra pectin.

2 lemons,
wash to remove wax or residue

2 oranges,
wash to remove wax or residue

2 pounds carrots,
peeled and shredded (4 cups)

2½ cups sugar

Peel the lemons and oranges, slice in half, and remove the seeds. Chop the halves into smaller pieces and process in a food processor fitted with the steel blade until only fine bits remain.

In a large heavy-bottomed saucepan, combine the lemons, oranges, shredded carrots, sugar, and 4 cups water and bring to a simmer over medium heat. Simmer for 30 minutes, stirring occasionally, until the marmalade is thick and syrupy.

HOW TO CAN IT: Using a wide-mouth funnel, ladle the hot marmalade into 6 sterilized half-pint mason jars, leaving ¼ inch headroom. Wipe the rims clean with hot water and place rubber lids and screw tops to seal. Turn upside down for 10 minutes to vacuum seal. Let cool and label.

HOW TO STORE IT: Store in a cool pantry or dark cupboard away from direct light. Best if used within the year, yet will keep longer.

➳ MAKING JAM

Recipes for jam should come with a warning label: "Danger, habit-forming process ahead. May result in eating more fruit and sugar than is good for you." Because once we get started, we're hopeless. Instead of bringing home a few quarts of berries to share with the family, fruit comes into the kitchen by the armful. Julia Child's advice to exercise moderation in everything is tossed aside when fresh berries are in season.

While other people are waving flags at the Fourth of July town parade, we celebrate by scouring the woods for wild berries or filling flats at a pick-your-own farm. Once home, the canning kettle is dusted off and the mason jars come up from the basement.

Making jam may appear easy, and for the most part it is. But we are reminded of what a neighbor once said about the art of preserving: "It is like learning to drive a car on the ice—it's a little tricky at first, but then once you get the hang of it, it is easy." And the rewards? Sticky and delicious.

BETTER HOMEMADE KETCHUP

Makes 5 PINTS

*O*nce you try this chunky and sweet ketchup, redolent with simmered spices that give it extra depth, you'll find it hard to go back to the oversugared commercial brands. Make this when tomatoes are abundant at the end of summer, and you just may have enough to get a family through the winter. You can make it with a 28-ounce can of chopped tomatoes if fresh aren't available, but the flavor will not be as good. We think you'll be surprised by how complex and delicious ketchup can be!

8 ripe red tomatoes
(4 pounds)

1 large yellow onion, quartered

2 tablespoons olive oil

2 teaspoons kosher salt

1 cinnamon stick

1 bay leaf

5 whole cloves

5 cardamom pods, crushed

1 star anise

10 whole black peppercorns

½ cup firmly packed light
brown sugar

½ cup apple cider vinegar
or white vinegar

1 teaspoon Hungarian paprika

Freshly ground black pepper

Bring a large pot of water to a boil. Cut a small X on the bottom (opposite the stem end) of each tomato. Drop them into the boiling water and cook for 30 seconds. Lift out the tomatoes with a slotted spoon and drop them into a bowl of ice water. With a sharp paring knife, slip off the skins and trim out the stem end and any blemishes. Chop the tomatoes into quarters.

Transfer the tomatoes and their juices to a food processor or blender, and process until totally smooth. Take out ¼ cup and set aside in a small bowl. Add the onion to the food processor and process again until smooth.

Heat the oil in a large nonreactive stockpot or Dutch oven (bigger than you think, as this will splatter) over medium heat. Add the tomato-onion puree and salt and stir well to blend. Cook for 8 to 10 minutes, letting the puree reduce and soften.

Cut a small square of cheesecloth (or use a mesh tea ball) and tie up the cinnamon, bay leaf, cloves, cardamom, star anise, and peppercorns into a bundle. Add the spice bag to the simmering puree, along with the reserved pureed tomato, brown sugar, and vinegar. Reduce the heat to low and simmer for about 25 minutes, uncovered, giving the puree an occasional stir.

Keep an eye on the pot—when it's done, the ketchup should be slightly thinner than commercial ketchup. This may take a little longer than 25 minutes, depending on your tomatoes. Stir in the paprika and pepper, taste for seasoning, and adjust as needed. Let the ketchup cool and remove the spice bundle. At this point, you can pour the ketchup directly into sterilized mason jars and chill, or process the ketchup for longer storage.

HOW TO CAN IT: Using a wide-mouth funnel, ladle the hot ketchup into 10 sterilized half-pint mason jars, leaving ¼ inch headroom. Wipe the rims clean with hot water and place rubber lids and screw tops to seal. Turn upside down to vacuum seal. Process in a hot-water bath for 20 minutes. Remove, let cool, and label.

HOW TO STORE IT: Refrigerated, homemade ketchup will keep for at least 2 months. Canned, it will keep in a cool, dark place for up to 6 months.

GINGER-PEACH CHUTNEY

Makes 6 PINTS

————— ◆◆ —————

Sweet, with the summer flavor of ripe peaches and an undertone of warm spiciness that only ginger can provide, this chutney will turn simple grilled chicken into a gourmet meal. A condiment that is made from fresh fruits and plentiful spices, chutney is an excellent digestive. It simmers on the stovetop for almost an hour until it reaches a glossy sheen; packed into jars and stored for several months, it builds up intense flavor. We make this recipe every August and find that it makes just enough to get through the winter until it becomes peach season again.

2 cups packed
dark brown sugar

2 cups apple cider vinegar

1 large yellow onion,
halved and thinly sliced into
half-moons (1 cup)

1 fresh cayenne pepper,
seeded and minced

1 fresh jalapeño,
seeded and minced

1 tablespoon
pickling or kosher salt

1 tablespoon
yellow mustard seeds

4 pounds ripe (not overly ripe)
peaches (about 8 peaches)

1 cup dried cranberries
or currants

½ cup finely chopped
crystallized ginger

In a large stockpot, bring the sugar and vinegar to a boil over medium-high heat, stirring to dissolve the sugar. Stir in the onion, cayenne and jalapeño peppers, salt, and mustard seeds. Reduce the heat to medium and cook at a brisk simmer for 10 minutes.

Meanwhile, bring a large stockpot of water to a boil, and gently immerse the peaches. Remove them after 1 minute, drain, let cool slightly in a colander, and slip off the skins. Over a large bowl, pit peaches and cut them into slices and then into roughly ½- to 1-inch chunks. (You should have about 6 cups chopped peaches.) Drain the excess juice that collects in the bottom of the bowl (it is a wonderful sweet nectar for the cook to drink!) and add the peaches to the simmering vinegar brine. Stir in the cranberries and the ginger.

Continue to simmer over medium-low heat for about 45 minutes, stirring occasionally, until the peaches and the brine take on a glossy look. Take care not to overcook the peaches, because they will cook again once the canning jars are processed, and it is best to have chunks remain.

HOW TO CAN IT: Using a wide-mouth funnel, ladle the hot chutney into 6 sterilized 1-pint mason jars, leaving ¼ inch headroom. Wipe the rims clean with hot water and place rubber lids and screw tops to seal. Turn upside down to vacuum seal. Process in a hot-water bath for 10 minutes. Remove, let cool, and label.

HOW TO STORE IT: Store the chutney on a shelf in a cool, dark place for at least 3 months to allow the flavors to meld and ripen.

Looking for a spicy, complex, chunky, sweet-and-sour condiment? Try chutney. Chutney is concocted from fresh fruit, ginger, hot chiles, and spices, and it is simple to make. You can follow a recipe (like our Ginger-Peach Chutney recipe at left), or keep basic proportions in mind—two cups sugar, two cups vinegar, and eight cups sliced or chopped fruit—and wing it. Add grated fresh ginger, raisins or cranberries, and black mustard seeds to impart a depth of flavor that will elevate the chutney beyond a simple relish.

Good chutney demands more time than creativity, and can take an hour of simmering before it reaches the glossy, thick consistency that signals readiness. Like good wine, chutney gets better with age, and can be served fresh, or sealed in canning jars and set on the shelf for at least three months. Serve it as a side with poultry or dabbed on a cracker with a slice of Cheddar cheese.

BRYANT HOUSE
MAPLE BARBECUE GLAZE

Makes 3 HALF-PINTS

*C*hef Glen Gourlay from the Bryant House Restaurant at our Weston store shared his recipe for maple BBQ glaze, and what a recipe it is! Great to baste pork chops, chicken, and pork shoulder, or to mix into pulled pork, it's sweet and spicy and simple to make, cooking down to a fragrant sauce in just under an hour. Store in the refrigerator and liberally slather on any meat before grilling. This recipe makes enough for one large chicken, plus a little more. You can make a double batch and can it to enjoy anytime you feel like grilling.

3 tablespoons vegetable oil

1 yellow onion, diced (1 cup)

1 (1-inch) knob fresh ginger, peeled and minced (2 teaspoons)

3 cloves garlic, smashed

½ teaspoon cayenne pepper

¼ teaspoon freshly ground black pepper

1 cup apple cider vinegar

6 ounces tomato paste

½ cup soy sauce

¼ cup sesame oil

1½ cups pure maple syrup

3 tablespoons mustard powder

⅛ teaspoon dried thyme

2 teaspoons kosher salt

In a large stockpot, heat the oil over medium heat. Add the onion and sauté until it becomes translucent, about 10 minutes, then add the ginger, garlic, cayenne pepper, and black pepper. Cook for 5 minutes more, then stir in the vinegar, tomato paste, soy sauce, sesame oil, maple syrup, and ½ cup water.

Stir with a whisk to break up the tomato paste and continue to simmer over medium heat until the liquid is smooth. Add the mustard, thyme, and 1 teaspoon of the salt and simmer over low heat for 30 minutes.

With an immersion blender, puree the sauce directly in the pot until smooth. Alternatively, transfer it to a blender in batches and puree until smooth—be careful, as the sauce will be hot. Taste and add the remaining 1 teaspoon salt if needed. At this point, you can transfer the sauce to a large mason jar and refrigerate, or process the sauce for longer storage.

HOW TO CAN IT: Using a wide-mouth funnel, ladle the hot BBQ sauce into 3 sterilized half-pint mason jars, leaving ¼ inch headroom. Wipe the rims clean with hot water and place rubber lids and screw tops to seal. Turn upside down to vacuum seal. Process in a hot-water bath for 20 minutes. Remove, let cool, and label.

HOW TO STORE IT: The sauce will keep in the refrigerator for up to 2 weeks. Canned, the sauce will keep in a cool, dark place for up to 6 months.

HOT PEPPER JELLY

Sweet and spicy hot pepper jelly is not for toast, but is quite versatile, as it's both sweet and hot. We love the way this cooks up so easily and we always have a jar on the pantry shelf. Serve over mild soft cheese, Cheddar, or cream cheese or add to a vegetable stir-fry for a quick burst of flavor.

You can vary the hot pepper varieties according to what you have growing in the garden or what you find at the farmers' market, but keep in mind that the peppers have to be hot! When the pot starts to boil with the vinegar and the peppers, be prepared for a fiery fragrance to come alive. It will tame to a sweet-natured jelly by the time it is packed into jars.

12 mixed hot peppers (habanero, serrano, and jalapeños)

4 yellow, green, or red bell peppers, seeded and chopped (about 1 cup)

2 cups apple cider vinegar

6 cups sugar

1 (6-ounce) pouch liquid pectin

Trim the tops off the hot and sweet peppers, remove the seeds, and coarsely chop into small pieces. (You might want to wear plastic gloves for handling the hot peppers' seeds; at the very least, wash your hands thoroughly with soap and water when done.) Place peppers in a food processor fitted with the steel blade. Pulse gently, leaving small chunks. Measure out 3 cups of the peppers and juice.

In a deep saucepan, combine the vinegar and sugar and bring to a boil, stirring to dissolve the sugar. Add the 3 cups peppers and bring to a full rolling boil. Stir in the liquid pectin, bring back to a rolling boil, and stir for 1 full minute. Remove from the heat.

HOW TO CAN IT: Using a wide-mouth funnel, ladle the hot jelly into 6 sterilized half-pint mason jars, leaving ¼ inch headroom. Wipe the rims clean with hot water and place rubber lids and screw tops to seal. Turn upside down for 10 minutes to vacuum seal. Let cool and label.

HOW TO STORE IT: Store in a cool pantry or dark cupboard away from direct light. Best if used within the year, yet will keep longer.

GREEN TOMATO
AND PEPPER PICCALILLI

Makes 6 PINTS

———— ◆◆ ————

Piccalilli is a lovely vegetable relish that can be served with hot dogs or hamburgers, used as a topping for meat loaf, or blended with mayo to make a nice tartar sauce for fish. This recipe originates from Betty Foster, a renowned cook in the Weston valley, who left a legacy of wonderful recipes to her daughters, one of whom was the head chef at the Bryant House Restaurant for many years. We also found piccalilli recipes in Delia's and Mildred's notebooks, and all were very similar and used the same key ingredient: green tomatoes.

Like most pickle recipes, this can take two days to prepare, but really doesn't take much time at all to actually cook. Once you've started making pickles and taste the difference between homemade and store-bought, this recipe may become part of your late summer routine. If it does, know that you can easily double it to make enough for friends and family.

6 pounds green tomatoes, coarsely chopped into bite-size pieces

3 large green bell peppers (or a mixture of red and green), seeded and coarsely chopped (4 cups)

4 large yellow onions, halved and thinly sliced into half-moons (4 cups)

½ cup kosher salt

2 cups packed brown sugar

2 cups granulated sugar

½ teaspoon ground cloves

½ teaspoon ground cinnamon

½ teaspoon ground allspice

½ cup yellow mustard seeds

2 cups apple cider vinegar

In a very large stainless-steel bowl, layer all the vegetables with the salt. Cover with a kitchen towel and let stand at room temperature overnight or for several hours. This takes the moisture out of the vegetables.

In the morning, drain the vegetables in a large colander, wash out the bowl, and return the vegetables to the bowl. In a food processor fitted with the steel blade, pulse the vegetables in batches to a medium-fine chop; be careful not to turn them to mush! Transfer to the colander again to drain out excess liquid.

In a large stockpot, combine the sugars, spices, mustard seeds, and vinegar and simmer until the sugar has dissolved. Add the chopped vegetables and simmer over low heat for 2 hours, stirring occasionally with a wooden spoon. You'll know it is ready when the piccalilli still has some liquid, yet not too much, and looks glossy.

HOW TO CAN IT: Using a wide-mouth funnel, ladle the hot relish into 6 sterilized 1-pint mason jars, leaving ¼ inch headroom. Wipe the rims clean with hot water and place rubber lids and screw tops to seal. Turn upside down to vacuum seal. Process in a hot-water bath for 10 minutes. Remove, let cool, and label.

HOW TO STORE IT: Store in a cool pantry or dark cupboard away from direct light. Best if used within the year, yet will keep longer.

West River farmers' market, Londonderry.

CHAPTER 9

The COOKIE and CANDY JARS

T HE CANDY COUNTER AT THE VERMONT Country Store in Weston looks much the same as it did when Vrest opened the doors in 1946. Big glass jars filled with candies the colors of the rainbow line the shelves, and boxes of fudge, brittle, and chocolates crowd the counters. Licorice, striped candy puffs, Mary Janes, Bonomo Turkish Taffy—all the candies of your youth tempt you everywhere you look. Remember the little brown bags you filled and the tiny red pencils to mark the price? The Vermont Country Store still has them. The memories all treats evoke make them taste even sweeter.

COOKIES, BROWNIES, FUDGE, and BRITTLE

Vermont Sweet Memories

THE TASTE OF HISTORY

THE RECIPE FOR MAPLE BONBONS, A TRADI-tional Vermont sweet, has been passed down through the generations of Mildred's family. My mother's mother got the recipe from her mother, who got it from hers, who got it from hers. The Hamilton-Wilcox women passed this recipe down orally, teaching and demonstrating from woman to woman to woman from the mid-1800s until 1975, when my mother finally wrote it down.

Making maple bonbons involves boiling maple syrup to a certain temperature while beating and then spooning it out quickly. This is a two-person job: one person to spoon it onto waxed paper, the other to press a nut in the middle—a perfect recipe for a mother and daughter or two friends on a late afternoon. As a child, Mildred's job was to gather the butternuts from the tree on the farm, dry them in the attic over the winter, hammer out the meat, and finally, when the big day came, to press the dried nut firmly into the center of each maple bonbon.

To eat one of these maple bonbons is to ingest the DNA of a farmwoman in Vermont from 1861, who just might have been sending a batch to a son fighting in the Civil War. After all, Vermont sent a higher percentage of its men to that war than any other state. Imagine a weary soldier biting into this little piece of heaven, this big taste of home.

–LYMAN ORTON

Mildred and her mother, Maria Wilcox, selling maple bonbons in front of the Wilcox farm, 1920.

TIMELESS TREAT

HOREHOUND CANDY WAS VREST ORTON'S FAVOR-ite, and he would always slip behind the counter and put a few "slugs" (as they were known) in his pocket before heading upstairs to his office. He was a prac-tical man, and he appreciated that the Store's hore-hound is made from the real herb and soothes the throat if hoarse, sore, or scratchy. But he also grew up in a country store, and perhaps the flavor of hore-hound is one he remembered from before gummy bears, worms, and frogs, satellite wafers, and Ba-zooka bubble gum.

WHEN VREST ORTON DECIDED TO OPEN THE VERmont Country Store, he traveled back to North Calais to the country store where his father, known as G.L., had started in business to buy back some of its shelving and fixtures. He found an almost-deserted hamlet, and not a trace of the store.

Another store in town, however, had bought some of the fixtures from G.L.'s store, and the shopkeeper remembered Vrest as a boy. They spent the day visiting stores in the area, tracking down and buying all the fixtures they could find that came from the old red clapboarded store where Vrest had sat in the evenings listening to veterans tell tales of the Civil War.

Vrest was heartened to find so many of the old fixtures and shelving to use in his Weston store. But one find was particularly sweet. "I was most happy to find," he writes in his *The Story of The Vermont Country Store*, "the actual curved glass candy case which I had, as a small boy, pressed my nose against to see the goodies inside."

GRANDMA'S BEST BROWNIES

Makes 24 BROWNIES

W*hy even think about boxed brownies when these are so easy to make (and the mixing bowl so delicious to lick)? This recipe is simple and straightforward—no coffee, no chips, just pure, plain, soft, and chewy chocolate brownies, the way Grandma would make.*

One thing we may do a little differently than Grandma, however, is to line the pan with parchment paper or foil to make it easy to lift the brownies out of the pan and transfer them to a cutting board to slice into individual portions. It's key to let the whole thing cool before cutting, which means you have to wait...which may be the hardest part about making these always-perfect brownies.

12 tablespoons
(1½ sticks) unsalted butter,
plus more for the pan

1¼ cups cake flour,
plus more for the pan

Nonstick cooking spray
(optional)

1 cup walnuts

6 ounces unsweetened
chocolate, finely chopped

2 cups sugar

4 large eggs

1 tablespoon
pure vanilla extract

½ teaspoon salt

½ teaspoon baking powder

Preheat the oven to 350°F. Lightly butter and flour a 13 × 9-inch baking pan, or coat with nonstick spray. Cut two sheets of parchment paper to fit inside the pan with an overhang on each side, and place crosswise in pan.

Spread the walnuts on a baking sheet and toast in the oven until fragrant, about 15 minutes. Let cool and coarsely chop. Keep the oven on.

In the top of a double boiler over simmering water (or in the microwave), melt the butter and chocolate, stirring occasionally until smooth. Pour the chocolate mixture into the bowl of a stand mixer fitted with the whisk attachment and beat in the sugar with the mixer on low speed. Add the eggs one at a time, mixing until each is incorporated before adding the next, then add the vanilla.

In a measuring cup or bowl, stir together the flour, salt, and baking powder and gradually add it to the chocolate batter, mixing until smooth.

Transfer the batter to the prepared baking pan, sprinkle with the walnuts, and bake for 30 to 35 minutes. Test with a wooden skewer inserted into the center of the brownies; if it comes out clean, they're done. Remove from the oven, lift the brownies out of the pan and onto a cutting board, and let cool completely before slicing.

AUNT DELIA'S
GINGER MOLASSES COOKIES

Makes 48 COOKIES

———◆———

Ginger cookies have been standard New England fare for decades. We found Aunt Delia's Ginger Molasses Cookie recipe in several books, always handwritten by different cooks in the family. Her recipe called for 3 ¼ cups whole wheat flour, no eggs, and a light hand with the spices. We lightened it up and added more ginger and other spices, and a crunchy dusting of sugar. You'll find them tempting as an afternoon snack or with a bowl of vanilla ice cream. Better yet, stuff ice cream inside two cookies to make a spicy, sweet ice cream sandwich.

2 ¼ cups unbleached
all-purpose flour

2 teaspoons ground cinnamon

2 teaspoons ground ginger

½ teaspoon ground cloves

2 teaspoons baking soda

½ teaspoon salt

1 cup packed
light brown sugar

1 cup (2 sticks) unsalted
butter, at room temperature

1 large egg,
at room temperature

⅓ cup molasses

½ cup turbinado or
other coarse sugar

Preheat the oven to 350°F. Line two baking sheets with parchment paper.

In a small bowl, stir together the flour, cinnamon, ginger, cloves, baking soda, and salt.

In the bowl of a stand mixer fitted with the paddle attachment, cream together the brown sugar and butter until light and fluffy. Add the egg and beat until blended. Scrape down the sides of the bowl and add the molasses. With the mixer on low, add the dry ingredients and mix until just blended. The batter will be thick and sticky.

Into a small bowl or onto a plate, pour out the turbinado sugar. Using a tablespoon, scoop out a spoonful of dough. Roll it between your palms into a 1-inch ball and then roll it in the turbinado sugar to coat. Place on a prepared baking sheet and repeat with the remaining dough, setting the cookie dough balls about 2 inches apart. For a flatter cookie, press the tops of the dough balls with a fork to flatten them slightly. Or keep them rounded, and they will develop the familiar crack in the top as they bake.

Bake the cookies for 12 to 14 minutes, or until they are golden brown. Transfer to a wire rack to cool.

Get THAT STICKY STUFF Out

Need to measure something sticky, like molasses or peanut butter? Fill your measuring cup with hot water, then dump it out and don't dry the cup. Fill the cup with the sticky stuff and it will slide right out, making cleanup easy.

HOMEMADE FIG NEWTONS

———— •••• ————

Fig Newtons are such a satisfying cookie, one you can almost feel holy about eating, since figs are so nutritious. When you make them yourself, though the process is more complicated than simply buying a package off the shelf, the reward is a far more delicious cookie than the commercial brand. The dough has a hint of orange zest, which, combined with the fig, gives it a sophisticated flavoring. To give them that familiar soft texture, the fresh-baked cookies steam in a plastic bag, which may seem odd, but really works! To avoid sticky dough, plan ahead: Make the dough and the filling the night before, and chill it thoroughly before rolling it out.

1½ cups unbleached all-purpose flour, plus more for dusting

1 teaspoon baking powder

¼ teaspoon kosher salt

10 tablespoons (1¼ sticks) unsalted butter, at room temperature

⅔ cup packed dark brown sugar

1 large egg

2 teaspoons pure vanilla extract

Zest of 1 orange

1 pound dried Turkish figs, cut into small pieces

In a medium bowl, whisk together the flour, baking powder, and salt and set aside.

In the bowl of a stand mixer fitted with the paddle attachment (or by hand), beat the butter and brown sugar until light and fluffy, 3 to 5 minutes. Add the egg, vanilla, and orange zest and beat until combined. Add the flour mixture and mix until well blended. The dough will be very soft. Scoop it out onto a piece of plastic wrap, shape it into a disc, and refrigerate overnight to chill.

In a medium saucepan, combine the figs and ½ cup water and bring to a boil. Cover and boil until the figs have absorbed all the water. If your figs are very dry and tough, you may need to use more water and simmer longer to get the figs to soften. Transfer the figs to a food processor fitted with the steel blade and pulse, scraping down the sides of the bowl occasionally, until the mixture is completely smooth. Let cool.

Scoop the fig filling into a pastry bag or a resealable plastic bag with one corner cut off, 1 inch on an angle.

Preheat the oven to 325°F.

Place a large piece of parchment or waxed paper on your work surface and flour it liberally. Divide the dough into four equal pieces. Place one piece on the parchment paper and return the other three pieces to the refrigerator.

Loosely shape the dough into a rectangle by squaring it on the work surface, then gently rolling with a floured rolling pin, stopping frequently to make sure it isn't sticking to the parchment, and adding more flour to keep it from sticking. Roll it into a long rectangle, about 4 inches wide by 12 inches long by ½ inch thick, and trim the edges with a knife to even it up.

(Continued)

Pipe the filling in a thick strip down the center of the dough rectangle. Dip your fingers into water and press the filling to flatten it a bit.

Fold one side of the dough over the filling, then the other. Press down on the seam to close it. Flip the cookie roll over, seam side down. Carefully transfer it to a baking sheet and refrigerate while you repeat this step with the other three pieces of dough, adding rolls to the baking sheet.

Once the baking sheet is filled, bake for 20 minutes or until the cookie rolls have begun to lightly brown around the edges. Remove from the oven and with a large spatula, transfer them to a cutting board, and cut the rolls into 2-inch cookies. Immediately place the cookies inside large resealable plastic bags in a single layer and close the bags for about 30 minutes. Remove the cookies from the bags and allow them to dry on a wire rack for 30 minutes, then place them in an airtight container. They will keep at room temperature for up to 2 weeks, or put them in a plastic bag and pop them in the freezer.

Keeping BROWN SUGAR Soft

Store your brown sugar in the freezer to keep it from going stale. Take it out a couple of minutes before you need it, and you're ready to go! A slice or two of apple or a slice of bread or even a couple of marshmallows in your brown sugar container overnight will soften it, too, thanks to the additional moisture.

∾ MILDRED'S COOKIE CUTTERS

One of our most cherished keepsakes is a bag filled with the cookie cutters our grandmother Mildred used in her kitchen for many years. Made of real tin, with faded red wooden handles, they'd be considered "vintage" now, but for our grandmother they were holiday tools of the trade for more than half a century.

Once a year, we pull the bag out of a drawer and empty the bells, wreaths, holly leaves, and gingerbread men onto the counter for Christmas cookie-making time, our most delicious family tradition. The gingerbread man cutter gets a workout, as nothing says Christmas to us quite as perfectly as the combination of nutmeg, cinnamon, clove, molasses, and frosting. We stamp out little men and ladies in our family assembly line with such abandon that invariably we run out of pans and are forced to eat icing while the cookies bake.

Let's make one thing clear: These are not intended for hanging from the Christmas tree as handmade ornaments; they are made to be devoured. We do save a few batches for gift-giving and relative-placating, but frankly, this is a tradition that feeds our bellies as much as our souls.

—ELIOT ORTON

CHOCOLATE-COVERED PUFF CANDY (BRITTLE)

Makes ABOUT 1½ POUNDS

———◆———

Maybe you know puff candy by a different name. In different areas around the world it also goes by sponge candy, honeycomb, sponge toffee, cinder toffee, hokey pokey, fairy food, or sea foam. No matter the name, the candy is basically toffee that has baking soda added at the end of cooking, which causes a chemical reaction and gives the candy the porous, spongelike look it's famous for.

This is an easy recipe for those just beginning to make candy, but be sure to invest in a candy thermometer to ensure it reaches the proper temperature. You can use nonstick cooking spray to grease the baking dish and parchment paper if you prefer. Keep the candy refrigerated after you've dipped it in chocolate to keep the texture. Puff candy is also the key ingredient in the Angel Food Crunch Cake (page 267), and what makes it sublime.

---

4 tablespoons (½ stick)
unsalted butter

1 cup sugar

1 cup dark corn syrup

1 tablespoon white vinegar

1 tablespoon baking soda

2 teaspoons
pure vanilla extract

12 ounces good-quality dark
chocolate, chopped

Grease an 8 × 8-inch baking dish with 2 tablespoons of the butter. Cut two pieces of parchment paper larger than the pan, and place in pan crosswise, so that the parchment paper hangs over on all four sides. Generously grease the paper with the remaining 2 tablespoons butter.

In a heavy-bottomed 2-quart saucepan, combine the sugar, corn syrup, and vinegar and clip a candy thermometer to the side of the pan. Cook over medium-high heat, stirring with a wooden spoon, until the mixture reaches 300°F on the candy thermometer, 10 to 15 minutes. You will smell the change as it reaches temperature, and you can test it by dropping a bit into cold water—when ready, it will turn brittle.

Remove the pan from the heat and stir in the baking soda and vanilla. It will bubble quite a bit while cooking, and then settle down once the baking soda is added. Stop stirring after the baking soda is combined to allow it to form bubbles.

Pour the candy into the prepared baking pan and don't move the dish until the candy is fully set, about 30 minutes. Remove the candy from the pan and break it into 1- to 2-inch pieces.

Melt the chocolate in a microwave or in the top of a double boiler over simmering water. Gently brush off any small crumbs on the candy, drop it in the chocolate, and remove it with a fork to let the excess chocolate drip off. Place pieces on a wire rack over a parchment paper–lined baking sheet to harden. Refrigerate until ready to serve.

MILDRED'S MAPLE BONBONS

Makes 24 BONBONS

W hen a native Vermonter friend popped one of these little morsels in his mouth, he said, "I'm tasting my childhood." If you have ever bought maple sugar candy as a souvenir from the Store, you will recognize the same sweet creamy flavor when you taste these family "heirloom" maple bonbons. We'd like to tell you how long they last, but they're eaten so fast around here we don't know for certain. We did manage to hide one batch (keep them covered on the counter or in the freezer), and they were still delectable weeks later.

1 cup dark amber maple syrup

2 cups sugar

1 cup heavy cream

½ teaspoon
pure vanilla extract

½ cup pecan or walnut halves

Combine the maple syrup, sugar, and cream in a heavy 2-quart saucepan and attach a candy thermometer to the side of the pan. Heat slowly over medium heat, stirring frequently with a wooden spoon to keep from burning, until the mixture comes to boil. Keep stirring until the temperature reaches 236°F, or soft ball stage (if you drip some into cold water, it will form a soft ball). This may take up to 15 minutes—keep a close eye on it so it does not go beyond, or it may turn into a hard candy instead!

Remove the pan from the heat and let the mixture cool to the point that you can touch the candy and it is still warm but does not burn. Transfer the mixture to the bowl of a stand mixer fitted with the whisk attachment, add the vanilla, and beat the mixture until it just begins to thicken and lose its gloss. This will take only a few minutes and can also be done by hand, beating with a whisk. Be careful to watch the consistency to note the change from glossy to not, since overmixing will give it a grainy texture.

Line a baking sheet or your counter with a piece of parchment paper. While the candy is still very warm, form it into balls. Wear thin cotton cooking gloves if you have them, or lightly butter your hands. Using 2 teaspoons, scoop the candy with one spoon and push it out onto the paper with the other. With your hands, roll it into a ball and then lightly press to form an oval. Press a pecan on top and set aside to cool completely. (If you have chocolate or candy molds in the shape of a maple leaf, place a pecan in the mold and, instead of forming balls, spoon the warm candy evenly over. Cool completely before popping out of the molds.)

If you are making these with a child or a friend, like the Wilcox family did, have one person spoon the candy directly into the other person's hands to roll, place on the paper, and press. When all the candies are made, both need to press the nuts on before the candy gets hard.

BUTTERNUTS

Hardly any butternut trees remain in Vermont, but there was one near our home in Weston in 1950 and my mother and I collected the sticky-shelled nuts in the fall as she used to do as a child, laid them out in the attic to dry over the winter, and, come sugaring season in March, retrieved them to make maple bonbons. Then came the tough part.

Cracking a butternut is really hard, requiring a sharp hammer blow then picking out the meat. It takes time, precision—hitting the nut off center sends it across the room—and patience, as the inside looks like a brain and the meat's in the pockets. This young boy was neither precise nor patient, although my precision, at least, has improved over the years.

—LYMAN ORTON

SALTED CARAMEL BUTTERMILK FUDGE

Makes ABOUT 48 PIECES

———◆◆———

The Orton family has been selling all flavors of delicious fudge for decades in the Store. Chocolate is everyone's favorite flavor, although there are serious maple-walnut fans. The Orton Family Fudge is so delicious we wanted to come up with a recipe for a flavor not offered, one worthy of the Orton name.

Melt-in-your-mouth smooth thanks to the buttermilk, this fudge is toasty caramel topped with a hint of finishing salt. It's the type of fudge that will keep you standing at the kitchen counter, taking little slices repeatedly, swearing you'll have "just one more." The recipe is remarkably easy. We line the loaf pan with parchment paper, which makes it easy to slice thin and gives it a natural and practical wrapping to keep it fresh longer. Not that it will last that long.

2 cups sugar

1 cup buttermilk

8 tablespoons (1 stick) unsalted butter

2 tablespoons dark corn syrup

1 teaspoon baking soda

1 teaspoon pure vanilla extract

½ teaspoon Maldon salt or other flaky finishing salt

In a large saucepan, combine the sugar, buttermilk, butter, corn syrup, and baking soda and clip a candy thermometer to the side of the pan, making sure it does not touch the bottom of the pan. Cook over medium heat, stirring continuously to keep the mixture from overflowing, until the mixture reaches 200°F.

Using a pastry brush dipped in hot water, wash down any sugar crystals that have formed on the sides of pan. Continue to cook until the syrup reaches soft ball stage, between 234° and 240°F. Test by dropping ½ teaspoon of the fudge into ice water. It should easily form a ball, but flatten in your hand.

Remove the pan from the heat and gently stir in the vanilla, but then do not stir until the syrup cools to about 200°F, or sugar crystals will form. Transfer to the bowl of a stand mixer fitted with the paddle attachment, or use a handheld mixer over the pan, and beat the fudge until thickened and no longer glossy. It will become lighter in color, too.

Line a small 3½ × 6-inch loaf pan with two pieces of parchment paper, laying them crosswise so they overhang the pan on all four sides. Pour the fudge into the pan and quickly sprinkle the Maldon salt over the top before it sets. Store in an airtight container in the refrigerator and thinly slice "as needed."

⌐ CANDY LESSONS IN MATH AND HONOR

In our store, we have a sign above the counter that says, "Add up your penny candy and tell the clerk the total." Each kind of candy has a price posted—say, 2 for 5 cents, 3 for 25 cents, 10 cents each, and so on—so kids really have to concentrate when selecting several kinds to be sure they come up with the correct total owed. It makes me smile to watch the expressions on their faces as they focus on what they want and how much it costs.

My dad put that sign up when I was a kid, and frequently I see parents point it out to their kids, telling them about the times they visited our stores when they were young and made their candy purchases. The prices are different today, but many of the candies are the same: root beer barrels, jawbreakers, juju fruits, red hot dollars, Wilbur Buds, candy buttons.

Every once in a while a twelve-year-old boy will plop down a bulging bag of candy in front of the clerk and say, "Fifty cents' worth!" I love watching the clerk peer over her glasses at the youngster, saying nothing. Suddenly the kid retreats with, "Well, maybe I better recount it."

What a wonderful—and effective—way to teach math and honor.

—LYMAN ORTON

OATMEAL LACE COOKIES

Makes 24 COOKIES

———— ◆◆ ————

This cookie surely must have been one of Aunt Delia's favorites to make, and for good reason. It is delectable in every way, and the buttery, nutty flavor is the perfect complement to a bowl of Wilcox maple-walnut ice cream. These lace cookies have a nice crunch, and since they are a little crumbly, they are not the grab-and-go variety, but demand to be eaten sitting down with a plate. Civilized.

So take your time, enjoy them with a pot of tea, or bring a plate to a friend. They could transport you back to Grandmother's table. And while you should take some time savoring them, they bake up quickly and require only a single saucepan, so the cleanup time is next to nothing.

¾ cup pecan pieces

6 tablespoons (¾ stick) unsalted butter

¾ cup rolled oats

½ teaspoon salt

¾ cup sugar

¼ cup unbleached all-purpose flour

2 tablespoons milk

Preheat the oven to 325°F.

Line a rimmed baking sheet with parchment paper and spread the pecans evenly on the baking sheet. Toast in the oven for 15 minutes, until fragrant and lightly browned. Remove from the oven. Keep the oven on, and leave the parchment paper on the baking sheet after you spoon off the nuts in the next step.

In a medium saucepan, melt the butter over medium heat. Turn off the heat and stir in the oats, pecans, and salt. Stir and let sit for 10 minutes. With a wooden spoon, stir in the sugar, flour, and milk until combined to form a thick batter.

Scoop out 2 tablespoons at a time and press the batter onto the parchment paper–lined baking sheet. Leave 2 inches between the cookies, since they will expand as they bake. Dip a spatula into water and flatten the cookies. Bake for 20 to 22 minutes, until golden. Remove and let cool on a wire rack.

❧ THE ESSENTIAL WHISK

The Vermont Country Store carried French whisks made of tinned steel in the 1950s, but the whisk only caught on in America when Julia Child (a Vermont Country Store customer) spread the word when she used one on the pilot of her television show in 1963 to whisk eggs for an omelet. Now, in the kitchen utensil section of the Store, wire whisks of all shapes and sizes pop up from ceramic jars.

Which whisk should you choose? Depends on what you're making. Here's a list of the many types out there and for what they're best suited:

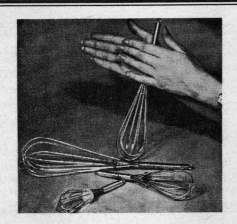

Our Genuine Wire Whisks

Indispensable for mixing and beating; for scrambling and stirring; for whipping (you roll it between two hands); can be hung up. Our set 4 sizes: 6, 8, 10, 12 inches. The set of FOUR. #645. $1.50* *Weight ½ lb.*

French whisk: Similar to the balloon whisk, but longer and narrower. An all-purpose whisk, but good at scraping the edges of pans, so especially good for making lump-free sauces.

Flat whisk: Also called a roux whisk, it looks like a balloon whisk with fewer loops that's been flattened. Use for making a roux or for pan sauces in shallow skillets.

Spiral whisk: What many of us use to make gravy at Thanksgiving. Since it continuously makes contact with the bowl or pan, it's terrific for making sauces, vinaigrettes, and, of course, gravy.

Ball whisk: This looks more like a kid's science toy than a kitchen tool, with its individual wires with ball bearings on the ends. Easier to clean and superb for aerating, this whisk makes whipping egg whites by hand a breeze.

Coil whisk: Instead of stirring around the bowl or pan, you pump this whisk up and down while it stays in one place or you twirl the handle between the palms of your hands. Use to lift sauces or thick mixtures from the bottom of a pan or to blend ingredients in a deep bowl.

Cage whisk: A balloon whisk with a sphere cage inside, which holds a ball bearing for weight. Especially good for blending thick mixtures into a silky texture, it is the best whisk for whipping up luxurious whipped cream.

Balloon whisk: Probably the one you have in your kitchen, it comes in many sizes, from tiny to ridiculously large. Use to mix eggs, whip cream, or mix dry ingredients together in lieu of sifting.

DATE NUT SQUARES

Makes SIXTEEN 2-INCH SQUARES

———◆◆◆———

Dried fruit, such as dates and prunes, was a staple item in many old farm kitchens, and for good reason. It was adaptable to making a quick bread or cookies, and fresh fruit was not always available, so the advantage of having something relatively healthy yet still sweet enough to serve as a dessert was a real bonus.

Discovering this easy-to-make recipe in the Orton/Wilcox recipe archives put a whole new twist on date nut squares, and they have now become the gold standard for any picnic or afternoon treat. The soft, luscious filling is not overly sweet, and with an oat topping, they just could be the healthiest of all cookies.

FILLING

1 cup walnuts

1 tablespoon unsalted butter

3 cups chopped pitted dates (1 pound)

¼ cup sugar

BARS

1 cup packed dark brown sugar

1 cup (2 sticks) unsalted butter, at room temperature

1¾ cups unbleached all-purpose flour

1½ cups quick-cooking oats

½ teaspoon salt

MAKE THE FILLING: Preheat the oven to 350°F. Place the walnuts in a small baking dish, being careful not to crowd them, and toast in the oven for 15 minutes. Remove the walnuts and finely chop them. Raise the oven temperature to 400°F. Lightly grease an 8 × 8-inch baking pan with the butter.

In a medium saucepan, combine the dates, sugar, and 1½ cups water and cook over low heat for about 10 minutes, stirring occasionally, until smooth and thickened. Let cool for 5 minutes, then mix in the walnuts. Set aside.

MAKE THE BARS: In the bowl of a stand mixer fitted with the paddle attachment (or by hand), mix together the brown sugar and butter until smooth and well combined. In a separate medium bowl, mix together the flour, oats, and salt and stir with a wooden spoon (or your clean hands) until crumbly. Add the flour and oat mixture to the butter mixture and beat gently until blended. The mixture will be crumbly and coarse.

Press two-thirds of the crumb batter evenly over the bottom of the greased pan. Spread the filling evenly over the top. Top with the remaining crumb batter and press lightly.

Bake for 25 to 30 minutes, or until light brown. Let cool for 5 minutes in the pan on a wire rack. Cut into four rows in one direction and then cut four perpendicular rows while still warm to make sixteen squares.

LEMON SPONGE CUSTARD CUPS

Serves 6

———◆———

These little gems come out of the oven like a crustless lemon meringue pie, with lemon custard that pools at the bottom waiting for your spoon. A classic lemon pudding cake baked into individual baking cups, these are easy to make and impressive to serve, and are a perfectly light, tart-sweet dessert for a summer meal.

2 tablespoons unsalted butter, at room temperature, plus more for the ramekins

1 cup granulated sugar, plus more for the ramekins

3 large eggs, separated

¼ cup unbleached all-purpose flour

½ teaspoon salt

Zest and juice of 2 lemons (1 to 1½ tablespoons zest and 6 tablespoons juice)

1½ cups whole milk

Confectioners' sugar, for dusting

Preheat the oven to 350°F. Butter six 6-ounce ramekins or individual soufflé dishes and lightly sprinkle them with granulated sugar. Tip out any excess sugar.

In the bowl of a stand mixer fitted with the whisk attachment, whip the egg whites until stiff. Transfer to another bowl and set aside. In the same bowl, cream the butter with the granulated sugar, then add the flour, salt, and lemon zest and juice. Slowly add the egg yolks and then stir in the milk until well combined.

Gently fold the egg whites into the mixture with a large spoon or rubber spatula. Spoon the batter into the prepared ramekins and place them in a roasting pan. Pour boiling water into the pan to come halfway up the sides of the ramekins.

Bake for 45 minutes. Remove the ramekins from the roasting pan and let cool completely or chill overnight. Run a knife around the inside edge of each ramekin and flip each one onto an individual plate; dust with confectioners' sugar and serve.

REVERSE CHOCOLATE CHIP COOKIES

Makes 15 COOKIES

For chocolate lovers, these are the ultimate big dark cookies, decorated with chunks of white chocolate, just like the ones Mildred would make for her clan when they came to visit. A change from the traditional chocolate chip, this is a solid cookie that does not crumble easily, which makes it ideal for packing in a lunch box or a care package to ship. It's our favorite cookie to take on a hike in the woods, or for quick energy—love that hit of chocolate and coffee caffeine—when we're feeling more ambitious and climbing a summit.

It's a quick cookie to make and requires no blenders or mixers. You can do all the stirring and mixing in one saucepan, reducing the cleanup time. These are easy starter cookies for kids to make: Just omit the coffee; it's not essential, but it does take the chocolate flavoring up a notch for a serious grown-up energy cookie.

---

1 cup (2 sticks)
unsalted butter

1 cup granulated sugar

½ cup packed
dark brown sugar

2 large eggs

2 teaspoons
pure vanilla extract

1 cup unsweetened
cocoa powder

2 tablespoons instant coffee
(optional)

2 cups unbleached
all-purpose flour

1 teaspoon baking powder

½ teaspoon salt

1 cup white chocolate chips or
chunks of white chocolate

Preheat the oven to 350°F. Line a baking sheet with parchment paper.

In a large saucepan, melt the butter over medium heat. Turn off the heat and stir in both sugars, the eggs, and the vanilla. Stir with a wooden spoon to combine.

In a medium bowl, whisk together the cocoa powder, instant coffee (if using), flour, baking powder, and salt. Stir into the melted butter mixture and, with a wooden spoon, beat to blend into a thick dough. Add the chocolate chips and stir again to evenly distribute.

Using a tablespoon or a smallish ice cream scoop, drop the dough onto the prepared baking sheet, leaving space in between the cookies for them to expand. Flatten them slightly with the palm of your hand.

Bake for 12 minutes. Let cool on a wire rack.

ORTON BROS.

COOKIE BUTTONS

SMALL IN STATURE,
BIG IN FLAVOR

ZESTY LEMON

NET. WT. 6oz. (170G)

➤ WHICH BROTHER IS WHICH?

The company bakery where Vermont Common Crackers are made also cooks up Orton Brothers Cookie Buttons, completely natural little cookies light on sugar and packed with taste. Customers at the Store like to sample each flavor, and to guess which brother is which on the childhood photos on the box.

HINT: The bottom photo shows Gardner, Eliot, and Cabot today.

CHAPTER 10

The CAKE and PIE SAFE

With its wire or pierced-tin sides and backs, the pie safe—once ubiquitous in Vermont kitchens—allowed air to circulate so that pies and cakes could sit on its shelves happily, flies and rodents kept at bay. Pies were once a staple for all meals, fueling the workday on the farm, and pie recipes crowd the old recipe notebooks of the Wilcox and Orton women, along with scores of cakes and crisps. Because women baked together and passed their knowledge on by word and deed, the archival recipes are as sparse on directions as they are plentiful.

PIES, CRISPS, COBBLERS, and CAKES

{Vermont Stories as American as Apple Pie}

MILDRED'S PIES

WHILE MILDRED LOVED WHOLE-GRAIN BREADS and muffins, she could also bake wonderful pies. Along with her assortment of birch rolling pins she kept pie weights, a crust crimper, and "pie birds," essential—if toylike—tools of pie craft we grandsons found marvelous.

Mildred's seasonal specialties were pecan, pumpkin, mince, and apple. She sometimes made a graham-style crust, toasty and robust, with plenty of butter and shortening and enough salt to bring out the flavor, and was a stickler that her pastry crusts be flaky. Her fillings were unique, as Vermont maple syrup often replaced a decent portion of the granulated sugar normally called for in a baked dessert recipe. In that respect, her pies were wholesome—as were her disdain for store-bought crusts and "jar fillings" and her energetic bias against white flour.

For her apple pies, Mildred preferred tart heirloom varieties long vanished in the supermarket era: Baldwin, Maiden's Blush, Northern Spy. Mottled and deformed, these sorry-looking specimens belied intense flavor as only back meadow apples can, for that is where she procured them.

Local apples can be inconvenient and unreliable. Some years prove miserable for the trees; those with an early spring thaw followed by a hard frost nourish then destroy young buds, and with them goes the whole season. Other years favor us with the confluence of mild weather and moderate rain, yielding brilliant fruit. By early fall we must race the deer and birds for the best pick, for they love apples with a ruthless efficiency that home gardeners know all too well. Once

Ella Orton picks apples for pie.

the apples hit the ground, the season is over. I will long remember a sparkling blue September day, a long ride into Weston on my bicycle, and a big apple tree named "Old Hopeful" alongside Route 100. I'd never seen it produce a single apple. Must have been an epic season, because that year its branches bowed to the soil with enormous golden apples. Took no time to ditch the bike, hop the fence, and fill my shirt with ten pounds of ludicrously perfect fruit. I rode like a shirtless Santa Claus to my grandmother's house and presented her with the bounty. She was delighted. It was the finest year for apple pie we ever had.

—CABOT ORTON

COBBLERS, CRISPS, CRUMBLES, BUCKLES, BETTYS– WHAT'S THE DIFFERENCE?

THE NAMES FOR OUR FAVORITE FRUIT DESSERTS change depending on region, but here's the take from a Vermont point of view:

Brown Betty: Dating back to Colonial times, a Betty's fruit is layered and topped with bread crumbs combined with sugar and butter.

Buckle: Fruit is folded into a cakelike batter or layered on top of that batter; a buttery streusel is sprinkled over the batter before baking.

Cobbler: Fruit baked in a deep dish with sweet biscuitlike dumplings on top that sink into the fruit.

Crisp: Fruit baked with a sweet, crumbly, and crunchy streusel-like topping that (traditionally) excludes oats.

Crumble: Fruit baked with a sweet, crispy topping that includes oats crumbled over the fruit.

OFFICIAL STATE PIE OF VERMONT

SINCE THE APPLE IS THE OFFICIAL VERMONT fruit, it's no surprise that Apple Pie is the official state pie. The surprise is who proposed the legislation: a third-grade class in Fairfax, in 1999. While learning about state symbols, the kids discovered there was no state fruit, so they researched which fruit was grown the most in Vermont: the apple. Then the students decided the state should have a state pie, too, and polled their schoolmates and then all third graders in the state. Apple pie was the definitive favorite.

After their state representative came to the class to explain how an idea becomes a law, he sponsored the legislation, and the students traveled to Montpelier to testify before the Agriculture Committee. After the bill passed, Governor Howard Dean came to the school for a big celebration, signing the bill into law while students cheered. Served that day? Apple pie, of course, baked by the cafeteria staff.

FARMHOUSE CIDER APPLE PIE

Makes ONE 9-INCH PIE; *Serves* 8 TO 10

W̲hen it comes to apple pies, the ingredients have to be just right. The apples you use will make the difference between a soft, mushy filling and one that holds a little shape and has a crisp, tart bite. Seek out cooking apples, such as Cortland, Gravenstein, Jonagold, or Newton Pippin, even a good crisp McIntosh.

The crust also has to be perfect. All of the old recipes, including Mildred's, call for lard or shortening, which easily blends into the flour to make a flaky crust. We prefer a pure butter crust, and the key is to make sure the butter is chilled and the water is icy cold, a critical step in the way the dough comes together. Before you start, chill ½ cup water with three ice cubes and let sit for 5 minutes.

Our secret ingredient, boiled apple cider, is what makes this apple pie stand out. It's sold in the Store, but if you don't have it, go ahead and make the pie without; it will still taste fantastic, just a little less intensely apple. An old-fashioned apple peeler-corer-slicer, also sold in the Store, can take an apple down to thin, peeled slices in less than 10 seconds!

TWO-CRUST PIECRUST

2½ cups unbleached all-purpose flour, plus more for dusting

½ teaspoon salt

1 teaspoon sugar

1 cup (2 sticks) unsalted butter, cut into pieces

⅓ to ½ cup ice water

MAKE THE CRUST: In a food processor fitted with the steel blade, pulse together the flour, salt, and sugar. With the machine running, add the butter one piece at a time, until it is fully incorporated and the mixture looks like cornmeal. With the machine running, add the ice water, 1 tablespoon at a time, until the dough pulls together into a ball (you may not need all the ice water). Scoop out the dough and press together all the tiny floury bits, then divide it in half and lightly press down to form two discs. Wrap each in plastic or place in a resealable plastic bag and refrigerate for at least 30 minutes.

Lightly flour the counter or a marble board and roll out one piece of the dough, starting from the center and working your way to the edges. Roll the dough into an 11-inch disc, about ⅛ inch thick, and slide it into a 9-inch pie pan, leaving an inch or so to drape over the edge. Roll out the remaining dough into a 9-inch disc and set it aside until the pie is filled.

Preheat the oven to 375°F.

MAKE THE FILLING: In a large bowl, toss the apples thoroughly with the lemon juice. Add vanilla, sugar, cinnamon, nutmeg, cloves, and salt. Sprinkle the cornstarch over everything, toss to coat, and heap the apples into the bottom crust. Pour the boiled cider evenly over the apples and dot evenly with the butter.

Moisten the edges of the bottom crust, and gently place the top crust over the apples. Trim and crimp to make a decorative edge.

MAKE THE GLAZE: Beat the egg yolk with the milk, and brush the shell with the mixture using a pastry brush, which will give it a nice golden crust. Cut designs or small slits into the top shell for steam to vent. In a small bowl, combine the cinnamon with the sugar. Sprinkle the pie with cinnamon sugar and bake for 55 to 60 minutes, until the apples are tender and the crust is golden.

❧ HOME-BAKED HOLIDAYS

Here in Vermont, the holidays are announced by candles in the windows, garlands of lights on the bushes, and pies in the oven. Our family has always baked prodigiously throughout the season. Cakes and cookies vie for counter space. Frosting is applied in extravagant quantities. More whipped cream is eaten than spread. Sound nutrition is rendered powerless against chocolate in all its forms.

Our mother's maple meringues look perfectly innocent on the tray, weightless little dollops that whisper sugary indulgences to the forlorn dieter. As with armies, their strength lies in numbers. A single meringue proves harmless as a scout, probing one's resolve; many together form brigades of sweet calories, battering the gates of willpower like a Viking siege engine.

By contrast, mince pie seems downright wholesome, practically a health food. Certainly, the apples and raisins occupy space we might otherwise fill with chocolate pudding. Mince was the venerable New England specialty our grandmother Mildred baked every November, vapors of cinnamon and nutmeg its potent calling card. Children don't tend to crave this.

In my view, pumpkin pie is the vital "bridge" dessert, conveying young diners from petulant fixation with banana crème and vanilla butterscotch toward mature enjoyment of unfamiliar textures such as custard or cooked cherries, and tolerance of recipes containing clove.

—CABOT ORTON

THE CAKE AND PIE SAFE

FRESH CHILLED BLUEBERRY PIE

Makes ONE 9-INCH PIE; *Serves* 8 TO 10

We love a hot pie straight from the oven, but every now and again, it's nice to change it up and serve a pie that is chilled, especially on a hot summer evening. Served with flavored whipped cream, it is a little slice of heaven.

You'll find this is one of the simplest pies you can bake. It has just one crust, a bottom that is sturdy and truly holds in the juice. If you want to buy a prebaked crust, that's okay, because this pie is all about the fruit. We simmer fresh berries and add them to the filling, and the blueberries puff up and are quite succulent. The recipe works best with fresh berries, but you can combine frozen with fresh, and even mix and match the fruit, using raspberries, blueberries, and strawberries. You can't really go wrong with any type of berry when it comes to a fruit pie.

CRUST

1½ cups unbleached all-purpose flour, plus more for dusting

½ teaspoon salt

1 stick (4 ounces) unsalted butter, cold, cut into ⅛-inch pieces

3 to 5 tablespoons ice water

MAKE THE CRUST: In a food processor fitted with the steel blade, pulse together the flour and salt. With the machine running, add the butter, one piece at a time, until it is fully incorporated and the mixture looks like cornmeal. With the machine still running, add the ice water, 1 tablespoon at a time, just until the dough pulls together into a ball (you may not need all the ice water). Scoop out the dough and press together all the tiny floury bits, and light press down to form a disc. Wrap in plastic or place in a resealable plastic bag and refrigerate for 1 hour (or longer, if you are baking the pie another time).

Preheat the oven to 375°F.

On a lightly floured surface, roll out the dough, starting from the center and working your way to the edges. Roll the dough into an 11-inch disc, about ⅛ inch thick, and slide it into a 9-inch pie pan. Trim the excess edges and crimp with your fingers or a fork to make it pretty, leaving it slightly draping over the edge.

Prick the bottom of the pastry with a fork and line with parchment paper. Fill the paper with pie weights or dried beans and bake until the crust begins to color around the edge, 25 to 30 minutes. Remove and let cool slightly before adding the filling.

(Continued)

PIE FILLING

½ cup granulated sugar

½ cup packed light or dark brown sugar

3 tablespoons cornstarch

½ teaspoon salt

2 pints fresh blueberries (4 cups)

2 tablespoons unsalted butter

Juice of 2 lemons (¼ cup)

WHIPPED CREAM (OPTIONAL)

1 cup heavy cream

¼ cup granulated sugar

½ teaspoon pure vanilla extract

1 teaspoon grated lemon zest

MAKE THE FILLING: In a medium saucepan, combine ⅓ cup water with the granulated sugar, brown sugar, cornstarch, and salt. Cook slowly over medium-low heat, stirring continuously, and bring to a boil to dissolve the sugars. Add 2 cups of the blueberries and keep stirring until the mixture begins to thicken and turn clear and glassy, about 4 minutes. Remove from the heat and stir in the butter and lemon juice. Gently fold in the remaining 2 cups blueberries. Let cool slightly, and then pour or spoon the filling into the prebaked piecrust and refrigerate until ready to serve.

MAKE THE WHIPPED CREAM (OPTIONAL): In the bowl of a stand mixer fitted with the whisk attachment, combine the cream, sugar, vanilla, and lemon zest. Whip the cream until peaks form.

Serve the pie with several heaping tablespoons of whipped cream, if desired.

IT'S ALL ABOUT THE CRUST

I don't recall a single filling of my mother's pies, because for Mildred, it was all about the piecrust. She was always fussing about the crust: Do it fast, keep the butter and lard cold, don't overhandle it, don't overstir, don't overroll it. Nowadays people buy piecrusts at the supermarket without bothering to read the ingredients. Mildred was a stickler for good ingredients handled correctly, and always produced a flaky crust. Try creating a flaky crust out of whole grains—now that's a real feat.

—LYMAN ORTON

GLAZED PEAR TARTE TATIN

Serves 6 TO 8

This piecrust bakes on top of the fruit, keeping the filling moist during cooking. Flip the hot rustic tart onto a plate, and serve. It's not as sweet as a traditional pie, but plenty flavorful! And it tastes even better reheated the next day for breakfast or as an afternoon snack. Make sure to arrange the fruit artistically, because when you flip it over to serve, that's what you'll see. It's a gorgeous and impressive presentation.

PÂTE BRISÉE SINGLE CRUST

1¼ cups unbleached all-purpose flour

½ teaspoon salt

8 tablespoons (1 stick) unsalted butter, cold, cut into small pieces

¼ cup ice water

FRUIT FILLING

8 Bosc pears

Juice of 1 lemon (3 tablespoons)

1½ cups sugar

8 tablespoons (1 stick) butter

½ teaspoon salt

MAKE THE PÂTE BRISÉE: In a food processor fitted with the steel blade, combine the flour and salt; pulse to combine. Add the butter and pulse until the mixture resembles coarse crumbs, about 10 seconds. (To mix by hand, combine the dry ingredients in a large bowl, then cut in the butter with a pastry blender.)

With the machine running, add the ice water, 1 tablespoon at a time, just until the dough holds together without being wet or sticky (you may not need all the ice water). Do not process for longer than 30 seconds. Test by squeezing a small amount of the dough together; if it is still too crumbly, add a bit more water.

Turn out the dough onto a clean, floured work surface and divide it in half. Shape it into flattened discs, wrap them in plastic wrap, and refrigerate for at least 1 hour, or up to overnight.

Roll out the pâte brisée into a 10-inch circle, about ⅛ inch thick; transfer to a baking sheet and chill until firm, about 30 minutes.

Preheat the oven to 400°F.

MAKE THE FILLING: Peel, halve, and core the pears and transfer to a large bowl. Toss with the lemon juice and set aside.

In a large high-sided skillet with a tight-fitting lid, combine the sugar and 6 tablespoons water. Bring to a boil over medium-high heat; cover and cook until the mixture begins to thicken and turn amber around the sides. Uncover and gently swirl the pan to caramelize evenly. Remove from the heat and stir in the butter and salt. Add the pears in a single layer to the caramel, and return the mixture to the heat, turning the pears occasionally until they are tender, 10 to 15 minutes. Remove from the heat and let cool.

(Continued)

THE CAKE AND PIE SAFE

Transfer the pears to a 9-inch cake pan, arranging them cut side up in two layers. Pour three-quarters of the caramel sauce evenly over the pears, reserving the rest for serving. Place the pâte brisée crust over the pears and tuck in the edges to enclose the pears in the pan. Set the pan on a baking sheet and bake for about 25 minutes, until the pastry is golden.

Let cool for 10 minutes. Place a rimmed serving platter over the pan, and quickly and carefully invert the pan and the platter together. Pour the remaining caramel over the tarte and serve.

The Church on the Hill in Weston.

SUMMER FRUIT COBBLER

Serves 6

◆◆

During the summer, a combination of berries and peaches celebrates one of the great culinary matches, brightening palate and plate. To serve a crowd, we top the fruit with biscuits in a classic cobbler. Our buttermilk biscuit topping has a touch of cardamom to accent the juicy fruit, and the cornmeal adds a slight pleasing crunch. We bake the berries first, so the topping stays light and airy. For potlucks or parties, this recipe can easily be doubled.

FILLING
½ cup sugar
1 tablespoon cornstarch
⅛ teaspoon ground cinnamon
⅛ teaspoon salt
2 pints fresh blueberries
6 ripe peaches, peeled, pitted, and sliced into sections
1 pint fresh raspberries or blackberries
Zest and juice of 1 lemon (2 to 3 teaspoons zest and 3 tablespoons juice)

BISCUIT TOPPING
1 cup unbleached all-purpose flour
2 tablespoons cornmeal
¼ cup sugar, plus 2 teaspoons for sprinkling
2 teaspoons baking powder
¼ teaspoon baking soda
¼ teaspoon salt
4 tablespoons (½ stick) unsalted butter, melted
½ cup buttermilk
½ teaspoon pure vanilla extract
½ teaspoon ground cardamom
⅛ teaspoon ground cinnamon

Vanilla ice cream, for serving (optional)

Preheat the oven to 375°F.

MAKE THE FILLING: In a large bowl, stir together the sugar, cornstarch, cinnamon, and salt. Add the blueberries, peaches, and raspberries and mix gently until evenly coated. Stir in the lemon juice and zest and transfer to a 9-inch glass pie pan. Place the pie pan on a baking sheet and bake for about 25 minutes, or until hot and bubbling throughout.

MAKE THE BISCUIT TOPPING: In a large bowl, whisk together the flour, cornmeal, ¼ cup of the sugar, the baking powder, baking soda, and salt. In a smaller bowl, whisk together the melted butter, buttermilk, and vanilla. In another small bowl, stir together the remaining 2 teaspoons sugar, the cardamom, and the cinnamon and set aside until the berries come out of the oven.

A few minutes before the fruit emerges from the oven, stir the buttermilk mixture into the flour mixture, stirring gently until just combined and no dry pockets remain.

Remove the hot, bubbling fruit from the oven and raise the oven temperature to 425°F. Spoon out eight equal portions of the biscuit topping and place them evenly over the hot fruit, spacing them at least ½ inch apart. Sprinkle each with a little of the cinnamon and cardamom sugar and bake until the filling is bubbling and the biscuits are golden brown and cooked through, about 15 minutes. Let cool slightly before serving with vanilla ice cream, if desired.

GINGERBREAD
WITH LEMON CURD

Serves 12

◆◆◆

The aroma of freshly baked gingerbread often filled Lyman Orton's home growing up, as it was one of Mildred's favorites. To him and to many of us, a whiff of gingerbread instantly whisks us back in time, evoking holiday, warmth, home.

Inspired by Mildred's recipe, ours takes the ginger aspect up a notch with the addition of crystallized ginger, which gives the bottom of the cake a sweet, sticky layer. The batter will seem thin to you, but you'll be surprised how it bakes up into a moist and spicy cake. Serve with lemon curd (or whipped cream), and don't forget a pot of hot tea or a big glass of ice-cold milk.

1 tablespoon unsalted butter,
at room temperature,
for the pan

2 cups unbleached
all-purpose flour,
plus 1 tablespoon for the pan

2 teaspoons baking soda

1 teaspoon ground ginger

1 teaspoon ground cinnamon

1 teaspoon ground cloves

½ teaspoon fine sea salt

1 cup sugar

1 cup unsulphured molasses

1 cup vegetable oil

3 large eggs,
at room temperature

1 cup boiling water

½ cup finely chopped
crystallized ginger

Lemon Curd (recipe follows),
for serving

Preheat the oven to 350°F and position a rack in the center. Lightly butter and flour a 9 × 13-inch baking pan, tapping out any excess flour.

In a medium bowl, sift together the flour, baking soda, ginger, cinnamon, cloves, and salt and set aside.

In the bowl of a stand mixer fitted with the whisk attachment, beat the sugar, molasses, oil, and eggs on high speed until well combined, about 2 minutes. Slowly add the flour mixture, and then add the boiling water. Gently mix to make a smooth, thin batter.

Evenly spread crystallized ginger in the bottom of the prepared pan. Pour the batter gently over the ginger and place the pan in the oven. Bake for 45 minutes, until the cake springs back when pressed in the center. Let cool for 10 minutes, then serve warm with lemon curd alongside.

LEMON CURD

Makes ½ CUP

6 tablespoons (¾ stick)
unsalted butter, at room
temperature

1 cup sugar

2 large eggs

2 egg yolks

Juice of 4 lemons (¾ cup)

Zest of 1 lemon (1 tablespoon)

Lemon curd is easy to prepare, except for one pesky problem: It sometimes winds up with bits of cooked and curdled egg. Because the egg whites cook at a low temperature, they're more prone to coagulation when combined with the lemon. Fear not! These will smooth out as the butter melts, producing a smooth, silky curd, ideal for topping gingerbread or adding to tarts or cookies. Be sure to use only real lemons for an authentic lemon taste.

In the bowl of a stand mixer, beat the butter and sugar for 2 minutes until blended. Slowly add the whole eggs, then the egg yolks. Beat for 1 minute. Mix in the lemon juice. (The mixture will look curdled, but it will smooth out as it cooks because the butter will melt.)

Transfer the mixture to a medium saucepan and cook over low heat until it looks smooth. Turn up the heat slightly and stir continuously with a whisk until the mixture thickens. Be careful not to let the mixture boil! If you want to check it with a thermometer, it should read 170°F.

Remove the curd from the heat. Stir in the lemon zest, transfer to a small bowl or jar, and cover with plastic wrap or a lid. Chill the curd in the refrigerator. It will keep in the refrigerator for a week or in the freezer for 2 months.

THE CAKE AND PIE SAFE

☙ WHAT'S WITH ALL THE CAKES?

Going through the recipe archives from the Wilcox, Hamilton, and Orton families reveals a surprising concentration on cakes. Spice cakes, sponge cakes, angel cakes, devil cakes, prune cakes (so many prune recipes we were concerned for the family's digestion!), fudge cakes, nut cakes, jam cakes. There were, of course, maple cakes and buttermilk cakes. One can see why a Betty Crocker booklet called the 1920s "the beginning of the real cake era."

The 1930s saw even wider cake popularity, aided perhaps by a 1931 booklet from, self-servingly, K. C. Baking Powder that declared that cakes were "an exceedingly well balanced food product" "no longer considered too rich for daily consumption."

Cakes have been around since ancient Egypt, but those were more breadlike, sweetened with honey and studded with dried fruit, spices, and nuts. It wasn't until the middle of the nineteenth century that the cake as we know it today—refined white flour, sugar, baking powder—made an entrance. The Orton recipe archives attest to just what a grand entrance it was!

LEMON POUND CAKE
WITH POPPY SEEDS

Makes ONE 8½ × 4½-INCH LOAF; *Serves* 8 TO 10

—◆◆◆—

Pound cake is one of those wonderfully simple cakes that can be served without frosting, yet is also divine with a chunky fruit syrup, toasted and smeared with butter, or sliced into many layers and spread with chocolate frosting. This cake is not overly sweet, and is rich, moist, dense, and soft. The poppy seeds add a very subtle texture, a little surprise crunch. Why not make this cake with the egg yolks left over from the Angel Food Crunch Cake (page 267)? Did Grandmother Wilcox make two cakes at a time for this reason?

2 sticks (1 cup)
unsalted butter, melted,
plus more for the pan

½ cup unbleached all-purpose
flour, plus more for dusting

⅔ cup sugar

7 large egg yolks

2 large eggs

Zest of 3 lemons

Juice of 1 lemon
(3 tablespoons)

½ cup cornstarch

¼ cup poppy seeds

Preheat the oven to 350°F and position a rack in the center. Butter and flour an 8½ × 4½-inch loaf pan.

In the bowl of a stand mixer fitted with the whisk attachment, beat the sugar with the egg yolks and whole eggs on medium-high speed until the mixture is pale yellow and very fluffy, about 8 minutes. Beat in the lemon zest and juice. In a separate bowl, whisk together the flour and the cornstarch, then add it to the egg mixture. With the mixer running on medium speed, slowly pour in the slightly cooled melted butter. Stir in the poppy seeds.

Pour the batter into the prepared pan. Bake for 60 minutes, or until the cake pulls away from the sides of the pan and a cake tester inserted into the center of the cake comes out clean. Let cool in the pan on a wire rack for 15 minutes. Invert the cake onto the rack and let cool completely before serving, at least 30 minutes.

THREE-LAYER COCONUT CAKE
WITH SEVEN-MINUTE FROSTING

Makes ONE 3-LAYER FROSTED CAKE; *Serves* 10 TO 12

O*f all the recipes we found in the Orton archives, we were most fascinated by the cakes. Most of the recipes listed ingredients only, and we can only assume that the techniques for making cake were passed down from generation to generation, daughters standing in the kitchen alongside mothers or grandmothers.*

Most of the recipes reflected a frugality, using only one or two eggs, until we found this recipe in Mildred's cookbook collection. We've added more egg whites to give it a lift, and detailed the step-by-step instructions to give you as much help as we can, in the hopes that your cake is successful and worthy of passing down to the next generation.

Basic white cake can be dressed up with layers of lemon curd or jam. Since we like the taste of coconut, we've added coconut extract and coconut between each layer. Play with it, and make up your own favorite special-occasion cake.

1½ cups (3 sticks) unsalted butter, at room temperature, plus more for the pans

4½ cups white (non-rising) cake flour, plus more for the pans

8 large egg whites

2¼ cups sugar

1 teaspoon pure vanilla extract

1 teaspoon coconut extract

2 teaspoons baking powder

1 teaspoon salt

1 cup whole milk

8 cups Seven-Minute Frosting (recipe follows)

1 cup shredded sweetened coconut

Preheat the oven to 350°F. Butter three 9 × 2-inch round cake pans and dust with flour, tapping out any excess flour.

In the bowl of a stand mixer fitted with the whisk attachment, beat the egg whites until frothy. Add ¼ cup of the sugar and continue to beat until stiff and glossy peaks form, about 4 minutes. Transfer to a large bowl.

Fit the mixer with the paddle attachment and in the same bowl, beat the butter with the remaining 2 cups sugar until light and fluffy, about 4 minutes. Blend in the vanilla and coconut extracts.

In a medium bowl or large measuring cup, sift together the flour, baking powder, and salt. With the mixer on low speed, add the flour mixture in three parts, alternating with milk and beginning and ending with flour; beat until the batter is just combined, being careful not to overbeat.

With a rubber spatula, gently fold one-third of the egg white mixture into the batter until combined, then fold in the remaining egg white. Stir to incorporate, being careful not to overmix.

Divide the batter evenly among the prepared pans, smoothing the tops with the rubber spatula. Bake for 30 to 35 minutes, or until a cake tester inserted into the centers comes out clean. Transfer the pans to wire racks to cool, then invert the cakes onto the racks to cool completely, top sides up.

(Continued)

TO FROST THE CAKE: Make the cake layers level by trimming the tops with a serrated bread knife. Place one layer on a serving plate, cut-side up. Spread 2 cups of the frosting on the first layer, all the way to the edge. Place another layer on top, cut side up, and top with more frosting, spreading it all the way to the edge. Place the final layer on top, cut side down, and spread the remaining 3 cups frosting over the entire cake, swirling to cover. Press the coconut evenly over the cake. (The coconut can be lightly toasted in a preheated 350°F oven, if desired.)

SEVEN-MINUTE FROSTING

Makes ABOUT 8 CUPS

1½ cups sugar

2 tablespoons light corn syrup

6 large egg whites

1 teaspoon pure vanilla extract or coconut extract

This makes a thick, creamy frosting, without all the butter of a traditional buttercream, and holds a nice peak for the coconut. To heighten the coconut flavor, substitute coconut extract for the vanilla. If you have a handheld mixer, you won't have to transfer to a stand mixer.

In the top of a double boiler, or in a heatproof bowl set over a saucepan of simmering water, combine the sugar, corn syrup, egg whites, and ¼ cup water. Stirring frequently with a whisk, cook until the mixture registers 160°F on an instant-read thermometer, about 2 minutes.

Transfer to the bowl of a stand mixer fitted with the whisk attachment (or beat in the pot or bowl with a handheld mixer). Beat the mixture on high speed until glossy and voluminous, about 5 minutes. Beat in the vanilla.

∾ A FEW TIPS TO MAKE SURE YOUR CAKE IS A SUCCESS

When buttering pans, always use room-temperature (softened) butter instead of melted butter.

To give the cake volume, be sure the butter and sugar are well blended and creamy before you add the other ingredients.

Add the flour or milk in batches, alternating to keep the batter from deflating.

If the cake calls for beaten egg whites, fold them in until they are just incorporated—don't overmix.

For even baking, always rotate the pans inside the oven halfway through the baking time.

To keep the cakes from cracking on the top, let the cakes cool for 20 minutes in the pan on a wire rack before inverting.

ANGEL FOOD CRUNCH CAKE

Serves 12

———◆———

Eliot Orton's wife, Julie, brought this recipe with her when she moved to Vermont from Quebec, as it has always been the cake she makes for every birthday for friends and family. She could not find the candy that is key to this recipe in any U.S. stores, until she learned from Eliot that it was available only at The Vermont Country Store. Made by one company in Buffalo, the Chocolate-Covered Puff Candy is not sold in the Store between April and October because it melts and gets too soft to ship. You'll always find a couple of bags in the Ortons' freezer, though, just in case.

You can make this scrumptious cake in minutes if you use a pre-bought cake and buy a bag of candy from the Store. Just go to the last paragraph of the recipe and follow from there. We prefer to make the angel food cake from scratch, for both the ethereal lightness and the satisfaction. We've included a from-scratch recipe for the candy, too (see page 227), in case you have a special occasion that falls during the summer months and you can't get the candy from the Store.

Assemble the cake just before serving to keep it white; otherwise, the candy blends into the frosting and turns it a lovely caramel color. Either way, this cake has to be one of the best-tasting cakes ever made, between the airy texture and hint of vanilla and the crisp candy frosting. It will linger in your memory until the next birthday.

---

12 egg whites (1½ cups),
at room temperature

1¼ teaspoons cream of tartar

2 teaspoons
pure vanilla extract

½ teaspoon salt

1½ cups sugar

1 cup plus 2 tablespoons
cake flour

2 cups heavy cream

1 cup crushed Chocolate-
Covered Puff Candy (page
227)

Preheat the oven to 325°F. Line the bottom of a tube pan with parchment paper cut to fit.

In the clean, dry bowl of a stand mixer fitted with the whisk attachment, beat the egg whites with the cream of tartar. Start on a low speed and beat until frothy, then increase the speed and beat until stiff peaks form, which can take about 10 minutes. (If you have a copper bowl, use it! It will cut this time in half.) The egg whites should be able to stand upright. Add the vanilla and mix just to blend.

In a medium bowl, whisk together the salt, sugar, and flour, or sift together to give the batter more air. With a rubber spatula, gently fold the dry ingredients into the egg whites. Pour the batter into the tube pan and bake for 50 to 60 minutes, or until a skewer inserted into the cake comes out clean.

Turn the pan upside down to cool, with a funnel or bottle in the hole of the tube pan. Let cool for 1 hour.

(Continued)

THE CAKE AND PIE SAFE

Ella, Julie, and Leo Orton frost their special occasions cake.

In the bowl of a stand mixer fitted with the whisk attachment, slowly whip the heavy cream. The more slowly you whip the cream, the thicker it will become. Remove the bowl from the mixer, and with a plastic spatula, fold the crushed candy into the cream.

Run a skewer between the pan and the cooled cake and turn the cake out onto a plate, right side up. Frost the cake all over with the whipped cream frosting. Serve immediately for a lighter-colored cake. If the frosting is made in advance, it will start to turn a tawny brown from the melting chocolate and caramel candy bits, but it will still taste delicious!

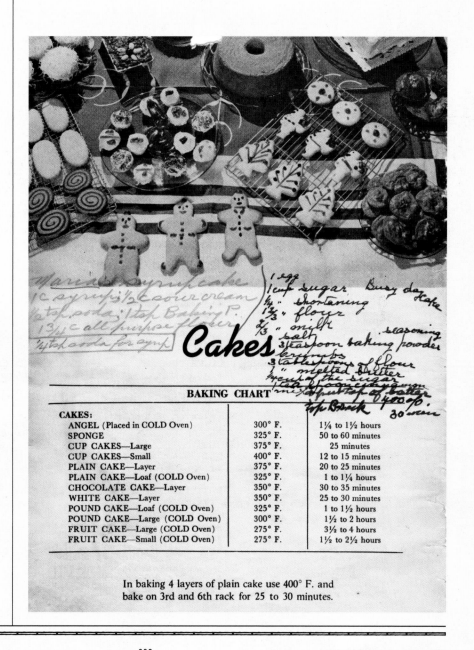

Cakes

BAKING CHART		
CAKES:		
ANGEL (Placed in COLD Oven)	300° F.	1¼ to 1½ hours
SPONGE	325° F.	50 to 60 minutes
CUP CAKES—Large	375° F.	25 minutes
CUP CAKES—Small	400° F.	12 to 15 minutes
PLAIN CAKE—Layer	375° F.	20 to 25 minutes
PLAIN CAKE—Loaf (COLD Oven)	325° F.	1 to 1¼ hours
CHOCOLATE CAKE—Layer	350° F.	30 to 35 minutes
WHITE CAKE—Layer	350° F.	25 to 30 minutes
POUND CAKE—Loaf (COLD Oven)	325° F.	1 to 1½ hours
POUND CAKE—Large (COLD Oven)	300° F.	1½ to 2 hours
FRUIT CAKE—Large (COLD Oven)	275° F.	3½ to 4 hours
FRUIT CAKE—Small (COLD Oven)	275° F.	1½ to 2½ hours

In baking 4 layers of plain cake use 400° F. and
bake on 3rd and 6th rack for 25 to 30 minutes.

NOT YOUR GRANDMOTHER'S FRUITCAKE

Makes FOUR 9 × 5-INCH LOAVES

Many of us have not-so-fond memories of fruitcakes that contained dried candied citrus peels and artificially dyed fruit pieces that would arrive in a round tin. This is not that fruitcake. We promise.

When buying naturally dried fruit, buy in bulk from a health food store for the best price and to avoid the preservatives often used to keep dried fruit soft. It takes awhile to chop all the fruit, so invite friends to make this recipe in your kitchen and share the bounty.

We've learned that the two keys to a really good fruitcake are good ingredients and time. Make this in late summer or at least eight weeks before Christmas, and store it in a cool, dry basement or in the back of the refrigerator. For a lovely holiday gift, wrap a loaf in fresh cheesecloth topped with a sprig of holly.

5 pounds mixed dried fruit (such as currants, golden raisins, dates, apricots, cherries, figs), cut into raisin-size pieces

½ pound walnuts (1 cup), coarsely chopped

½ pound pecans (1 cup), coarsely chopped

2 cups brandy or bourbon, plus more as needed

2 cups (4 sticks) unsalted butter, at room temperature, plus 1 tablespoon for greasing

4 cups unbleached all-purpose flour, plus more as needed

2 teaspoons ground cinnamon

1 teaspoon ground allspice

2 teaspoons baking powder

¾ teaspoon salt

2½ cups packed dark brown sugar

½ cup honey

10 large eggs, at room temperature

Place the fruit and the nuts in a large bowl. Add 1 cup of the brandy to cover. Let the fruit and nuts soak up the liquor for a few hours, or overnight.

Preheat the oven to 250°F. Butter and flour four 9 × 5-inch loaf pans.

In a medium bowl, combine the flour, cinnamon, allspice, baking powder, and salt. Add half this mixture to the fruit and nuts and mix well until it coats everything. Set the rest aside.

In the bowl of a stand mixer fitted with the paddle attachment, cream together the butter, sugar, and honey until fluffy, about 3 minutes. Add the eggs, one at a time, beating well after each addition. Add the remaining flour and blend until all is incorporated.

In a small bowl, whisk together the apricot nectar, heavy cream, and lemon juice. Use a rubber spatula to fold this into the batter until smooth. Pour the batter over the fruit and nuts and mix until fully combined. This takes some muscle and a couple of minutes. Divide the batter among the prepared pans, filling them almost to the top of the pans, as this cake does not rise much. Smooth the tops with a rubber spatula.

Bake for 3 hours, rotating the loaves around the oven halfway through, then check with a toothpick for doneness (it will come out clean). Remove from the oven and let cool in the pans.

(Continued)

1 cup apricot nectar (available in a specialty food store)

½ cup heavy cream

Juice of 1 small lemon (2 tablespoons)

½ cup orange-flavored liqueur (such as triple sec or Cointreau)

While the cakes are cooling, cut four pieces of cheesecloth large enough to wrap around each of the loaves. In a small bowl, combine the remaining 1 cup brandy and the triple sec, add the cheesecloth pieces, and let them soak in the liquid.

Once the cakes are cool, wrap each in a piece of the liquor-laced cheesecloth and place back into the loaf pan. Evenly pour any remaining liqueur over the tops, and wrap in plastic wrap or place in a large resealable plastic bag. Tuck away in a corner of a cool basement or the back of the refrigerator.

Allow the fruitcake to sit for a minimum of 4 weeks—it needs time to get dense and hard. Continue to pour more brandy over the top every week, to keep them moist. You can taste the cake after 1 week, but it will only get better with age.

BY THE BOOK—THE GOOD BOOK

We were curious to find in Maria Wilcox's recipe notebook a recipe for Scripture Cake, with ingredients listed with Bible verse references. While hers cheated a bit by actually writing the ingredients, most Scripture Cake recipes we saw had just the Bible verse, leaving cooks wondering just what was 3½ cups Exodus 29:2?

Back in the day, women would bake this cake to serve to a new pastor in town (and subtly test his scripture knowledge), or to bring to a church supper. An early form of a trivia game, perhaps, or a sweet way to instill Bible verses into young helpers, the Scripture Cake is best made with a recipe that "cheats," like Maria's, or with a King James Bible at your side! (As for Exodus 29:2: "And unleavened bread, and cakes unleavened tempered with oil, and wafers unleavened anointed with oil: of wheaten flour shalt thou make them.")

Scripture cake

3½ cups flour — 1 Kings 4 - 22
1 " butter — Judges 5 - 25
3 " sugar — Jeremiah 6 - 20
2 " raisins — 1 Samuel 30 - 12
2 " figs — 1 " " 30 - 12
1 " almonds — Numbers 17 - 8
1 " water — Genesis 24 - 17
6 eggs — Isaiah 10 - 14
1 tablespoon honey — Exodus 16 - 31
pinch salt — Leviticus 2 - 13

follow: - Solomon's advice for making good boys and girls and you will have good cake.
Proverbs 23 - 14

MOCHA FUDGE CAKE

Serves 12

— ◆◆ —

Here's where we separate the true chocolate lovers from the rest. With a hint of coffee in the fudgy frosting and two ways of chocolate delivery in the rich, moist cake, this concoction may catapult you directly into chocolate heaven.

If you want to take it down a notch, you can eliminate the chocolate chips from the recipe. We've tried it both ways, and here's our take: If you're going to frost the cake in any other manner (we sometimes serve it as two cakes, with whipped cream and fresh berries on top of the single layers), the chips are key. If you're slathering the layers with this intense frosting, you may prefer the smoother finish and slightly less sweet taste of the cake without the chips. Your call. No matter which way you choose to make it, this cake is a standout.

¾ cup (1½ sticks) unsalted butter, plus more for the pans

6 ounces unsweetened chocolate

6 large eggs

3 cups sugar

½ teaspoon salt

2 teaspoons pure vanilla extract

1½ cups unbleached all-purpose flour

1½ cups semisweet chocolate chips (optional)

4 cups Mocha Fudge Frosting (recipe follows)

Preheat the oven to 350°F and position a rack in the center. Grease two 9 × 1½-inch round cake pans with removable bottoms with butter, or, if you're using regular cake pans, line the bottoms with parchment or waxed paper cut to fit.

In a small saucepan, melt the butter and unsweetened chocolate over low heat. Stir until smooth and combined, then let cool to lukewarm. In a large bowl, whisk the eggs until golden, then add the sugar, salt, vanilla, and the melted chocolate mixture. Stir in the flour and chocolate chips (if using).

Pour the batter evenly into the prepared pans. Bake for 35 to 40 minutes. You can control how moist the cake is by the amount of time it bakes. If you like a more cakelike and less fudgy cake, keep it in the oven for the longer period of time. You can tell when the cake is done by the puffiness on top with a few circular cracks. Let the cakes cool in the pans on wire racks, then invert onto the racks. Wrap them well if you're not frosting them the same day.

TO FROST THE CAKE: Trim the cake layers to make them even. Place one cake layer on a cake plate, cut side up, and spread some of the frosting over the top. Top with a second cake layer, cut side down, and spread the frosting over the top and then around the sides to completely cover the cake. With a knife, make decorative little waves. Ta-da!

MOCHA FUDGE FROSTING

Makes 4 CUPS

1¼ cups sugar

2 tablespoons espresso powder or instant coffee granules

1 cup heavy cream

5 ounces unsweetened chocolate, finely chopped

8 tablespoons (1 stick) unsalted butter

1 teaspoon pure vanilla extract

Combine the sugar, espresso, and heavy cream in a small but deep heavy saucepan; the mixture will boil up during cooking. Bring to a boil, stirring continuously. Reduce the heat and simmer, stirring continuously, for 6 minutes. Remove from the heat and add the chopped chocolate; stir until melted and well combined. Stir in the butter and vanilla until well combined and smooth.

Chill until the mixture begins to thicken. Beat with a wooden spoon until thick and creamy.

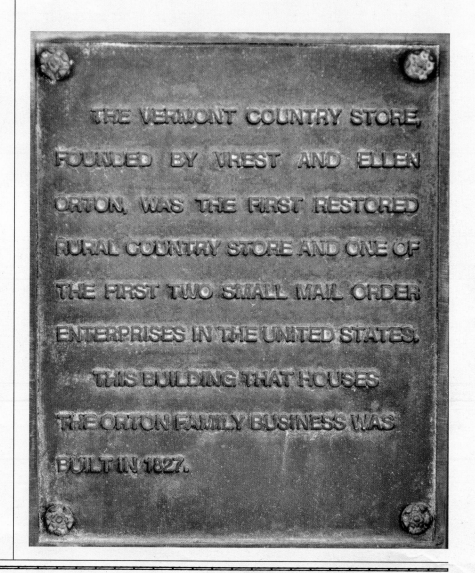

CHAPTER 11

VERMONT, *A* WAY *of* LIFE

ERMONT IS AN ODD AND WONDROUS STATE, at times ornery and freethinking, always intimate in scale and charming in landscape, with covered bridges and villages (like Corinth, left) straight out of Currier & Ives that real people call home. Here we've gathered a bit of Vermont lore to amuse and enlighten. We invite you to visit our state, either in person or through the pages of this book. You may experience a sense of "coming home" that Vermonters do when returning across the border. Something changes in the landscape, in the air—and maybe in ourselves. We roll down the window and breathe deeply.

Mildred, Vrest, Lyman, and Jeremy heading for the Weston rope tow, circa 1949.

A FEW OLD VERMONT SAYINGS

What you don't say won't ever hurt you.

It's better to wear out than rust out.

It's nice to sit and think
but sometimes it's nicer just to sit.

You can't always judge a cow by her looks.

Paul Orton chats up customers in 1947.

VERMONT FACTS

Independent Republic: 1777–1791

Fourteenth state: 1791

Tree: Sugar Maple

Animal: Morgan Horse

Insect: Honeybee

Flower: Red Clover

Beverage: Milk

Bird: Hermit Thrush

40 Gallons of Sap = 1 Gallon Syrup

Highest: Mount Mansfield 4,293 feet

Lowest: Lake Champlain 95 feet

Population: Second smallest state

Area: Sixth smallest state

Average Weston Snowfall: 10 feet a year

Vermont is the only state in the nation that doesn't have a single building taller than 124 feet.

A HISTORY OF VERMONT FIRSTS

FOR A SMALL STATE, VERMONT CAN BOAST A bushel of firsts, among them:

The **first shot fired in the Revolutionary War** to shed British blood was by Solomon Brown from New Haven, Vermont, at the Battle of Lexington in 1775.

Vermont was the **first state to abolish slavery.** Actually, slavery was specifically abolished before Vermont was a state, in the constitution of our Independent Republic adopted on July 8, 1777. (It became the fourteenth state in 1791.)

The **first marble quarry in the United States** was established in South Dorset, Vermont, run by a man fittingly named Underhill.

The **first fishing spoon lure** was invented in 1830 by Julio Buel of Castleton, Vermont.

The **first electric motor** was invented in 1834 by Thomas Davenport of Brandon, Vermont.

The **first person to use laughing gas** as an anesthetic for pulling teeth was Horace Wells of White River Junction, Vermont, in 1844.

The **first postage stamp** used in America was made in Brattleboro, Vermont, in 1846.

The **first Boy Scout troop** was organized in Barre, Vermont, in 1909 by William F. Milne.

The **first U.S. ski lift**, a simple rope tow powered by a Model T Ford engine, started pulling skiers uphill and shredding mittens in the process in January 1934 in Woodstock. The much more skier-friendly J-bar lift was also invented in Vermont by Fred Pabst at Bromley. The first ski chairlift was used on Vermont's Mount Mansfield in 1940.

Vermont was the **first state in the nation to enact a total ban on billboards**, in 1968.

Vermont was the **first state to legalize civil unions** (2000) and the first to legalize same sex marriage (2009).

Vermont passed the nation's **first GMO food labeling law** in 2014.

THE FIRST PLATFORM SCALE WAS INVENTED BY one of our ancestors, Thaddeus Fairbanks, in 1830 in St. Johnsbury, Vermont. This new, more accurate scale made it possible to weigh heavy objects without hoisting the entire load. The platform scale had huge ramifications for business, but also, in a small way, transformed everyday life. Hunters could accurately weigh their kill and, once the scale was reduced and made portable, cooks could accurately weigh their chickens, vegetables, and flour.

By the end of the nineteenth century, Fairbanks scales were the best-known American product in the world, sold throughout England, Europe, China, Cuba, the Caribbean, South America, India, and Russia. They even became the official scale of the United States Postal Service!

What scale was used on the space shuttle *Apollo*? Weighed in Muhammad Ali for the Fight of the Century against Joe Frazier? Was the official scale of the 2002 Winter Olympics? Fairbanks, all.

We're proud to have a connection with one of the nation's oldest industrial manufacturing companies, started in 1824 in Vermont and run by three brothers and still going strong. Come see our Vermont Scale Museum—the largest extant—assembled by our father, Lyman, at the Weston store.

—GARDNER ORTON

KISSING BRIDGES

VERMONT HAS MORE COVERED BRIDGES PER square mile than any other state, more than one hundred, a living reminder of how old-timers put up bridges to last. When Vrest Orton was chairman of the Vermont Historic Sites Commission, he convinced the Army Engineers to save an 1872 covered bridge in Townshend, Vermont, from being destroyed for a dam project. Years later it was reassembled at The Vermont Country Store in Rockingham, where it sits today.

When you visit the Rockingham store, you'll notice a sign telling of Vermont's Kissing Bridges. The story is that the bridges were covered to provide a secret place for one to court—although the reality, far less romantic, is that the wooden bridges would last three times as long if covered in harsh Vermont weather. Some romantic native Vermonters still stop in the middle of a covered bridge to kiss when cycling or driving through. We've even had couples get married at the Rockingham Kissing Bridge!

A VERMONTER'S RIGHT *to* DRY

Here, Lyman Orton speaks on behalf of "The Right to Dry" provision on the statehouse lawn in Montpelier, June 4, 2009. The law passed, and now all residents in the state have the right to dry their laundry on a clothesline. "There is nothing more consistent with [a Vermonter's] heritage of practicality, frugality, and common sense than hanging laundry on a clothesline and allowing nature to dry it with zero use of energy," Lyman said in his testimony to the legislature. "It's about our heritage, our culture, and our social interaction. We pride ourselves on small-town character. We don't live exclusively; we live inclusively, and that means airing our clean *and* dirty laundry!"

THE FREEMAN'S OATH

BEFORE YOU REGISTER TO VOTE FOR THE FIRST time in Vermont, you have to appear before the town clerk, raise your right hand, and answer in the affirmative to this oath called for in our constitution. Read it a few times and ponder its meaning.

> You solemnly swear that whenever you give your vote or suffrage, touching any matter that concerns the state of Vermont, you will do it so as in your conscience you shall judge will most conduce to the best good of the same, as established by the Constitution, without fear or favor of any person.

DRIVE INTO WESTON, LIKE MANY VERMONT VIL-lages, and you'll come smack upon an acre of land known as the Village Green. When Weston was incorporated in 1799, the center of the village was a lowly frog pond, then a dump for the local tanneries, then a meadow for grazing cows owned by surrounding homeowners. In 1886, by an act of the Vermont Legislature, the nonprofit Farrar Park Association was created, and the following year the Trustees, nine Weston women, received by gift that same circular piece of land. The bylaws of the Association prohibited games being played, as the intent was a village green to be used for quiet reflection and as a gathering place.

Over the years, the Trustees, always all women (a tradition rather than a legal requirement), planted saplings, erected a wooden bandstand and granite war monument, and circled the area with a green iron fence. The saplings grew into towering sugar maples and many a visitor to The Vermont Country Store sits for a bit beneath the sheltering canopy.

Each December a local artist decorates the bandstand with garlands and bows in a masterpiece of elegant understatement. On Christmas Eve anonymous villagers ring the Green with luminary candles and their radiant glow slows every passing car to a crawl. As much as the world changes, the Green shows what doesn't change.

Our grandmother tended that Green with a cadre of other fierce women, affectionately referred to as the Nine Old Ladies, for six decades. Could be because she lived on it, could be because she was an avid citizen, could be because the Store was across the Green and, until she died at ninety-nine, she walked its paths nearly every day. Could be because she was a Vermonter down to her bones, generations deep, and you take care of the people and places that sustain you.

—CABOT ORTON

We turned and took one farewell look at Weston.
This was America. This is America. This will always be America.

—*THE SATURDAY EVENING POST,*
"The Happy Storekeeper of the Green Mountains," 1952

Bandstand on the Village Green, Weston

Lyman, Eliot, Gardner, and Cabot Orton, Proprietors.

ACKNOWLEDGMENTS

From ELLEN AND ANDREA: Writing *The Vermont Country Store Cookbook* has been an extraordinary pleasure for us, but it wouldn't have happened without the collective vision of a great many who contributed to the book you hold in your hands.

First, we'd like to thank the Orton family for preserving the past, trusting us with their stories, and allowing us to mine the family archives so we could develop recipes with Mildred looking over our shoulder. (When we discovered a recipe for ice cream scribbled on the back of an envelope with a penny stamp and a 1909 postmark, we knew this book would work.) Lyman's editing skills kept us honest, Cabot's memory sparked delightful stories, Gardner shared a magical moment, and Eliot served as point person for the family, strategizing with us, weighing in on the look and feel of the book, and solving any issue before it became a problem.

Many members of The Vermont Country Store team deserve our deepest thanks for their tremendous encouragement and indispensable aid, especially CEO Chris Vickers, who saw the possibilities, Donnel Barnum, for her inestimable help with archive materials and photographs, and Lynda Corbett, Chelsea Nye, and Deb Bradder, for their supporting roles.

Deepest thanks go to our editor, Karen Murgolo, for her enthusiasm and vision, for giving us much freedom, and for gently shaping so many ingredients into such a beautiful feast. Also to our agent, Colleen Mohyde, for providing the opportunity to write this book, for her constant attention throughout the process, and for her unflagging faith that it would get done.

We are especially grateful to photographer Matthew Benson and his creative team, Nora Singley, Sara Abalan, and Leslie Stockton, who sculpted our recipes into magnificent works of art. Shot in the historic Orton family home on the Village Green, this imaginative, exacting, and fun team deserves the highest praise on every level. A nod of gratitude to Bennington Potters for lending us some of the beautiful handmade pottery you see in this book. And to Jim Szabo, who tirelessly searched the attics and corners of The Vermont Country Store for the perfect prop, and Chef Glen Gourlay, who offered us tasty recipes from the Bryant House.

Special thanks go to the recipe testers, Nancy Benoit, Joanne Prouty, and Becky Moore, for their professionalism, good cheer, and knowledge of food. Without their wonderful, indefatigable enthusiasm and attention to detail, we might never have met our tight deadline.

Feeding family and friends is at the heart of why we wrote this book. With gratitude and love, we wish to thank all of our good friends and family who have been on this journey with us for the past year, who have supported us from appetizers through dessert.

From ELLEN: I am ever grateful to my friends and family who shared recipes and good times around the table. My special thanks are for my mother, Deborah Ecker, and my grandmothers, Barbara Ecker and Helen Stark, who instilled the basics of how to set an attractive table and of the pleasures of cooking and entertaining. As always, my deepest thanks go to my children, Molly and Sam, who have embraced our family's love for cooking and eating well. I also extend my appreciation to Andrea, my coauthor, for the pleasure of stepping back in time with old photos, stories, and recipes.

From ANDREA: My thanks to my coauthor, Ellen, whose quest for perfection brought these recipes to the table. Undying gratitude goes to my husband, Rob, who keeps me on an even keel through every challenge and eats anything I cook up. Thanks also to my beloved mother, whose myriad virtues did not include being an inspiring cook, forcing me to discover for myself the wonders of complex tastes; and to my father, who introduced me to travel and fine food. And to the joys of my life, Jessica and Zachary, who have themselves become fine cooks and finer human beings.

Horse-drawn sleigh behind The Vermont Country Store in Rockingham.

PHOTO CREDITS

———◆◆———

INDEX

ABOUT THE AUTHORS

ELLEN ECKER OGDEN is a well-known food and garden writer and kitchen garden designer who lives in Vermont. She writes for such magazines as *Eating Well*, *Organic Gardening*, and *Country Gardens*, among others. Her kitchen garden designs have been featured in the *New York Times*, the *Boston Globe* and *Martha Stewart Living*. Her books include *From the Cook's Garden*, *The Vermont Cheese Book*, and *The Complete Kitchen Garden*, featuring designs and recipes for cooks who love to garden. www.ellenogden.com

ANDREA DIEHL is a writer and editor with more than thirty years in the communications business. Her varied work background includes managing all brand messaging for The Vermont Country Store, writing speeches for the president of Princeton, handling PR for a U.S. Attorney, and writing about her great passion as food editor of the *Philadelphia Daily News*. She holds a BA from Williams College, a masters of education from Antioch, and an MFA from Bennington College in Writing and Literature, and lives in southern Vermont. www.iDiehlCommunications.com

THE ORTON FAMILY is the proud owner of The Vermont Country Store, founded by Vrest and Mildred Orton in 1946. Today it is run by their son Lyman and his sons Cabot, Gardner, and Eliot, seventh- and eighth-generation Vermonters, and fourth- and fifth-generation storekeepers.